Divided by Faith

Divided By Faith

Evangelical Religion and the Problem of Race in America

Michael O. Emerson
Christian Smith

OXFORD
UNIVERSITY PRESS
2000

OXFORD
UNIVERSITY PRESS

Oxford   New York
Athens   Auckland   Bangkok   Bogotá   Buenos Aires
Calcutta   Cape Town   Chennai   Dar es Salaam
Delhi   Florence   Hong Kong   Istanbul   Karachi
Kuala Lumpur   Madrid   Melbourne   Mexico City
Mumbai   Nairobi   Paris   São Paulo   Singapore
Taipei   Tokyo   Toronto   Warsaw
and associated companies in
Berlin   Ibadan

Library of Congress Cataloging-in-Publication Data
Emerson, Michael O., 1965–
Divided by faith : evangelical religion and the problems of race
in America / Michael O. Emerson, Christian Smith.
p.   cm.
Includes bibliographical references and index.
ISBN 0–19–513140-1
1. Race relations—Religious aspects—Christianity.
2. United States—Race relations.
3. Evangelicalism—United States.
I. Smith, Christian (Christian Stephen), 1960–
II. Title.
BT734.2.E48 2000
261.8'348'00973—dc21   00-036743

5 7 9 8 6 4

Printed in the United States of America
on acid-free paper

To Joni, my love.
M.O.E.

For Stan, who helped start all of this.
C.S.S.

❀

Contents

Preface   *ix*

Introduction   1
Religion and the Racialized Society

1   Confronting the Black–White Racial Divide   5

2   From Separate Pews to Separate Churches   21
Evangelical Racial Thought and Practice, 1700–1964

3   Becoming Active   51
Contemporary Involvement in the American Dilemma

4   Color Blind   69
Evangelicals Speak on the "Race Problem"

5   Controlling One's Own Destiny   93
Explaining Economic Inequality Between Blacks and Whites

6   Let's Be Friends   115
Exploring Solutions to the Race Problem

7   The Organization of Religion   135
and Internally Similar Congregations

8   Structurally Speaking   153
Religion and Racialization

9   Conclusion   169

Appendix A   *173*
Appendix B   *179*
Notes   *183*
Bibliography   *197*
Index   *209*

Preface

To learn more about American life, this book examines the role of white evangelicalism in black–white relations. Our argument is that evangelicals desire to end racial division and inequality, and attempt to think and act accordingly. But, in the process, they likely do more to perpetuate the racial divide than they do to tear it down. We base our argument on historical analyses of the movement and race relations, a national survey and hundreds of face-to-face interviews with contemporary evangelicals and other Americans, and an examination of the role that the structure of U.S. religion plays in racial division and inequality.

We have taken it as our charge to tell as honest, accurate, rigorous, and enlightening a tale about our topic as possible. In so doing, we were led to move beyond the old idea that racial problems result from ignorant, prejudiced, mean people (and that evangelicals are such people). This is simply inaccurate, and does not get us far in trying to understand why racial division in the United States persists. We also move beyond the idea that race issues continue merely because dominant groups attempt to consciously defend their economic privilege. Instead, we explore the ways in which culture, values, norms, and organizational features that are quintessentially evangelical and quintessentially American, despite having many positive qualities, paradoxically have negative effects on race relations.

Michael Emerson principally authored this book, so any shortcomings in the book are principally his. For all that is positive about this work, but none that is negative, we wish to thank the many people and institutions who contributed in a myriad of ways to this project. We must thank the thousands of people who agreed to telephone interviews, and the hundreds of people around the country who allowed us to come to their homes for interviews. We are truly appreciative. A grant from the Pew Charitable Trusts afforded us the resources to interview people, meet together as a research team, and reduce our teaching loads, providing us time to write. We thank Joel Carpenter for his vision, expert assistance, and support of this project. Further, we thank Bethel College, Rice University, and the University of North Carolina. We also extend our appreciation to our department colleagues. They supported the writing of this work with their encouragement, especially Jim Hurd and Harley Schreck, who had to work more so that this book could be written. They are true friends.

A special thank-you to the Pew Young Scholars, led by Wade Clark Roof, and the Center for the Study of Religion and American Culture. They not only encouraged this project, but were willing to critique its earlier forms as well.

Many people have contributed by commenting on portions of this book, including Patricia Chang, Roger Finke, Stephen Hart, and Mark Noll. We are thankful for their sharp readings and helpful suggestions. Others contributed to the overall argument of the book, especially Sally Gallagher, Paul Kennedy, Dan Olson, Mark Regnerus, and Johan Sikkink. Their input was much needed. We also appreciate the assistance and advice of our editor, Cynthia Read.

Two research assistants—Robyn Minahan and Rachel Laustsen—did wonderful work tracking down sources, making phone calls, looking up information, and other tasks too numerous to mention. Their work was invaluable. So too was the work of Chelsea DeArmond, who put this manuscript into readable form and gave us helpful stylistic assistance.

This book could not have been written without the expertise and time of Tim Essenberg, Leo Gabriel, Greg Keath, Karen McKinney, and Scottye Holloway and the great people of Ambassadors. We are grateful for your wisdom, spirit of friendship, and willingness to cross barriers. You have taught far more than you can know.

Our families are most important of all. Thank-you to our extended families: Mom, Dad, Rick and Karin, and Ann. Our very biggest thank-you to our immediate families: Joni, Anthony, Josiah, Leah, Sophia; Emily, Zachary, Erin, and Caroline. Thank you for keeping us focused on the right priorities, and for your love.

Houston, TX   M.O.E.
August 1999   C.S.S.

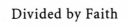

Divided by Faith

Introduction

Religion and the Racialized Society

I do not imagine that the white and black race will ever live in any country upon an equal footing. But I believe the difficulty to be still greater in the United States than elsewhere. An isolated individual may surmount the prejudices of religion, of his country, or of his race, and if this individual is a king he may effect surprising changes in society; but a whole people cannot rise, as it were, above itself. A despot who should subject the Americans and their former slaves to the same yoke, might perhaps succeed in commingling their races; but as long as the American democracy remains at the head of affairs no one will undertake so difficult a task; and it may be foreseen that the freer the white population of the United States becomes, the more isolated will it remain.

Alexis de Tocqueville, *Democracy in America (1835)*

This book is a story of how well-intentioned people, their values, and their institutions actually recreate racial divisions and inequalities they ostensibly oppose. It is a narrative of how some of America's core values and assumptions and its reliance on market principles contradict and work against other esteemed values. To tell this tale of paradox, we explore the connection between two of the most dynamic, controversial, long-standing, and unique aspects of American life—evangelical religion and black–white race relations.

As a nation, Americans have devoted extensive time and energy discussing religion and race. Questions like, "What is the proper place of religion?" "What is the role of race?" "In what direction is each heading and what does this mean for us as a nation?" are studied and debated by public officials, religious and racial group leaders, scholars, the media, and "people on the street."

But the connection between the two, especially religion's role in the racially divided United States, is grossly under-studied. Some historical accounts exist, and tend to argue that religion has done little to overcome the racial divide.[1] These are good works, but we are left with vital questions unanswered. Why does religion have so little impact? Why does it sometimes buck this trend, being a powerful agent of racial change, for example, with the Civil Rights movement? What is religion's role now? And, more broadly, what can we learn about the American experiment itself from religion and race relations?

When we turn to contemporary analysis, the paucity of connections between religion and race is stark. Race-relations scholars almost completely avoid the role of religion. Simple religion indicators like frequency of worship attendance occasionally find their way into explanations of racial views, but these are exceptions. Far more commonly, religion is simply ignored. And among those studying religion, reflections on religion's role in challenging or buttressing the racial divide are likewise scarce.

Overdue, then, is a careful consideration of the connection between religion and race relations. We undertake such a consideration by focusing on a dynamic brand of American religion—Protestant evangelical Christianity—and a major fault line of American racial division—the black–white divide.

WHO ARE EVANGELICALS?

Many American values—freedom, individualism, independence, equality of opportunity, privacy, and the like—derive largely from the confluence of evangelical Protestant Christianity and Enlightenment philosophy, within the context of conditions encountered in the new world.[2] Like a smoothly blended soup, the flavors of American values so well combined these traditions that both evangelical Christians and secularists could ladle from the same kettle. Historically, evangelical Protestantism was an "insider" religion, and was the mainstream religion for the first century and a quarter of American history. And today, apart from their orthodox faith values, evangelicals remain integrated in American society.[3] They work in all occupations, live in every region of the country, are married, single, young, old, have children in public schools and private schools, have incomes and education comparable to other Americans, and are Republicans and Democrats.

So what unites evangelicals, who along with other conservative Protestants represent approximately one-quarter of Americans?[4] Although they are a mosaic socially, politically, economically, and regionally, they share the defining features of the evangelicalism movement.[5] In contrast to those who might cite human reason, personal experience, tradition, or individual preference as conclusive authorities for truth, evangelicals hold that the final, ultimate authority is the Bible. Stemming from this, evangelicals believe that Christ died for the salvation of all, and that anyone who accepts Christ as the one way to eternal life will be saved. This act of faith is often called being "born again" and is associated with a spiritually, and often more broadly, transformed life. And of course, true to their name, evangelicals believe in the importance of sharing their faith, or evangelizing.[6] Evangelicals, as we employ the term here, are also those who call themselves such.[7] That is, we asked people their primary religious identity—for example, Catholic, mainline Protestant—and define evangelicals in part as those who said their primary religious identity is evangelical.[8] Evangelicals come from all ethnic and racial backgrounds, but nearly 90 percent of Americans who call themselves evangelicals are white. This book focuses primarily, but not exclusively, on white evangelicals.

Just as important for our purposes, evangelicals believe in "engaged orthodoxy." By engaged orthodoxy we mean taking the conservative faith beyond the boundaries of the evangelical subculture, and engaging the larger culture and society. To be sure, for many non-evangelical Americans, this is controversial. For evangelicals, however, this engaged orthodoxy is part of their very identity. Evangelicals want their traditional faith to offer solutions to pressing social problems, such as race relations.

In recent years, evangelicals, or at least some of their leaders, have been highly active in the area of race relations, calling for nothing less than a complete end to racial strife and division, a tearing down of the "dividing wall of hostility."[9] A June 23, 1997, front-page story in the *Wall Street Journal* called evangelicals "the most energetic element of society addressing racial divisions." From the Promise Keepers movement, to local actions, to "the Memphis Miracle," in which the formerly all-white Pentecostal Fellowship of North America disbanded to create the cross-racial Pentecostal churches of North America, to America's best-known evangelical, Billy Graham, saying that "racial and ethnic hostility is the foremost social problem facing our world today," evangelicals appear to be applying their concept of engaged orthodoxy to one of the United States's most vexing social problems. *Divided by Faith* is an assessment of evangelicalism in black–white relations.

1

Confronting the
Black–White Racial
Divide

While I was sitting at a stoplight a few blocks from my [Emerson's] home in Minneapolis, reflecting on the recent rash of drive-by shootings in the area, three African-American teens clad in the urban uniform of the day—baggy pants and shirts, jewelry, and Fila basketball shoes—crossed the street in front of me. I was the only white in the area and on seeing me these young men abruptly stopped, turned, and faced me. The middle one drew up his hands, positioned as if holding a pistol, to mock-shoot me. After taking aim and pulling the imaginary trigger, complete with a kickback motion from the force of the weapon, he blew the imaginary smoke off his finger. Confidently smiling, as if to say it would be that easy, they turned and walked away. I sat there, frozen.

My highly educated colleague James, an African American who recently moved to a new state, was driving from work, which is in a nearly all-white, well-to-do suburb, to his home in another nearly all-white, well-to-do suburb. About a mile after he left work, a police car began to follow him. It followed him all the way to his suburb. "Why are they following me?" James thought, and as they continued to trail him, "Why don't they pull me over?" The police continued to follow him to his street, and even to his home.

When James had pulled into his driveway, the police blocked the driveway entrance to the street, turned on the police car lights, and ordered him, over the loudspeaker, to get out of his car with his hands away from his body. Neighbors peered out their windows, and those outside stopped their activities to observe their new neighbor and the unfolding scene. Although frustrated, angry, and very embarrassed, he did as he was told. The white police officers got out to search and question him. After a few minutes they told him they were sorry for the inconvenience and he was free to go. It turned out it was merely a case of mistaken identity; they thought he was someone else wanted for a serious crime. James asked why they had to follow him all the way to his home, resulting in embarrassing him in front of his neighbors and likely reinforcing stereotypes about black men. He never did get a clear answer.

Since that incident, which took place about a year ago, the police stopped James twice more. In both instances, it turned out to be a case of mistaken identity. The same thing, he told me, has happened all his life, no matter where he has lived. Curiosity raised, I asked other African Americans if they had ever experienced anything similar. Nearly everyone I asked had. My colleague and neighbor Walanda told me she had been pulled over by the police in a posh suburb, home to upscale shopping, four times, and no longer goes there.

Why do these incidents happen? Why do we think it worthwhile to mention the race of those involved? Although interpretations of these events may vary, few readers familiar with the United States will have trouble answering these questions. For race is intimately tied to the American experience. It is what Swedish researcher Gunnar Myrdal called "an American dilemma."[1] Others have gone further, describing it as indivisible from American life.[2] Few subjects are as persistent, as potentially emotionally explosive, or as troublesome as race in America.

But the impact of race is not captured only by incidents such as those just described. It takes more benign forms as well. The race problem is not confined to prejudice or unfair treatment by some individuals. To focus solely on these when considering American race relations is to miss the broader picture.

For example, prejudice does not account for an experience I [Emerson] had while doing research for this book. I called to interview Chauntel Adams, an African-American woman. After two rings, a man, likely her husband, answered.

"Hello," I said, "this is Dr. Michael Emerson. Is Chauntel there?"

"Just a minute."

He cupped his hand over the phone receiver to keep me from hearing his next words, but, as is often the case, I heard anyway.

"Chauntel, the phone."

"Who is it?" came her reply, obviously from another room.

"I don't know," he responded, "some white guy."

Beyond this man's ability to accurately identify my race from just two short sentences uttered over a phone is the fact that my race had meaning. What meaning it had was not entirely clear, but the fact that it mattered was obvious. Yet, despite its meaning, it did not necessarily entail prejudice.

So how do we capture the meaning of race in America? In this book, we use the term "racialized society." Not only, we argue, is it a more useful term than prejudice or racism, but it provides a framework by which to guide our inquiry. In the post-Civil Rights United States, the racialized society is one in which intermarriage rates are low, residential separation and socioeconomic inequality are the norm, our definitions of personal identity and our choices of intimate associations reveal racial distinctiveness, and where "we are never unaware of the race of a person with whom we interact."[3] In short, and this is its unchanging essence, a racialized society is *a society wherein race matters profoundly for differences in life experiences, life opportunities, and social relationships.* A racialized society can also be said to be "a society that allocates differential economic, political, social, and even psychological rewards to groups along racial lines; lines that are socially constructed."[4]

To say that racial categories are socially constructed is, for many, a new way to think about race. After all, usually Americans can clearly identify people according to their race, and do so based on physical rather than social characteristics. But to say that race is socially constructed does not mean physical differences are not readily apparent. Rather, we say that race is socially constructed for at least two different reasons. First, only certain physical characteristics are used to classify people. Foot size and ear shape are not used by Americans to classify people by race, even though people vary on these physical characteristics. Second, race is socially constructed insofar as selected physical characteristics have social meaning. On meeting someone for the first time, Americans often assume that a white person is middle class or higher. They also often assume that a black person or an American Indian is lower class. They may or may not be correct in their assumption, but race is socially constructed at these points because selected physical characteristics are associated with selected social characteristics. The social construction of race is highlighted by the fact that the way groups of people are defined changes. In the United States, Irish and Italian Americans were once viewed as distinct, and inferior, racial groups. Today, they are classified as white Americans of Irish or Italian ethnicity.

To understand that race in the United States is socially constructed is necessary for understanding the racialization perspective. Although it may seem odd to many Americans, who are socialized into the reality of race from an early age, "race" as a social construct arose in the sixteenth and seventeenth centuries to justify the overtaking and enslaving of whole people groups.[5] It continues to exist only insofar as it is recreated. That is, races exist because a society is racialized. As we will explore, who people marry, where people live, political struggles, objective interests, and identities, among others, are all part of the racialized character of society, and the "structure" of racial formation.[6] Furthermore, due to the origins of the idea of race, the placement of people in racial groups always means some form of hierarchy. This is why we may define a racialized society, in part, as one that allocates differential rewards by race.

This is not to deny the importance of other divisions within racial groups, such as class or gender. Rather, this says race is an independent, fundamental cleavage within the United States. For example, Brooks and Manza examined the social cleavages—which they define as differences in political alignment among groups—of class, sex, religion, and race from 1960 to 1990.[7] For all years examined, they found that race was easily the largest social cleavage (followed by religion), and that the race cleavage had actually grown in magnitude since 1960.

But, in societies where race matters, we must be clear that the form of racial hierarchy and division varies. The form varies both between societies and over time within societies, as their economic system and other institutions change.[8] In the United States, roughly speaking, the form has changed from slavery, to "Jim Crow" segregation,[9] to the post-Civil Rights-era division.

A major problem in understanding race relations in the United States is that we tend to understand race, racism, and the form of racialization as constants rather than as variables. This view has grave implications. Racism, for instance, is often captured best in people's minds by the ideology and actions of the Ku Klux Klan: an overt doctrine of racial superiority—usually labeled prejudice—that leads to discrimination.[10] Based on this unchanging standard, racism is viewed as an irrational psychological phenomenon that is the product of individuals, and is evidenced in overt, usually hostile behavior. It is the driving force behind anything negative about race relations. Using this perspective, social scientists devise survey questions meant to measure the level of racism in a society, such as "Whites have a right to keep blacks out of their neighborhood," or "How strongly would you object if a member of your family brought a black friend home for dinner?" Based on this approach, they conclude that racism is declining, since a smaller percentage of people over time respond in a prejudiced fashion. The interpretation? Because racism is seen as driving racial problems, race matters less for shaping social life and life opportunities.

But things look different when we see that the form of racialization changes. Suppose we were still using a standard that was set in relation to slavery. Making the same assumption about racism that we do today, we would assume that slavery is the result of racism (even though, as noted above, racism was an ideology created to justify slavery, not vice versa). If we were designing ways to measure racism in the antebellum era, we might measure racism as the level of agreement with statements like, "Darkies are happier being slaves," "Colored people are more like children than adults," "Africans are not fully human," and "It is God's will that Anglos be masters, and Africans be slaves." If we used this unchanging standard, we would find that the farther removed from 1865, the smaller the percentage of people agreeing with such statements. Again, using present-day logic, we would conclude that racism and the race problem were declining, and indeed, say by 1955, we would conclude it had nearly disappeared.

But our hindsight is clear. By 1955, the problems of race and the racial hierarchy had not disappeared at all. The forms had changed to be sure, but so ever-present were the problems that major social movements and upheavals resulted. These upheavals ushered in a new era of race relations in the United States—the post-Civil Rights era. Our understandings of race relations, however, remain stuck in the Jim Crow era, leading us to mistaken conclusions—racism is on the wane, and racial division and the racial hierarchy are but historical artifacts. Rather than incorrectly examine race in the United States using an old standard, we must adapt our understanding and analysis to the new, post-Civil Rights era.

The framework we here use—racialization—reflects that adaptation. It understands that racial practices that reproduce racial division in the contemporary United States "(1) are increasingly covert, (2) are embedded in normal operations of institutions, (3) avoid direct racial terminology, and (4) are invisible to most Whites." [11] It understands that racism is not mere individual, overt prejudice or the free-floating irrational driver of race problems, but the collective misuse of power that results in diminished life opportunities for some racial groups.[12] Racism is a changing ideology with the constant and rational purpose of perpetuating and justifying a social system that is racialized.[13] The justification may include individual, overt prejudice and discrimination, but these are not necessary. Because racialization is embedded within the normal, everyday operation of institutions, this framework understands that people need not intend their actions to contribute to racial division and inequality for their actions to do so.

Saying that we need not intend our actions to be discriminatory for racialization to occur does not sit well with most of us. Yet, throughout American history, the racialized character of the United States has relied as much on its institutionalization as on people being individually prejudiced. Many slave owners were quite fond of their slaves and formed deep bonds, while the institution of slavery did the racializing. During the late 1930s and early 1940s, Swedish scholar Gunnar Myrdal traveled America in preparation for his monumental work on American race relations. In interviewing, he found many honest, good-natured people who told him that though the United States once had a race problem back during slavery times, it no longer did. Relations between the races were good and improving all the time, people were content, and society was functioning smoothly. Yes, a few racists were out there, and some of the things they did were dreadful, but those racists in no way represented the majority of people. Myrdal then pushed them a bit, asking about the gross inequalities and the segregation between races, and suggested that perhaps they themselves contributed to the problem simply by living according to socially defined ways, such as segregation. People were rather taken aback by this, and though they had not really thought about this before, they were sure this was not the problem. They then proceeded to offer a justification for the system.

Something similar, we argue, is what occurs today. Institutions and some of America's nonrace-based values reproduce racialization without any need for people to be prejudiced, as defined in the Jim Crow era. In fact, often the leaders in reproducing racialization in the post-Civil Rights era are those who are least prejudiced, as traditionally measured.

For example, as we show elsewhere,[14] highly educated whites, compared to less well-educated whites, are much less likely to say they are uncomfortable with black neighbors, less likely to say that they would move if African Americans moved to their neighborhood, and more likely to say that they would consider moving to neighborhoods where African Americans live. The implication is clear. Based on what the well educated say, they should be less segregated from blacks than are other white Americans. But when we looked at where whites actually lived by educational level, even after controlling for many other factors, such as income, college-educated whites are actually more segregated from black Americans then are whites with less education. We also uncovered the exact same pattern for taking children out of public schools. Although highly educated whites express significantly more openness to their children attending racially integrated schools, when we look at their actual practices, they are significantly more likely to take their children out of public schools as the percentage of African Americans increases, again even after controlling for other differences. Their children are thus actually more likely to attend racially homogenous schools.

Why this pattern? It is not because well-educated whites are more prejudiced in the traditional sense. Rather, it is because they are better able to follow core American ideals—in this instance, a nice home in a quiet neighborhood with parks and good schools. In the racialized United States, this means ending up in "whiter" neighborhoods and schools. To reproduce racialization does not require "racism" or "prejudice" as they are typically defined.

In fact, the racialized society is reproduced in everyday actions and decisions. These are seen, as in past eras, as normal and acceptable, at least by white Americans.[15] As one example, although many Americans believe residential segregation by force of law is wrong (the Jim Crow method), they accept residential segregation by choice (the post-Civil Rights method). The methods differ, but the results—reproducing racialization—are the same.[16] Choice and freedom are two of the dominant American values that today maintain the racialized society. Contemporaries may view these values as the realization of America's destiny, but these values are at the same time now essential tools in dividing people along socially constructed racial lines.

IS THE UNITED STATES REALLY RACIALIZED?

When we speak of the racialized society, we mean primarily the black–white divide (or in some cases, the black–nonblack divide). This is not to suggest that other races and ethnicities in the United States do not matter, only that the gulf between American blacks and whites is generally more vast and the history longer in comparison to others. Noted race relations scholar Thomas Pettigrew argues that the African American–European American divide is unique "not only in the United States but in the world at large."[17] Further, for the Americans we interviewed, the black–white issue was clearly the one race issue at the forefront of their minds. And indeed, if we follow the definition of a racialized society, it is largely a black–white divide (or again, in some cases, black–nonblack). We can see this black–white divide by examining, among others, intermarriage rates, residential patterns, economic inequalities, health, dialects, racial classification, musical expressions, media reactions to controversial music, television viewing habits, and where Americans worship.

Consider, for one, racial divisions in marriage. Although up-to-date intermarriage rates are often difficult to obtain, due to scarce and incomplete records, careful estimates have been calculated. Studies of West Coast communities found that for marriages involving at least one Japanese American, 50 percent involved a non-Japanese American.[18] For Chinese Americans, estimates range from 20 to 45 percent marrying outside their group; and about 30 percent of married Korean Americans are married to non-Korean Americans.[19] Depending on how American Indian ancestry is measured, anywhere from 40 to 78 percent of married American Indians have non-Indian spouses.[20] But for blacks and whites, well over 90 percent of those who marry do so within their own racial group. Despite a doubling of the black–white marriage rate since 1980, only about 1 percent of black women and 3 percent of black men are interracially married.[21] All told, black–white marriages constitute less than one-half of one percent of existing marriages.[22] Clearly, when it comes to marriage, the black–white divide is the largest.

Residential integration and segregation studies continually show that the degree of segregation between blacks and nonblacks is far greater than between any other two racial groups in the United States.[23] Further, outside the South, the greater the percentage of African Americans in an area, the greater the level of segregation.[24] In other words, because limited contact with African Americans is preferred by most other Americans,[25] increasingly higher levels of segregation are needed as the proportion of African Americans increases. What is more, unlike other groups, whose level of segregation declines with increased socioeconomic status, no strong pattern emerges for African Americans.[26] Segregation is not merely separation but, in the contemporary United States, is hierarchical. Residential segregation by race, researchers show us, isolates African Americans, and concentrates poverty and social problems in their neighborhoods. This is more evidence of a black–white racialized society.

Economic inequality between blacks and whites is pervasive. Occupationally, white Americans tend to be concentrated in the prestigious, better-paying jobs, while black Americans tend to be clustered in low-prestige, lower-paying jobs. Black Americans are also much more likely to be unemployed. The current approximate ratio of two unemployed blacks for every one unemployed white has held nearly constant since 1950. In fact, the unemployment disparity is actually larger today than in 1950. Moreover, the method used for calculating unemployment underestimates the disparity, as the unemployed are only those without jobs who have actively sought a job within the last four weeks. Those who have simply dropped out of the workforce, often called discouraged workers, are not counted as unemployed. When we examine the percentages of discouraged workers by race, we again find a higher percentage of blacks than whites.

Average incomes of African Americans have always been less than the average income of white Americans. As of 1994, the median income of blacks was 62 percent that of whites. This was essentially unchanged from nearly thirty years earlier—the median income of blacks in 1967 was 59 percent of that of whites.[27] Lower average incomes likely lead to greater poverty rates, and indeed this is the case. Whereas less than one in eleven non-Hispanic whites fall below the poverty line, nearly one in three blacks do.

Although income is the most common way to compare racial economic inequality, in their award-winning book, *Black Wealth/White Wealth*, Melvin Oliver and Thomas Shapiro argue that wealth—what people own minus what they owe—is actually the more important measure. It is wealth and not income, they claim, that "is used to create opportunities, secure a desired stature and standard of living, or pass class status along to one's children." Wealth therefore comes "closer in meaning and theoretical significance to our traditional notions of economic well-being and access to life chances." Their research finds stunning disparities in wealth between blacks and whites, disparities that remain vast even when accounting for differences in education, occupation, parent's occupation, income, family type, and other factors.[28]

Using unique data from the Survey of Income and Program Participation, they measure household wealth in two ways: (1) as net worth, which is all assets minus all debts, and (2) net financial assets, which is net worth minus equity accrued in a home or vehicle. What did they find? The median net worth of blacks is just 8 percent of that of whites—3,700 dollars compared to 43,800 dollars—and the median net financial assets, shockingly, is 0 percent of that of whites—zero dollars compared to 7,000 dollars.

Shifting their focus just to middle-class Americans, Oliver and Shapiro demonstrate the very shaky footing of the black middle class. For example, median net financial assets for college-educated whites are nearly 20,000 dollars; for college-educated blacks, just 175 dollars. Without an asset pillar to stand on, the black middle class relies almost exclusively on income and job security. As the authors discovered in interviews with white and black Americans, a downturn in the economy or a change in marital status quickly sends significant numbers of the black middle class into lower classes. Whites, with their far superior assets, are able to survive such disruptions with little overall class-status change. In this case, it is true that when white America gets a cold, black America gets pneumonia.[29]

Table 1–1 summarizes white and black disparities already mentioned. It also contains comparisons for those in executive, managerial, and professional occupations, which we label as upper-white-collar occupations. We show both those who are in such occupations now and a separate category for those household heads who are in upper-white-collar occupations and whose parent household head was also in an upper white-collar occupation. Regardless of the comparison, the conclusion is the same. The inequality is expansive. So expansive in fact that even if all homes and vehicles were taken from white Americans, they would still, on average, have greater net worth than black Americans. To see this, compare black net worth to white net financial assets in Table 1-1.

Table 1–1

White and Black Household Median Net Worth and Net Financial Assets by Selected Characteristics (in Dollars)

	Median Net Worth		Median Net Financial Assets	
	White	*Black*	*White*	*Black*
Overall	43,800	3,700	7,000	0
Upper White-Collar Occupation (UWC)	66,800	12,303	15,150	5
UWC & Parents' UWC	70,850	17,499	16,420	5
College Graduate	74,922	17,437	19,823	175

Net Worth = Assets *minus* Debts
Net Financial Assets = Net Worth *minus* Housing and Vehicle Assets
Source: Oliver and Shapiro (1995), Tables 4.4, 5.1, 5.7, and 6.6

Health, life, and even death are racialized. For example, a study conducted by physicians Mark Wenneker and Arnold Epstein examined all circulatory disease and chest pain patients admitted to hospitals in Massachusetts. Examining patients by age, race, and income, the researchers found that whites were 89 percent more likely to be given coronary bypass surgery than blacks.[30] A nationwide study of Medicare patients revealed an even higher disparity.[31] White Americans were three times as likely as black Americans to receive this surgery.[32] Without apparent intention, doctors discriminated against African Americans and in favor of white Americans in recommending surgery. Other areas of health also diverge by race. For instance, African-American babies die at a rate over *twice* the frequency of white babies, African-American mothers are four times more likely to die in childbirth than white Americans, and young African-American males are six times more likely to be murdered than are young white American males.[33]

Because "race" is socially constructed, it is contested and redefined. A continuous struggle in the United States concerns the classification of new immigrants. Light-skinned immigrants, originally classified as distinct racial groups,[34] came over time and through challenge to be reclassified as white, even while maintaining some ethnic distinctives. Among dark-skinned immigrants from Africa, Latin America, and the Caribbean, the struggle is to avoid being labeled "black."[35] We witness this process on a micro level. An influx of Somalians and other east African immigrants into the city in which I [Emerson] live provides occasion for contact, and I see and hear their struggle to avoid categorization as African American. On one occasion, a Somalian—far darker-skinned than the vast majority of African Americans—requested a ride from my friend, saying three times, "I am not black." The Somalian's assumption—that he would not get a ride if he was defined as black—was learned quickly. In an attempt to heighten his life opportunities, he contests classification as an African American.

Musical expression for much of American history has been race-based, with different genres (pop, blues, classical, jazz, country, hip-hop, contemporary Christian, gospel) often being associated primarily with either black or white Americans. Moreover, the lyrical content of songs often has different foci. Thus, in an analysis of controversial songs from respective teenage languages of rebellion—heavy metal ("white music") and rap ("black music")—sociologist Amy Binder found a stark difference in lyrical content. As an example, for songs with an anti-authoritarian theme, she writes: "While heavy metal music lyrics stake a claim for the autonomy of the young person against school and adult officials, anti-authoritarian rap asserts independence from the authority of the police and white power structures in general."[36]

And we are racialized not just in the music and lyrics, but even in the arguments used when debating their possible harmfulness. Again comparing heavy metal and rap music, Binder identified large contrasts in the print media's coverage.[37] On the one hand, cognizant of the racial implications, the media were more likely to defend the validity of rap music as an art form containing important messages than they were heavy metal music. Yet, when rap music was criticized, the media used a very different set of arguments. For anti-heavy metal arguments, the corruption of it listeners' values and behavior and the need for parents to protect their children accounted for two-thirds of anti-heavy metal arguments (compared to just 14 percent using these arguments against rap). For rap, two-thirds of the stories cited the danger to society. As Binder develops the contrast:

> Because most writers considered rap lyrics to be even more explicit than heavy metal messages, rap lyrics should have been framed as even more harmful to their young audience. Yet, rather than warning the American public that a generation of young black children was endangered by musical messages, the writers argued that the American public at large would suffer at the hands of these listeners as a result of rap music.[38]

She concludes by pointing out that the need for writers to employ racial rhetoric in making their arguments "reflects the degree to which race shapes our understandings of the world." [39]

We can even see the racial separateness of the racialized society in television viewing patterns. This "high frequency" American activity reveals much about our society. Of the twenty most watched shows among black viewers in the 1995–96 season, only two—*NFL Monday Night Football* and *ER*—were also among the top twenty with white viewers. *ER* made it only by the skin of its teeth, however; it was number 1 among whites, number 20 among blacks. The second most watched television show for whites was *Seinfeld*; for blacks it was 89th. The three most popular shows among African Americans—*New York Undercover, Living Single,* and *The Crew*—were barely on the Caucasian map, with *New York Undercover* ranking 122nd and the other two tied for 124th. Black and white Americans largely watch and identify with separate stars, shows, humor, drama, and more. Further, as the availability of shows primarily starring African Americans has increased, so too has the separation in viewing habits. [40]

Finally, the racialized society is evident in religious affiliation choices. According to religion and race scholars Lincoln and Mamiya:

> Seven major black denominations account for more than 80 percent of black religious affiliation in the United States. ... Moreover, the remaining 15 to 20 percent of black Christians are scattered among numerous small black sects, the Roman Catholic Church, and the mainline white Protestant denominations. *The overwhelming majority of the latter are in predominantly black congregations,* despite denominational affiliation with white communions [emphasis added]. [41]

Although estimates for whites are harder to find, we can make them confidently, given the simple fact that in the case of groups of unequal size, the larger group must by definition be more separated from the smaller group than vice versa. Because about 90 percent of African Americans attend predominately black congregations, at least 95 percent of white Americans— and probably higher—attend predominately white churches. [42] The list of evidence for racialization could go on and on.

Writing in the 1830s, Alexis de Tocqueville, a French aristocrat and a student of American life, noted that whites and blacks were really two foreign communities. He predicted that if and when the slaves were freed, the black–white divide would only grow more intense. In his words, the danger of conflict between the two groups "perpetually haunts the imagination of Americans, like a painful dream." More than 100 years later, Gunnar Myrdal, in a massive study of American race relations, came to the same conclusion. America was really a divided society, divided primarily by white and black. In 1968, the President's Commission, in studying the urban riots of the mid-to-late 1960s, wrote that we are two separate societies. In 1992, social scientist Andrew Hacker's book *Two Nations* made the same claim. The book, whose subtitle is "Black and White, Separate, Hostile, Unequal," argues that "America may be seen as two separate nations. Of course, there are places where the races mingle. Yet in most significant respects, the separation is pervasive and penetrating. As a social and human division, it surpasses all others" (p. 3). In 1993, reviewing the state of the unequal racial divide twenty-five years after the Kerner Report, the Eisenhower Foundation Commission concluded that the assessment of the United States as "two societies, one black, one white—separate and unequal ... [is] more relevant today" than in 1968. The United States is indeed a racialized society, always was in the past, and in many respects is becoming more so.

RELIGION AND OVERCOMING THE RACIALIZED SOCIETY

Because our racialized society often both produces and reflects hostility, disorder, unequal treatment, misunderstanding, conflict, violence, compromised life opportunities, and other social ills, our nation has historically, with varying degrees of intensity, searched for ways to overcome it. Many believe religion is a potential force for overcoming the racialized society. Nearly all religions have spoken out against racial and ethnic division, and Christianity is no exception. In fact, the hundreds of Christians we interviewed echoed this repeatedly. If anyone should be doing something about the racialized society and if anyone has the answers to the race problem, they said it is Christians. Their religion calls for it, and their faith gives them the tools and moral force needed for change. And, as we saw earlier in the chapter and will see in much greater detail in Chapter Three, contemporary evangelicals are indeed engaged in a concerted effort to overcome racial division.

Viewed sociologically, religion is a set of beliefs and practices focused on the sacred or supernatural, through which life experiences of groups and individuals are given meaning and direction.[43] By helping to explain and give meaning to life as experienced in the here and now, religion's initial and primary thrust is conservative. Put another way, by providing significance and purpose to life as it is, religion provides legitimization for the world as it is. Why do we have earthquakes? The gods are angry. Why do we live in different castes? Our earthly position is determined by the character content of our prior lives. Why did I survive this crash but others did not? It was God's will. Why am I a poor factory worker? Your reward is yet to come; question not the ways of Providence. For these reasons, some view religion as merely a supporter of the status quo. Karl Marx's description of religion as an "opiate of the people" is perhaps the best-known example of this perspective.

But this view of religion is incomplete. Within the very forces able to render religion a legitimator of the world are revolutionary impulses able to change the world. Because religion is oriented not toward the mundane but toward the sacred or supernatural, it establishes a perceived objective reality above and beyond space and time. This reality acquires an independent and privileged position to act, through its believers, back on the mundane world. The seeds of change are planted in the faith. As Smith writes, "In this way, the ultimate legitimator of the status quo can easily become its ultimate judge. This dual potential lies precisely in the ultimacy and distance that characterizes sacred transcendence itself."[44] In this light, the answer to "Why am I a poor factory worker?" may come to be, "You should not be a poor factory worker, and we must work to change your condition, for our faith demands it." This change might range from increasing the training of the worker to a radical critique of the entire economic system. Emboldened by the sacred, religion can be a powerful source for change. And indeed, as part of what we examine in Chapter Two, religion has been a source for change in American race relations, from abolition to the Civil Rights movement. Thus, religion can provide the moral force for people to determine that something about their world so excessively violates their moral standards that they must act to correct it. It also can provide the moral force necessary for sustained, focused, collective action to achieve the desired goal.

Nevertheless, we argue that religion, as structured in America, is unable to make a great impact on the racialized society. In fact, far from knocking down racial barriers, religion generally serves to maintain these historical divides, and helps to develop new ones. Although this may seem to contradict the preceding paragraph, it does not. The structure of religion in America is conducive to freeing groups from the direct control of other groups, but not to addressing the fundamental divisions that exist in our current racialized society. In short, religion in the United States can serve as a moral force in freeing people, but not in bringing them together as equals across racial lines. American religion is thus one embodiment of larger American contradictions. The following chapters develop this argument.

Our Methods

We rely on a variety of data sources in writing this book, including much primary data we collected ourselves. We conducted a national telephone survey of more than 2,500 Americans, using random sampling methods.

This provided us with quantitative data for tables and comparison purposes. But we wanted to go further. We wanted to go to the homes of evangelicals to meet them, interview them, and learn more about their lives. To accomplish this, we traveled to twenty-three states, interviewing nearly 200 (mostly white) evangelicals.[45] This provided us with a mass of rich, qualitative, contextualized, nationally representative data. In addition to these data sources we draw on the General Social Survey, an annually conducted national sample of Americans with a wealth of race questions. We also draw on a variety of other sources that inform the issue at hand.

WHERE WE GO FROM HERE

Before examining contemporary evangelicals' views on race, we set the scene in Chapter Two by looking at how Christians, particularly evangelicals, have thought of race in the past, and what sorts of actions they have taken to address racial issues. Chapter Three describes the activities of post-Civil Rights-era evangelicals. We then look in detail at contemporary evangelical racial views. We listen to their voices, and put their words into a theoretical context. We ask evangelicals about the race problem, about racial inequality, and about solutions. We analyze their responses in light of the racialization framework explained above. We will see that the cultural tools evangelicals use, and their degree of isolation from other racial groups, shape how they explain and negotiate race relations in the United States.

Drawing on what we learn from Chapters Two through Six, Chapters Seven and Eight examine the role of religion more broadly, and, due to the nature of our task, in a more theoretical and abstract manner than previous chapters. We first show, in Chapter Seven, how the organization of American religion leads to racially segregated congregations. In Chapter Eight, we argue that the very processes that make religion strong in the United States simultaneously contribute to racialization. No "racism" in the traditional sense is needed or intended. In understanding this, and the findings from the previous chapters, we come to learn more about the contradiction that is America.

2

From Separate Pews to Separate Churches

Evangelical Racial Thought and Practice, 1700–1964

We begin our quest to understand race and religion in America by venturing back to before the dawning of the new American nation. If history is our greatest teacher, then we are wise to attend to it. Starting in 1700, we will survey 265 years of history, bringing us to the passage of the Civil Rights Act. Our survey is necessarily quick. We only highlight key patterns and thoughts along the way.

Traversing history, we find some common markers. Because evangelicals view their primary task as evangelism and discipleship,[1] they tend to avoid issues that hinder these activities. Thus, they are generally not counter-cultural. With some significant exceptions, they avoid "rocking the boat," and live within the confines of the larger culture. At times they have been able to call for and realize social change, but most typically their influence has been limited to alterations at the margins. So, despite having the subcultural tools to call for radical changes in race relations, they most consistently call for changes in persons that leave the dominant social structures, institutions, and culture intact. This avoidance of boat-rocking unwittingly leads to granting power to larger economic and social forces. It also means that evangelicals' views to a considerable extent conform to the socioeconomic conditions of their time. Evangelicals usually fail to challenge the system not just out of concern for evangelism, but also because they support the American system and enjoy its fruits. They share the Protestant work ethic, support laissez-faire economics, and sometimes fail to evaluate whether the social system is consistent with their Christianity.

THE EARLY PROVINCIAL PERIOD: 1700–1730

Traditionally, white Christians paid little attention to slaves' souls. The pre-1700 views that black slaves were less than fully human, did not possess souls, and were incapable of learning, as well as simple indifference by white Christians all led to a lack of interest in proselytizing slaves. During the early provincial period in America, however, this began to change.

As we will see, for many Anglos, "Christianizing" slaves came to be seen as a Christian responsibility. However, outside of some Quakers and a few scattered others, almost no Anglos before the start of the eighteenth century—slave owner or not, Christian or non-Christian—questioned the validity of slavery as an institution. As historian Lester Scherer put it, "In Christian life and thought the accommodation with slavery was almost complete." Let us examine this more closely.[2]

From the European perspective, the settling of the vast "virgin" lands of North America required much effort. Many Anglos came to believe, once they saw its advantages, that slavery was indispensable for survival and for producing an agricultural surplus for export. In many eyes, originally in the South and to a lesser extent in the North, the growing prosperity of the provinces needed to move forward on the backs of African slaves. Christians certainly shared this view, and did not see slavery as harmful. According to one clergyman: "To live in Virginia without slaves is morally impossible." This perceived necessity for slaves influenced Christian doctrine on the issue. For white ministers and commoners alike, at least in the South and border states, "a deep feeling of the misery of life without enslaved blacks often provided the hidden premise of theological and ethical statements about slavery."[3]

Thus, more and more Africans were imported to the American colonies, such that during this period the African slave population grew at a rate three times faster than the population as a whole. By 1750, about 20 percent of the American population was African or of African descent (compared to about 13 percent today). The slaves' growing presence in and importance for "the American way of life" led to some changes in the thinking and activities of Christians: the new call to Christianize slaves and, fearful of revolts, an increased emphasis on order.

In a stance then seen as enlightened and humane, clergymen combined spiritual equality with temporal inequality. Some clergy began claiming that for Anglos to neglect the spiritual welfare of slaves revealed their ignorance of Christ, and shirked Christian responsibility. Cotton Mather, a New England Congregational minister and perhaps the best known of the early advocates for African-American Christianization, put it this way: "How canst thou Love thy Negro, and be willing to see him ly under the Rage of Sin, and the Wrath of God?" Mather was so convinced of this position that he published pamphlets on the need to Christianize, and in his home hosted the "Society of Negroes," a Sunday-night gathering of worship and a sermon meant to convert the attending Africans.

The push to convert slaves was not well received among many masters, or even among non-slave owners. Objections ranged from the older ideas that Africans did not have eternal souls to their inability to learn the Christian faith. But the major objections centered around preserving the social order. If slaves were Christianized, this could mean automatic freedom or slave revolts.

Originally unwritten was the rule that in accepting Christ and being baptized, the slave was freed not only from sin, but also from slavery. This was rather troublesome to the Anglos who thought about such things, as they felt it impossible to realize their vision without slave labor. The clergy, being part of the same sociocultural environment and eager to see Christianizing take place, quickly stepped in to refute and change this perceived custom. Their strategy was threefold. First, beginning as early as 1664, and increasingly during the first quarter of the eighteenth century, they encouraged several colonial legislatures to declare that slaves remained slaves even when baptized. They also had Anglican Bishop George Berkeley request a formal statement from Britain's Attorney General and Solicitor General. In 1729, both replied that baptism did not negate slave status within the British kingdom. Third, clergymen argued that Christian liberty in no way changed temporal bondage. In a widely distributed 1727 letter to American planters, Anglican Bishop Gibson declared that "Christianity, and the embracing of the Gospel, does not make the least Alteration in Civil Relations." Cotton Mather forcefully argued that the Bible did not give Christian slaves the right to liberty. Just as forcefully, he argued that neither the canons of the church nor the English constitution made a connection between Christianization and temporal freedom. Indeed, slavery was an advantageous institution: because the slaves were viewed as heathens, enslavement provided them "the opportunity to cast off their heathenism and embrace the Christian religion," with no concomitant change in temporal status.[4]

But some Anglos also objected that Christianization would lead to slave revolts. If slaves were Christianized, they would gain new, and in Anglos' minds, inappropriate attitudes that could be used to stir up revolts. Chief among these were insubordination, pride, and impudence. Again, the clergy countered with fast and decisive counterarguments. If slaves were Christianized, they argued, they would in fact adopt attitudes quite the opposite. They would be humble, gentle, hard working, and obedient. As the Presbyterian minister Samuel Davies said, "There never was a good Christian yet who was a bad Servant." And to ensure such a result, the clergy preached this to the Africans. Indeed, from what records exist, these ideas were even incorporated in baptismal vows. Ordained missionary Francis LeJau's baptismal vow for slaves, for example, read in part:

> You declare in the presence of God and before this congregation that you do not ask for the holy baptism out of any design to free yourself from the Duty and Obedience you owe to your Master while you live, but merely for the good of Your soul and to partake of the Graces and Blessings promised to the Members of the Church of Jesus Christ.

When a black freeman was to be hanged in 1721 for murdering his wife, Cotton Mather first gave a sermon. Turning to the slaves, he said: "There is a fondness for Freedom in many of you, who live Comfortably in a very easy Servitude." Because God had divinely ordained their places, he said, they must not try to alter it. They must view their position with humbleness, patience, and sweet contentment, for in return for serving their masters, all their needs were cared for. Pride is the enemy that led this black freeman down the wrong path, and it is pride that tempts slaves to desire the freedom God did not ordain for them. Then, just before the hanging, he told the slaves: "Pride goeth before Destruction."

But a few of the clergy went further. Not only did Christianity make slaves better slaves, they argued, it did not in any way hinder owners from using whatever means necessary to obtain compliance. When Bishop Gibson wrote on the issue, he declared that if a slave behaved badly, Christianity did not remove from masters "any proper Methods of enforcing Obedience." The church allowed any degree of "strictness and severity" necessary to maintain mastery. Whether their slaves were baptized or not, owners had the authority to determine the necessary punishment in instances of insubordination.

Thus, in an effort to garner support for Christianizing activities, the clergy not only reaffirmed the appropriateness of slavery as an institution, but gave it cosmic status, solidifying its position in America. Moreover, they unintentionally laid the groundwork for the more advanced nineteenth-century pro-slavery biblically-based doctrines. As theologian Ernst Troeltsch concluded, the "teachings and practice of the church constituted one of the main sanctions for [slavery's] perpetuation." [5]

White Christians, like others, craved order and feared chaos. In colonial America, order meant subduing one-fifth of the population for the good of the other four-fifths. Thus, white Christians partook in a whole range of activities to preserve order: "Christians along with others rode patrol, served as constables, administered the whippings, and generally maintained the private tyranny by which whites asserted their mastery." Just as significantly, in the effort to Christianize the slaves, the gospel came to be a significant force for social control. This influence flowered even further in the following century.

All the Christianizing discussion and efforts did not translate into many conversions among slaves until the middle of the eighteenth century. A few embraced the message, but the vast majority did not. The Christianization of slaves became more successful, however, with the introduction of revivalist evangelicalism.[6]

THE EVANGELICAL GREAT AWAKENING

Evangelicalism took firm root in America with the spread of the Great Awakening. Starting in the middle colonies in the 1720s under the influence of people such as Gilbert Tennent, it gained full force in the late 1730s and early 1740s when English evangelist George Whitefield traveled the provinces with his emotion-stirring revivals, garnering support from the learned Massachusetts minister Jonathan Edwards, among others. By all accounts, George Whitefield was a major force in early American history. Religious historian Sydney Ahlstrom deemed him the "hero-founder" of American evangelicalism, and according to historian George Marsden, "the first media star in American history."[7] According to sociologists Roger Finke and Rodney Stark, Whitefield "was quite simply one of the most powerful and moving preachers ever to hold forth."[8] Whitefield, it is said, could seize the attention of a crowd simply by pronouncing "Mesopotamia." Even the reserved rationalist Ben Franklin was entranced. Describing Whitefield's preaching as sweet music, he told of attending a sermon meant to raise funds for Whitefield's Georgia orphanage. As Franklin relates, "I perceived he intended to finish with a collection, and I silently resolved he should get nothing from me." He continued listening to the sermon, and as the sweet music of Whitefield's preaching played, he began to soften. After a full portion of brilliant, moving oratory, the author of the famous aphorism "A fool and his money are soon parted" wrote: "[Whitefield] finished so admirably that I emptied my pockets wholly into the collectors dish, gold and all."[9]

As the "founder" of American evangelicalism, George Whitefield is an important figure for our purposes. He embodies some of the contradictions we will see in present-day evangelicals—well-intentioned, but adapting the message to fit the sociocultural, racialized context—and he embodies early white evangelicals' views on race. Perhaps even more strongly than Cotton Mather, Whitefield supported the Christianizing of slaves. In 1740, in a widely circulated pamphlet, George Whitefield asked: Are your children "any way better by Nature than the poor Negroes? No, in no wise. Blacks are just as much, and no more, conceived and born in Sin, as White Men are. Both, if born and bred up here, I am persuaded, are naturally capable of the same [religious] improvement." When Whitefield conducted revivals, he preached to both whites and blacks. After revival meetings in Philadelphia in 1740, Whitefield wrote that "near fifty negroes came to give me thanks for what God had done to their souls" and that he had witnessed African Americans who were "exceedingly wrought upon under the Word preached." [10] The evangelical strain of Christianity was congenial to African heritages, with its emotive emphasis, its non-hierarchical structure, its stress on the superiority of the spiritual over the temporal, and its promise that the last shall be first. [11] As a result of the message shared by Whitefield and other evangelical preachers, "Negros began entering the churches in much larger and accelerating numbers." [12]

At the same time that Whitefield preached his message of radical equality in Christ, and shared the salvation message with slaves, he was a supporter of slavery. According to Wood, he was convinced that for the heathen Africans, "bondage was their best insurance for salvation." [13] What is more, in an open letter to planters in the colonies, Whitefield urged kinder treatment of slaves, but noted that cruelty can have the positive effect of heightening "the sense of their natural misery," thereby increasing receptivity to the Christian message.

Whitefield also shared a strong concern for the economic success of the colonies, particularly the newest, Georgia. Settled circa 1735 as the last of the English colonies, Georgia initially prohibited slavery. This was not due to any question about the propriety of slavery. Rather, it was due to the fear that the competition of slave labor might inhibit the immigration of Anglos, who were viewed as the only reliable defenders of the colony in the event of war. [14] Whitefield's orphanage was located in Georgia and he, like others, worried that it could not develop without slaves. He testified before Parliament in 1741 in support of the introduction of slavery in Georgia. In a published report, Whitefield asked for the use of slaves at the orphanage to which Ben Franklin had contributed his money. Highlighting the prospects for Georgia, he wrote that if the trustees "should see good hereafter to grant a limited Use of Negroes, it must certainly, in all outward appearance, be as flourishing a colony as South Carolina." He further petitioned for the introduction of slaves by arguing that God had created the Georgia climate for blacks, that the large investment in the colony would be lost without increased production, that the orphanage would not survive without the benefit of slaves, and, consistent with his calling, the unsaved would become saved.

Whitefield believed strongly in this last point. From his perspective, God allowed slavery for larger purposes, including the Christianization and uplifting of the heathen Africans. "How much better must their condition be, when disposed of in a [C]hristian country, where they are treated with mildness and humanity, and required to perform no more than that portion of labor which in some way or other is the common lot of the human race." [15] In 1747–48, when the orphanage he co-founded bought slaves (in defiance of the exclusion), Whitefield, according to Wood, became a slave owner himself. In 1749, in part due to the efforts of Whitefield, the slave exclusion was repealed. By that time, white Georgia Christians had united under Whitefield's message.[16]

Should any doubt the validity of their pro-slavery beliefs, anecdotal evidence from slaves could be mustered. For example, a slave named William Grimes, wanting to avoid joining a new master in Georgia, prayed that God would allow him to break his leg so he might be left behind. After striking the leg with an ax, and finding the leg fully intact, Grimes wrote: "I then prayed to God that if it was his will that I should go, that I might willingly." And go willingly he did. This was not an isolated example. As Frederick Douglass later wrote, "I have met many religious colored people … who are under the delusion that God requires them to submit to slavery and to wear chains with meekness and humility." [17]

Efforts to evangelize, we have seen, led Christians to support the wider racialized status quo. To challenge the very foundations of the larger system was simply not part of their worldview. Further, as Berger, among others, notes, the connection between cultural and religious legitimation is often strong.[18] To overturn slavery was seen as going against God's ordained pattern.

THE NEW NATION: 1770–1830

The Revolutionary War's seeds of change did more than lead to a revolt against the British motherland. The very ideology used to justify the war also resulted for some in a new perspective on slavery. It is not enough, it was argued, to Christianize slaves. The rhetoric and ideology used to muster support for the revolutionary war—both political and theological—made American slavery itself seem problematic to many. Indeed, in a few short decades, most northern states had outlawed slavery, and in 1808 slave importation was abolished nationwide.

As Revolutionary leaders such as deist Thomas Jefferson and evangelical Patrick Henry began to question the contradiction between the institution of slavery and the American rhetoric of a right to freedom from the "slavery" of British rule, other evangelicals began to see slavery as "an emblem of colonial iniquity" [19] and a sin against God. In 1770, a Baptist preacher in Massachusetts claimed that in permitting slavery, "We, the patrons of liberty, have dishonored the Christian name, and degraded human nature nearly to a level with the beasts." [20]

The reasons why evangelicals came to question slavery during this time are complicated. First were the emerging theological interpretations that race-based slavery was wrong. The logic of the Revolutionary War, with its rhetorical reliance on the natural rights of man, and the subsequent need to account for differences in humans by use of social explanations, as opposed to being simply created by God, were also significant. These factors channeled "the religious ideal of equality toward reconsideration of the Negro's external status." [21] Just as significant, the economic need to build a new land on the backs of Africans, never as strong in the North as the South, was now almost completely absent in the North and declining in the upper South. Changes in the mode of economic production and demand for slave labor allowed for a change in the view of slavery. Because the African-American population was quite small in the North, never greater than 3 percent during this time, the fear of revolts and "being overtaken" was not strong. Evangelicals who had theological doubts about the validity of race-based slavery rooted their objections in biblical terms. By situating their position within the cosmic order, and calling for repentance from oppression based on Old Testament themes, their developing antislavery appeals conveyed a sense of the supernatural that was absent from the arguments of most other critics. [22] Slavery must be challenged, or God would demand retribution.

Most early antislavery activists were typically religious. The first formally organized society against slavery was founded in the City of Brotherly Love in 1775, and the first national organization was founded in 1794. Just what was the stance of early antislavery activists? Historians of this era consistently mention certain dominant themes. Owing in part to their relatively high social standing and in part to their religious sensibilities, they were moderates and gradualists. They hoped to end slavery, but in due time. Thus, when proposals were made and laws were passed, they typically called for the freeing of the next generation of slaves or manumission at some future date or when slaves reached a certain age. The early slavery opponents had no intention of violating property rights, and were set on reimbursing slaveholders for loss of property. As the use of the term "property" indicates, they were not full-fledged egalitarians, continuing to see blacks as in-

ferior or as not part of American society. The early white abolitionists opposed slavery but not racialization. They were uncomfortable with these
strange Africans, and, to put it bluntly, wished them to go away. With, from
their perspective, benevolence in their hearts, they worked to make African
Americans literally go away through the colonization societies with the goal
of sending freed slaves to colonies in Africa.

The early antislavery activists were moderates and gradualists for another important reason. They believed that the mission of the church, seen
as evangelizing and discipling, must come first. Evangelicals of this time—
and most other Americans—held that by changing individuals, social
problems would eventually dissipate. Thus, only to emphasize abolishing
slavery directly was misguided. Jedidiah Morse, speaking at a celebration
for the 1808 abolition of slave trade, nicely captured the early abolitionist
perspectives. Although Africa was in "heathenish and Mahometan dark-
ness," God had enabled white men to transport those Africans who were to
receive Christ's freedom. "But since the blessed gospel now sheds its genial
influence on Africa, by the preaching of the missionaries of the cross, its na-
tives have no need to be carried to foreign lands, in order to enjoy its light;
and God hath shut the door against their further transportation." And what
of those remaining in temporal bondage in the United States? According to
Essig, "A direct and immediate assault on slavery was unnecessary, he believed, for it would be abolished gradually by the diffusion of gospel principles through America. ... In his enthusiasm for African missions, his stress
on evangelism at home, and his acquiescence to the prolonged existence of
slavery in America, Morse accurately mirrored attitudes that prevailed
among many white evangelicals in the North." [23] We therefore see, for example, that though the 1818 Presbyterian General Assembly said slavery
was "utterly inconsistent with the law of God," they also were sympathetic
to slaveholders, whom they perceived to be trapped in a moral dilemma
(and who of course were indeed caught in a moral dilemma, although one
of their own making). Thus, they recommended that slave owners support
the colonization society, give religious instruction, and, to the degree possible, avoid cruel treatment of slaves.[24] At this very same assembly, a decision
was also upheld to dispose of a Presbyterian minister due to his antislavery
views, largely because they were deemed too radical.

Early evangelical abolitionists were conciliatory in tone, not wanting to
raise too much ruckus for fear of hurting the main mission of the church
and upsetting the social order. "They avoided passionate denunciations or
the reciting of atrocity stories. They avowed that their plans were of a pacific
nature and that any opposition to slaveholders was opposition to a brother
rather than to an enemy," and seemed to go out of their way to win the es-
teem of southerners.[25] Indeed, so conciliatory were their tones, so mild

their requests, that many white southerners felt comfortable in the abolitionist movement. Not until the tones became stronger and the call for the
end of slavery more immediate, more directly threatening the southern
economic and social order, did many white southerners remove themselves
from abolitionist societies.

The success of the early movement was actually minimal and it lost mo-
mentum after the 1808 prohibition on slave importation. The quest for
changed hearts and more Christian behaviors was largely subverted by economic and political realities. "The Northern states had all but abandoned
slavery, it is true, but the chief reason had been the availability of a free labor
supply which made bonded labor unprofitable. The early abolitionists created no general sentiment against slavery." [26] In the upper South, where
antislavery sentiment was initially strong, "Both the churches and politicians soon found that they would lose their constituencies if they took a
strong stance. In the deep South, more economically dependent on the slavery system, abolitionism never had a chance." [27] In short, the "brotherly reconciliation approach" of the early abolitionists found itself overrun by
growing sectional divisions and economic interests. [28]

Thus, as the Revolutionary rhetoric faded, many white evangelicals saw
nothing intrinsically wrong with slaveholding, and believed that the more
obvious abuses of the system would dissipate with the conversion of masters and slaves. Further, they saw the push for major change as harmful to
the central mission of the church: "Many of these same figures regarded
antislavery agitation as the chief threat to the peace and prosperity of the
church. The evil of slaveholding had become a closed subject, an extrane-
ous issue, a highly sensitive matter, anything but a pressing concern." [29] This
too, however, eventually changed.

THE NATION DIVIDES: 1830–1865

In thinking on the millennium, the expected 1,000-year reign by Christ, the
idea was popular that Christians needed to pave the way for Christ's return.
This was fueled by the spread of theological postmillennialism, the belief
that society must move closer and closer to a pure Christian civilization
and, when it reaches near perfection, then Christ will indeed return. This
millennial expectancy and close connection with civilization fueled evangelical vigor to save the lost *and* to reform society, and movement toward
reform fueled millennial expectancy. These fed the desire to create a Christian America.

A Christian nation was one where not only individuals were Christian,
but Christian morality infused every sector and institution of an orderly society. Hopes ran high during the period that Christians, through the appli-

cation of Christian principles, could soon usher in the millennial period. However, in the evangelical pursuit for a Christian America, a sharp thorn gouged their sides:

> The Protestant forces displayed their most serious inner weaknesses in confronting the fact of slavery in America. Over the slavery issue, the evangelical crusade for a Christian America sharply divided. Evangelicals who shared much of the same Christian vision for their country encountered an obstacle that split them apart, and on the fundamental moral issue of human freedom.[30]

Evangelicals, directed and energized by the same faith in common pursuit of a Christian America, diverged in their definitions of what a Christian America was. Northerners came to see it as a society without slavery, southerners as a society with slavery. Several things hardened these positions. These included the fear of slave revolts, heightened by the 1831 Nat Turner insurrection in which nearly sixty Anglos were killed, the continued economic advantages of slavery in the South, and the rise of more radical abolitionists in the North.

In the 1830s, a new breed of abolitionists arose, many of whom were driven by evangelical fervor for a Christian America. This new generation of abolitionists differed from the earlier generation in significant ways. They stood for uncompensated emancipation, rejected colonization, and were "immediatists": "'We shall spare no exertions nor means to bring the whole nation to speedy repentance,' ran one of the resolutions adopted at the first meeting of the American Anti-Slavery Society in December of 1833 at Philadelphia. Thus did abolitionism take on a new character, a direct confrontation—not a flank attack—on slavery." [31]

The new abolitionists sounded a harsher note, calling slaveholders child-sellers, women-whippers, and thieves, and America a liar and a disgrace to humanity. They were more broad-based as well, enlisting the support of grassroots evangelicals. Theodore Weld adapted the revivalist techniques of his mentor, Charles Finney, to win converts to the cause. He traveled the country, holding "protracted meetings" climaxing in the "call to decision" to the antislavery cause, leaving behind new followers to uphold the cause.[32] As part of this broader movement, preexisting organizations such as tract and cent societies took up the antislavery cause. Cent societies, formed by church women, evolved from religious and benevolent organizations to workers for antislavery, obtaining one-cent-a-week pledges from congregational members for the movement.[33]

The new breed of abolitionists also differed in another significant way: they included free African Americans in their societies. Well-known figures, such as Frederick Douglass, Harriet Tubman, Sojourner Truth, and scores of others played vital roles in the movement. Free black Americans worked for slavery's demise as members in both white-dominated and separate black abolitionist societies, making financial contributions, working in the underground railroad, speaking, and writing. African American David Walker, a former North Carolinian who moved to Boston and became a member of the Massachusetts General Colored Association (and whose son was elected to the Massachusetts legislature in 1866), published David Walker's Appeal, a 76-page pamphlet that appeared in three editions in 1829 and 1830. Mincing no words, he said that blacks must and shall be as free as white Americans, asking white America, "Will you wait until we shall, under God, obtain our liberty by the crushing arm of power?" The pamphlet caused a major stir. It prompted North Carolina and Georgia to outlaw "incendiary publications" and led the governor of Georgia and mayor of Savannah to send protest letters to Boston's mayor. In the South, African Americans, many of whom regarded it as an inspired work, were sometimes arrested for distributing it. A contemporary author, Samuel J. May, wrote that "the excitement which had become so general and so furious against the Abolitionists throughout slaveholding States was owing in no small measure to... David Walker." [34] The pamphlets' reputation among southern whites, and some northern whites as well, was made even more infamous by the 1831 Nat Turner revolt.

As the rhetoric became more inflammatory and southerners dug in, trouble began in the abolitionist ranks. In 1839, a split occurred between the more radical and largely non-evangelical abolitionists, led by William Garrison, and the more moderate evangelicals, such as Arthur and Lewis Tappan. Moreover, a number of evangelicals disavowed the movement, including the leading revivalist of the time, Charles Finney. His positions, representative of many evangelicals, are worth exploring in more detail.

Finney's contribution to the abolitionist movement was substantial. He supplied the theological framework—stressing the need for the devout to engage in social reform—and the revivalistic impulse for opposition to slavery.[35] That is, he made opposition to slavery an aspect of Christian discipleship. Many of the prominent abolitionists were influenced by him. Finney not only preached the evil of slaveholding, but was one of the first to use his pulpit to prohibit slaveholders from taking communion, claiming that those who owned slaves were not Christians.

But his views were complicated by his primary concern for evangelism. Anything that interfered with this needed to be put aside. Finney came to see the abolitionist movement—with its increasingly inflammatory rhetoric, its focus first and foremost on slavery as a key sin, and its eventual mixing of antislavery with support for the amalgamation of the races—as a cause that had grown too big, and one that incorrectly relegated preaching the gospel to a secondary role. Simply put, abolition was a detriment to evangelism. Failing to convince abolitionists to mend their ways, Finney became estranged from the movement.[36] Lesick summarized his positions:

> Finney considered slavery a sin, but asserted that there should be no "diversion of the public mind" from the task of converting people and inculcating their minds with "the gospel." In addition, he believed racial prejudice was not a sin and that advocating "amalgamation" contradicted the goal of "benevolence," diverted public attention from the very real sin of slave holding, led to attacks on free blacks, and disrupted the churches.[37]

Here we see the complexity of thinking about racialized America. Finney's evangelical faith seemed to demand a degree of moderation on the issue and avoidance of issues that would hinder conversions and the unity of congregations. This gives us insight into the position of lay evangelicals in the North. If the well-educated and progressive Finney willingly spoke out against slavery, but not racial prejudice and segregation, it is reasonable to suppose that grassroots evangelicals, though perhaps viewing slavery as wrong, were often prejudiced, continued to view African Americans as inferior, and were generally opposed to integration of the races. Although calling for a people to be freed, they did not call for an end to racialization. This allowed for a new form of racial inequality to spring forth after slavery's demise. Specifically, by calling for an end to slavery but not racial division, the table was set for a large serving of Jim Crow.

Slavery was viewed by many as a separate issue from the larger race question, and most ordinary, lay evangelicals as well as the bulk of abolitionists easily made this distinction (some of the Lane Rebels, including Theodore Weld, were exceptions). Again Finney gives us insight. As he wrote to his formerly close but now estranged friend Arthur Tappan, a supporter of integration:

> You err in supposing that the principle of abolition and amalgamation are identical. Abolition is a question of flagrant and unblushing wrong. A direct and outrageous violation of fundamental right. The other is a question of prejudice that does not necessarily deprive any man of any positive right.[38]

As with his stance on slavery, Finney also applied his other racial beliefs. He opposed the election of black church trustees, claiming it was inexpedient. In his church, blacks and whites were segregated. Lewis Tappen, a leading evangelical abolitionist and member of Finney's New York City church in the early 1830s, was unable to succeed in allowing people to sit in church where they chose, regardless of color. He took issue with Finney: "Finding nothing could be done in a matter so near to my heart I left the church." [39]

Our present point is that although some of the more outspoken abolitionists were evangelical, most evangelicals were not outspoken abolitionists. Thus, on the whole, northern evangelicals did not differ from southern evangelicals in their racial views, except that they tended to oppose slavery. This was easily done, in that slavery did not exist in the North. They were thus not particularly visionary or radical on the matter.

> When immediate abolitionism reared its head in the major denominations in the 1830s and 1840s, moderate and conservative leaders in the North joined southerners in reaffirming that emancipation was not an essential part of the Christian gospel. Northern church leaders balked, however, when southerners demanded an explicit sanction on slaveholding, a demand which contributed to the sectional division of Methodist and Baptist denominations. Down to the eve of the Civil War, a number of northern evangelicals remained wedded to the idea that slavery would disappear as an indirect result of revivalism.[40]

The crevice of difference widened over time, as it led Methodists to divide by region in 1844, Baptists in 1845, New School Presbyterians in 1857, and Old School Presbyterians in 1861. Other denominations also experienced severe tensions, but without strong national constituencies were able to avoid formal division. With the splits came a hardened, more fully developed defense of positions that further expanded the divide. Cole and others have suggested that the religious language of moral righteousness, no compromise, and the placing of these issues in the timeless, changeless cosmic order deepened and widened the division.[41] Having here examined the northern abolitionists, we turn to a brief look at the southern slavery supporters.

Southern Evangelical Religion and Slavery: 1830–1865

Not until the second quarter of the nineteenth century, and largely in response to the new breed of abolitionists, did southern whites invoke the Bible and Christian ideals in a systematic defense of slavery.[42] In a mix of culture and religion, southern whites developed a variety of pro-slavery arguments. These arguments ranged from biblical, to charitable, to evangelistic, to social, to political. The Bible, the defenders argued, does not oppose slavery and in fact, by direct and indirect precept, supports it. Moreover, the chief mission of the church is evangelization and discipleship and slavery allows for the Christianization, spiritual growth, and humane treatment of people who otherwise would miss out on salvation. According to one argument, the curse of Ham, recorded in the book of Genesis, rendered Africans an inferior race, and it is a Christian responsibility to protect and provide for them. In light of their inferiority and inability to control themselves, slavery allows for social order, and limits crime and vice that would other-

Figure 2.1
Originally from Christian History, *vol. 11, no 1., page 24, 1992. Reprinted with permission of Christian History, a product of Christianity Today, Inc.*

WHY CHRISTIANS SHOULD SUPPORT SLAVERY
Key reasons advanced by southern church leaders

Many southern Christians felt that slavery, in one Baptist minister's words, "stands as an institution of God." Here's why:

Biblical reasons

▸Abraham, the "father of faith," and all the patriarchs held slaves without God's disapproval (Gen 21:9–10).

▸Canaan, Ham's son, was made a slave to his brothers (Gen 9:24–27).

▸The Ten Commandments mention slavery twice, showing God's implicit acceptance of it (Ex 20:10, 17).

▸Slavery was widespread throughout the Roman world, and yet Jesus never spoke against it.

▸The apostle Paul specifically commanded slaves to obey their masters (Eph 6:5–8).

▸Paul returned a runaway slave, Philemon, to his master (Philem 12).

Charitable and evangelistic reasons

▸Slavery removes people from a culture that "worshipped the devil, practiced witchcraft and sorcery" and other evils.

▸Slavery brings heathens to a Christian land where they can hear the gospel. Christian masters provide religious instruction for their slaves.

▸Under slavery, people are treated with kindness, as many northern visitors can attest.

▸It is in slaveholders' own interest to treat their slaves well.

Social reasons

▸Just as women are called to play a subordinate role (Eph 5:22; 1 Tim 2:11–15), so slaves are stationed by God in their place.

▸Slavery is God's means of protecting and providing for an inferior race (suffering the "curse of Ham" in Gen 9:25 or even the punishment of Cain in Gen 4:12).

▸Abolition would lead to slave uprisings, bloodshed, and anarchy. Consider the mob's "rule of terror" during the French Revolution.

Political reasons

▸Christians are to obey civil authorities, and those authorities permit and protect slavery.

▸The church should concentrate on spiritual matters, not political ones.

▸Those who support abolition are, in James H. Thornwell's words, "atheists, socialists, communists [and] red republicans."

— *The Editors*

wise occur. Further, Christians should obey the law, which permitted and protected slavery, and not get involved in merely temporal matters such as slavery abolition.

In the South, with the regional system of slavery and a much larger percentage of African Americans, whites and blacks actually had much more interpersonal contact than they had in the North. Unlike after the war, this included contact in churches, where "black and white co-worshippers heard the same sermon, were baptized into communion together, and upon death were buried in the same cemeteries." [43] In addition to hearing the same sermons that whites did, slaves often received a special sermon extolling them to perform well in their God-chosen role, for which they would be rewarded with eternal life. As Sarah Fitzpatrick, an elderly former slave, recounted in a 1938 interview:

> Us "Niggers" had our meetin' in de white fo'ks Baptist church in de town o' Tuskeegee. Dere's a place up in de loft, dere now dat dey built fer de "Nigger" slaves to 'tend church wid de white fo'ks. White preacher he preached to de white fo'ks n' when he git 'thu wid dem he preached some to de "Niggers." Tell em to mind dere master and behave dey self an' dey'll go to hebben when dey die.[44]

Not only did southern white Christians see slavery as acceptable and even commendable, but many owned slaves themselves. In fact, in the year before the Methodist split, 25,000 members owned 208,000 slaves; 1,200 Methodist clergy were slaveholders. From 1846 until the Civil War, every man who achieved the rank of bishop within the Methodist Episcopal Church, South, was a slaveholder.[45] Other southern denominations had similar profiles. Slavery was clearly part of the southern vision for an orderly and virtuous Christian America with limited central government. In their eyes, slavery was part of a Christian society purer than the aggressive and economically and socially oppressive North.

Thus, we see that the evangelical faith motivated racial beliefs and practices, but that the common faith was expressed within the dominant social milieu, giving it different emphases. According to Marsden, "social and economic factors made it easier for the dominant classes in the North to follow further what they professed concerning human rights than most white Southerners. White Southerners' social and economic circumstances forced them to emphasize the parts of their heritage that stressed the importance of good order." [46] Forrest Wood put the church's role even more strongly:

> Cynical though it may sound, it is not an exaggeration to submit that the critical fact in determining who opposed slavery and who supported it was, with every church that claimed a national constituency, a consequence entirely of

political and economic factors. All of the Christian conviction in the world could not dent the purse of one slaveholder.[47]

Ironically, with their slavery positions firmly entrenched, backed by evangelical vigor on both sides, and both working for a Christian America, war was the only resolution to a permanent schism between northerners and southerners. For years people had warned that not to resolve the slavery issue would lead to bloodshed. History proved them right.

NEW FORM, SIMILAR RESULT: 1865–1917

Nearly 100 years of working for abolition through changed hearts and voluntary means failed. Likewise, the extensive arguments showing slavery's consistency with the Christian mission convinced few northerners. It took war, the ultimate show of force and nonvolunteerism, to settle the slavery question. But as many suspected would be the case, the old slavery was, after a period of unsettledness, simply replaced with a new, in many ways similar, institution. Further, while northerners questioned and even challenged de jure segregation, their own lands were increasingly replete with de facto segregation, making their criticisms ring hollow and, indeed, limiting their critique.

Slavery as an institution ended with the war, but the former slaves remained. What should be done with "them" remained a question. As late as the month of his death, Abraham Lincoln was considering the idea of deportation. He asked Ben Butler, former union general and Massachusetts politician, to calculate the logistics of such a venture. Butler reported back:

> Mr. President, I have gone carefully over my calculations as to the power of the country to export the Negroes of the South and I assure you that, using all your naval vessels and all the merchant marine fit to cross the seas with safety, it will be impossible for you to transport to the nearest place ... half as fast as Negro children will be born here.[48]

The freedpeople were not leaving. The four million former slaves were now four million people without land, with few economic resources, without much formal education, without even cooking utensils, and surrounded by hostile people who wanted to prove the new era a mistake. Thousands died in the transition. In some areas, one out of every four African Americans died from disease, starvation, and killings.[49] Moreover, because of their dire circumstances, many soon became victims of a new type of peonage: sharecropping.

But before sharecropping came into full force, and before Jim Crow laws, came a remarkable period in American history called Reconstruction.

From the white Christian side, with a vigor akin to the abolitionists, north-ern church people organized agencies, raised funds, and sent educators and missionaries to the South to aid the former slaves. Schools were started, churches built, and hardships endured in the name, paternalistic to be sure, of "raising up the Negro." White southern church people, stung by war's loss, focused on rebuilding homes and society. Angry at northern interfer-ence, they did little to aid the cause.

For African Americans, despite their general economic poverty, the Reconstruction period was a time of remarkable involvement in public life:

> A former slave named Blanche Kelso Bruce was representing Mississippi in the United States Senate. Pinckney Benton Stewart Pinchback, young, charming, daring, was sitting in the governor's office in Louisiana. In Missis-sippi, South Carolina, and Louisiana, black lieutenant governers were sitting on the right hand of power. A black was secretary of state in Florida; a black was on the state supreme court in South Carolina. In these and other South-ern states, blacks were superintendents of education, state treasurers, adju-tant generals, solicitors, judges and major general of militia. Robert H. Wood was mayor of Natchez, Mississippi, and Norris Wright Cuney was running for mayor of Galvaston, Texas. Seven blacks were sitting in the [United States] House of Representatives.[50]

And this was just the tip of the iceberg. Blacks and whites were seen going to school together, and even in politics together. As northern reporter James S. Pike reported on his visit to the South Carolina House of Representatives: "The Speaker is black, the clerk is black, the doorkeepers are black, the little pages are black, the chairman of the Ways and Means is black, and the chap-lain is coal black." [51] This was a shock to white southerners, and northerners too. After hundreds of years of white domination, suddenly, within just a few short years, former slaves were holding seats of power.

In addition to the Fourteenth and Fifteenth Amendments, African Americans in the South were able to capitalize on their numbers. According to the 1860 census, African Americans constituted 35 percent of Virginia's population, 36 percent of North Carolina's, 44 percent of Georgia's, 45 per-cent of Florida's and Alabama's, 50 percent of Louisiana's, 55 percent of Mississippi's, and 59 percent of South Carolina's. Assuming voting along racial lines, these proportions made winning elections not only possible, but likely.

All this was too threatening for most white southerners, and for many white northerners as well. They feared for their way of life, their sense of group position, and their vision of a Christian America, which, as the lead-ing evangelical social reformer of the time, northerner Josiah Strong, clearly expressed, was to be an Anglo-Saxon society.[52] The former slaves were not properly Christianized nor educated to be holding elected offices and running the nation. More directly, the economic and cultural threat of the African Americans was very real, and southerners responded by instituting the increasingly harsh realities of the now well-known Jim Crow laws, designed to separate blacks from whites and subjugate blacks in social and economic life.[53] This was possible because northerners pulled out of the South and left the "race problem" to be solved by southerners.

White northerners largely abandoned the freedpeople due to political compromises, the immensity of the task, hostilities, declining interest, focus on overseas expansion, industrialization issues in northern cities, racial attitudes that were growing increasingly similar to white southerners' (including the influence of Social Darwinism), and a growing desire for national unity and reconciliation.[54] What differences existed in attitudes and actions between northerners and southerners, it can be argued, likely had much to do with the vastly smaller African-American population in the North compared to the South, who thus represented a substantially smaller economic and cultural threat.[55] By the 1890s, race had ceased to be an issue in national politics. By the turn of the century, an increasing number of white northerners' thinking on race was essentially that of the white southerner.[56]

Because the nineteenth century was dominated by evangelical Christianity—George Marsden estimates that over half of the U.S. population and 85 percent of Protestants were evangelical—it is likely that actions that occurred during this time were largely supported by evangelical Christians.[57] Indeed, this was the case. Almost immediately after the war, before the formal institution of Jim Crow segregation, African Americans in frustration left the white churches en masse to form their own churches. Denied equal participation in the existing churches, "the move toward racially separate churches was not a matter of doctrinal disagreement, but a protest against unequal and restrictive treatment."[58] Many white Christians saw the separation as positive and part of God's design. As one Virginia churchman put it: "No Christian ought to allow his conscience to be disturbed by the thought that he violates the unity of the Church by insisting on an independent organization for the colored race. The distinctions are drawn by God Himself."[59] Segregated churches also reduced the risk of the great taboo, interracial marriage. Although people of both races were Christian, it was believed that God made the races different, and so blacks and whites should be segregated. They were spiritual brothers, but not temporal neighbors. If more evidence was needed, many whites pointed out that the freedpeople preferred segregated churches because they had left voluntarily.[60]

Segregated churches were the bellwether to segregation in other spheres of life, which was incrementally instituted over the last twenty years of the nineteenth and first few years of the twentieth century. As new forms of segregation were made into law, southern evangelicals did not object. When they did speak on the issue, it was with approval. The well-known *Christian Advocate* of Nashville, for example, wrote in 1905:

> The negro leaders in the South and their injudicious friends up North who are making such an ado over "Jim Crow laws" quite overlook the fact that such laws do not discriminate against the blacks. They assign to the use for negroes certain seats in trolley cars, equally desirable with others, and certain sections of the railway cars, usually the same cars in which the whites ride. In these places under the law they have rights. Without such a law those rights would often be challenged.[61]

Some northern evangelicals did speak out, but not too loudly because their institutions were largely segregated as well. Southern and northern Christians were in unison, though, in condemning lynchings and mob violence of the rebel few. Such acts simply were not to be tolerated. Aside from these troubling events, southerners to be sure, and many northerners as well, believed race relations were running smoothly. As the *Alabama Baptist* put it in 1891: "The Southern whites and Southern blacks are getting along admirably, and always will, if blatant politicians keep hands off." [62]

What problems there were, most white Christians argued, rested largely with African Americans themselves. They did not yet know how to live as a free people, and had to be "trained in the way that they should go." They were largely poor and lacking education. Of special concern was their perceived lack of positive work habits and cleanliness, and their proclivity for crime and desire for interracial sexual relations. What the blacks needed was first to become Christians, and then proper instruction in self-discipline, moral control, and character building that came with being a Christian. If whites needed support for these views, the most influential African American of the time, Booker T. Washington, could be cited, and he often was.

Booker T. Washington was born of a white father and slave mother in 1856, although his white heritage was little spoken of. He was admired by almost all white Americans, who viewed him as embodying the American (and Christian) success story, and his views on race confirmed theirs. Born a slave, after emancipation he wanted to attend school, but poverty ruled that out. At the age of nine he began working, first in a salt furnace, then a coal mine. He remained determined to get a formal education, and at the age of sixteen enrolled in Hampton Institute, paying his way by working as a janitor. After joining the staff at Hampton, he was selected in 1881 to head up the newly formed Tuskegee normal school for African Americans. The school was but two small converted buildings, with no equipment and little money. By the time of his death in 1915, Tuskegee Institute was more than 100 well-equipped buildings with 1,500 students, almost 200 faculty members, and an endowment of nearly two million dollars.

Washington was beloved by white America for his racial views. In a famous speech at the 1895 Atlanta Exposition, he proclaimed that "in all things purely social we can be as separate as the fingers, yet one as the hand in all things essential to mutual progress." [63] Coming from this seemingly self-made Baptist African-American man, such words were music to the ears of white America. His Protestant-ethic approach to overcoming the race problem also made him exceedingly popular. He emphasized vocational training for students—such as carpentry, farming, and printing for the boys, and cooking, sewing, and related household skills for the girls—personal hygiene, good manners, character building, and required daily chapel attendance. Christian white America quickly made him the leading African-American spokesman for the rest of his life.

Booker T. Washington's views reflected those of white evangelical Christians. Namely, the race issue was not a major problem, and what problem there was largely laid at the feet of African Americans themselves. While W. E. B. DuBois and other prominent African Americans of the time were questioning Jim Crow and other forces that denied equality of opportunity, white evangelical Americans generally held that there was equality of opportunity. The key to success and the welfare of the society was for individuals to work hard and be disciplined. Christianity was an important component. The ethic was the gospel of work.[64]

Prominent at the same time as Washington were white evangelists D. L. Moody and, later, Billy Sunday. It is instructive that for these northern evangelists, social reform, which had been a central characteristic of evangelical thought since the 1830s, was dropped in favor of a nearly singular emphasis on personal piety.[65] The race issue was little on their minds. When Moody held revival meetings in the South, he did so on a segregated basis. When Billy Sunday followed after the turn of the century, he too held segregated revival meetings. All this confirms Reimers' and Myrdal's observations that the racial issue simply was not important to most white evangelicals and white Americans generally in the latter half of the nineteenth and beginning of the twentieth century.[66]

RENEWED CONCERN: 1917–1950

Several events centering around World War I changed this. In 1870, over 90 percent of African Americans lived in the South, and over 80 percent lived in the rural South. By 1910, this had changed little. Northern industries needed workers but immigrants from other lands filled these needs. With the coming of World War I, however, immigration slowed while the demand for labor increased. In a monumental change for African Americans and for American race relations, blacks began leaving the rural South in large numbers for northern (and southern) cities. And for the first time, white northerners, including evangelicals, began encountering African Americans in large numbers. They did not react well.

Through practices such as racial steering as well as violence, Northern whites during this period birthed the black urban ghetto, a quintessential urban feature of contemporary American society, as the solution to the rise in the urban black population. Racial violence increased in urban areas as whites fought to protect their jobs and neighborhoods. Between 1917 and 1921, one black home in Chicago was bombed, on average, every twenty days.[67] African Americans, often used as strikebreakers by northern industrialists, were viewed with contempt not only for their color, but also the economic threat they represented. Urban riots—at the time, whites attacking blacks—became a northern problem. Violence heightened in the South as well. The Ku Klux Klan resurged and black servicemen returning from World War I were even lynched while still in uniform. Suddenly, the racial issue became once again, in the eyes of whites, a problem.

White evangelicals (by this time, because of the modernist battles, perhaps more appropriately called fundamentalists) wanted to quell the racial problem, which they perceived as the inability of individuals to get along and excessive violence. In the 1920s and 1930s, an interracial movement was launched, affecting first the South, then the North. Because of the violence and threat of further violence in the North and the increased lynchings and resurgence of the Ku Klux Klan after the war, addressing race relations issues—but not the larger racialized social system—was urgent. Beginning in the South, the Commission on Interracial Cooperation was founded in 1919 (and continued until 1944). Like most such movements, the organization did not spring from the churches themselves but from church members. The Commission was part of a larger interracial movement in the 1920s and 1930s. Here, according to the writers of the time,[68] was a fresh wind in American race relations.

The goal during this period was to provide a better racial environment. As later scholars analyzed it, the movement had rather limited goals and was typically paternalistic. Still, for the time, it was a significant movement. It advocated an end to lynching, portraying African Americans in a more positive light, and better facilities, such as school buildings, for African Americans, though still within the context of segregation. Indeed, the Commission never attacked segregation itself, but simply strived to improve race relations and the lives of black Americans within the institutional context of segregation. Their activities included inviting leading African Americans to speak to white groups, and holding discussions between representatives of the races. After a few years of such activities, southern churches formally sanctioned the Commission.

Books and articles appeared in the same spirit as the Commission. Typical was a 1922 book by southern evangelical Robert E. Smith. In his preface, Smith informs his readers that he is the son of a slave owner and confederate soldier, loves the South, and will be buried in the South. And owing to his love for his native land, he exhorts southerners to take a fresh look at the race issue. His "fresh look" clearly reflects the more progressive evangelicals of the time, but also clearly reflects the limited goals and patronizing attitude. "We must," he writes, "move toward the light of altruism and brotherhood." Negroes are no longer an ignorant and servile race, but free Americans. The races are equal, he argues. The Bible supports this, and the Constitution supports this. So what in particular did he advocate? More enlightened understanding and more just treatment for "our sun-burned brothers." But this did not include ending segregation. In his words: "There is little difference of sentiment between the whites and the blacks on this point. Both races believe that a separate social life is most desirable and most practical."

Northern white Christians were also becoming involved in the interracial movement, although not as extensively as in the South. The Federal Council of Churches formed the Commission on Race Relations in 1921, and soon established an annual Race Relations Sunday, where white and black ministers exchanged pulpits. However, most formal efforts at addressing the race issue in the North during this period were engaged by mainline or theologically liberal Christians, not conservative Protestants, who were expending their energy on opposing secularization and the liberal agenda of mainline churches. Because the liberal agenda included race activities, conservative Protestants tended to shy away from addressing the race issue. As in the past, the activities in which they did engage were primarily missionary and educational.

The emergent racial difficulties in the North eventually quieted down, in the eyes of whites, thus requiring less attention. This "quieting down" was, as Massey and Denton outline, simply earlier racial violence giving way to more "civilized" forms of maintaining advantage and segregation, such as the formation of neighborhood "improvement" associations, zoning restrictions, the preemptive purchase of property that African Americans might buy, redlining, racial steering, and restrictive covenants.[69]

Much religious activism in this period also took the form of church pronouncements denouncing lynchings and other forms of inhumane personal treatment. Criticisms of Jim Crow segregation were still relatively infrequent however, and northern de facto segregation and the practices used to achieve the segregation were almost never criticized. Perhaps, as some have suggested, advocacy of the desegregation of American society was rare among religious activists due to the segregation within their churches and denominational structures.

The activities of commissions and nonbinding pronouncements of denominations do not tell us much about the views of ordinary Christians. It is likely that the masses, when they thought about the issue, supported the status quo, except perhaps to seek better treatment around the edges of the racialized system—for example, refraining from lynchings or at least holding a trial beforehand. Bits and pieces of evidence support this interpretation. A 1922–23 survey on southern views conducted by the Commission on Interracial Cooperation concluded: "The majority of the church people, ministers and laymen, have only a slight conviction as to the implications of Christianity to this field." [70] Researcher Frank Loescher concluded that "there is little evidence that the convictions of rank-and-file membership of Protestant denominations are greatly influenced by these official actions." [71] And a survey of Lutheran lay leaders found that many members held racial attitudes inconsistent with the church's official pronouncements.

Gunnar Myrdal, the Swedish social scientist brought to the United States by the Carnegie Corporation to study American race relations at the end of the 1930s and into the early 1940s, offers some keen observations on the thinking of the masses. He found that a common initial, superficial response to the race issue, from both white and black respondents, was that race relations were not a problem: "To be sure, it was not an unusual experience of the writer to be told confidently sometimes by the learned, but most often by the laity, that there is 'no Negro problem' in America and that, if there ever was one, it is solved and settled for all time and to the full satisfaction of both parties." [72] These thoughts were most often and most emphatically expressed in the Deep South, but were not entirely absent in the North. Myrdal also found that if he pressed people just a bit, the "no problem" consensus quickly collapsed. Thus, he concluded: "Nearly everybody in America is prepared to discuss the issue, and almost nobody is entirely without opinions on it. The opinions vary. They may be vague and hesitating or even questioning, or they may be hardened and articulate. But few Americans are unaware of the Negro problem." [73] Nearly everybody in America was prepared to discuss the issue, no matter where they lived or their level of contact with African Americans. And for African Americans, the problem was "all-important."

Still, in the North smaller percentages of African Americans, the rapid tempo of life, urbanization, industrialization, immigration, and de facto segregation all worked to push the race problem to a "back burner" for whites. Myrdal found among white northerners a great lack of awareness of the extent of racial discrimination. On hearing some of the facts, they seemed genuinely surprised at the level of discrimination and hardship. As for their views, "Most white Northerners seem to hold that the Negroes ought to stay on Southern land, and that, in any case, they cannot be asked to accept any responsibility for recent Negro migrants." [74]

For African Americans, Myrdal observed, once past the superficial, "no problems" etiquette, one found that the racialized social system was central, affecting their lives in a myriad of ways. "The Negro problem constantly looms in the background of social intercourse," [75] and "They sense how they are hampered and enclosed behind the walls of segregation and discrimination more acutely than might be expected." [76] As for formal actions by the black church to address the segregation and inequalities, it is well documented that until the 1950s black churches did not make significant challenges to the status quo. Instead, they offered an other-worldly vision and encouraged forbearance in the face of suffering and oppression.

On the whole then, after a short period of ferment, white evangelicals were quiet on the race issue, and black evangelicals were fairly silent as well. By the 1950s, however, black evangelicals began to speak out with a more organized voice. With World War II came new changes, particularly the acceleration of suburbanization and white flight in the face of continued black migration to northern cities. While in 1940 only one-third of metropolitan residents lived in suburbs, by 1965, the majority did. The end result, according to Massey and Denton, was that nearly all American cities with significant black populations—North, South, and West—had developed black ghettos.[77]

THE CIVIL RIGHTS ERA OF THE 1950S AND EARLY 1960S

The 1950s and early 1960s were a time of great contrast between the race-issue activities of white and black Christians. It is common knowledge that religious leaders from within black churches led the Civil Rights movement. While many played lesser-known parts in the beginning—such as the Reverend Vernon Johns and Morehouse professor Benjamin Mays—they opened the door for social action by Martin Luther King, Ralph Abernathy, and a host of other black Christian activists. In a movement centered and most successful in the South, black Christians called, protested, boycotted, and died for an end to Jim Crow segregation. The connection between religious faith and the social movement is a remarkable moment in American religious history, attesting to the power of religion to call for and realize change. In this case, the goal was freedom from oppression and unequal treatment, at least as expressed through the laws and practices of the South. When the movement moved north and attempted to address northern race issues, namely ghettos, it was largely unsuccessful. This different version of segregation and discrimination was not easily addressed by direct-action campaigns. Clear villains were difficult to identify, clear solutions difficult to implement. Still, this relatively short period of black Christian action led to monumental changes in the South.

In the white evangelical world, the story is quite different. Some whites did indeed participate in Civil Rights marches, freedom rides, and the like, but they were rarely evangelical Christians. Rather, they were northern liberal Christians, Catholics, Jews, and non-Christians. Southern evangelicals generally sided against black evangelicals on the segregation issue, and northern evangelicals seemed more preoccupied with other issues—such as evangelism, and fighting communism and theological liberalism. In fact, when we reviewed a central periodical of evangelicals, *Christianity Today*, from its founding in 1957 to 1965, we found, on average, less than two articles per year on race issues, despite this being a tumultuous period in American race relations history. The arguments that did appear were not consistent from article to article. For example, the first race article to appear supported Jim Crow segregation, while a later article opposed it. On the whole, in comparison to the thought and activities of contemporary black evangelicals, this mainly white evangelical periodical spoke little and, when it did speak, did so hesitantly. Indeed, *Christianity Today* actually received dispatches from one of its coeditors on the southern marches, but they "went unpublished for fear of giving the impression that civil rights should be part of the Christian agenda." [78]

As for the laity, they were probably even quieter on the race issue. William Martin notes, "Most evangelicals, even in the North, did not think it their duty to oppose segregation; it was enough to treat the blacks they knew personally with courtesy and fairness." [79] That is, they opposed personal prejudice and discrimination, but not the racialized social system itself.

This was certainly the view of the young, but exceedingly popular evangelist and evangelical leader Billy Graham. During his early years, similar to his forebears, he wanted very much to avoid the larger questions of race so as not to deter the main task of evangelism. Graham's southern crusades of the late 1940s and early 1950s were segregated. Constantly pressed on the issue by northern liberals and others, Graham was forced to speak: "In 1951, he tried to play both sides of the issue, announcing that he personally favored improved race relations but that organized reform efforts were likely to do more harm than good, especially since it seemed to him that communists and communist sympathizers were at the root of most such efforts." [80] He went on to state clearly that the races were equal, that race hatred was wrong, and that the answer to the race problem was Christian conversion and love.

Graham began a series of wavering actions on the race issue. In 1952, he held desegregated meetings in Washington, D.C.; a few weeks later in Houston, he accepted the local organizers' segregated seating terms. A short time later, he again held segregated meetings in Mississippi, but defied the governor's request for separate services. At the meetings, he criticized segregation, but when this upset white southerners, he told the local newspaper, "I feel that I have been misinterpreted on racial segregation. We follow the existing social customs in whatever part of the country in which we minister. As far as I have been able to find in my study of the Bible, it has nothing to say about segregation or nonsegregation. I came to Jackson to preach only the Bible and not to enter into local issues." [81] The following year in Chattanooga, Graham requested that the services be desegregated. When denied, he personally removed the ropes marking the black section. But a few months later in Dallas, he again accepted segregated seating.

After the *Brown v Board of Education* decision in 1954, Graham no longer permitted any form of enforced segregation at his meetings and in 1957 he began attempting to integrate his own organization racially. He even had Martin Luther King come to say an opening prayer at a crusade meeting in New York City that year. But Graham could not accept the methodology of Martin Luther King and the Civil Rights movement, having a deep abhorrence for public protest and favoring a gradualist approach to integration. He also did not believe in working to change laws, as he sincerely believed that laws could not change wicked hearts.

To understand this, we must account for the pre-millennial view that had come to dominate the American evangelical worldview and played a role in limiting evangelical action on race issues. According to this view, the present world is evil and will inevitably suffer moral decline until Christ comes again. Thus, to devote oneself to social reform is futile. The implications of this view were clearly expressed by Billy Graham. In response to King's famous "I Have a Dream" speech that his children might one day play together with white children, Graham, who had been invited but did not attend the 1963 March on Washington, said: "Only when Christ comes again will little white children of Alabama walk hand in hand with little black children." [82] This was not meant to be harsh, but rather what he and most white evangelicals perceived to be realistic. [83]

At the end of this period, white evangelicals were quiet, but opposed to individual racial prejudice and, in the North but not the South, tentatively opposed to the Jim Crow system. Still, churches were highly segregated, neighborhoods were highly segregated, urban riots in America's ghettos were reappearing, the black power movement was emerging, and the bumpy road over issues such as affirmative action was just beginning.

CONCLUSION

We have quickly covered an enormous period, moving from evangelicals deciding that slaves should be Christianized but that race-based slavery is perfectly compatible with the law of God, to tentative support in the North for the end of Jim Crow and equality of treatment. Few can survey this history and deny that there has been at least some progress, at least in some respects. Yet it is ironic that as racial thinking became more egalitarian, and as laws were passed and policies enacted meant to level the playing field, whites and blacks in many ways were growing farther apart. They had gone from separate pews to separate churches. And with the black power movement, blacks as well as whites began arguing that perhaps we are better off apart after all. In sum, as slavery receded, a formally segregated public sphere rose in its place. By 1964, as the formally segregated public sphere receded, an informally segregated private sphere began to rise in its place. Perhaps most ironic of all, at least in regions where there was co-residence, whites and blacks probably knew less about each other in 1964 than they had in centuries past. As Myrdal aptly foretold: "The younger generations [the leaders and persons who had come to power by 1964]... are less indoctrinated against the Negro than their parents were. But they are also farther away from him, know less about him and, sometimes, get more irritated by what little they see." [84] As the National Advisory Commission on Civil Disorders reported in 1968, in the aftermath of the Civil Rights movement, "our nation is moving toward two societies, one black, one white—separate and unequal." Racialization, although it changed in form, remained ever-present.

Over the centuries, religion was also at times used by white and black Christians to call for America to realize its ideals. Those ideals include equality and freedom. Freedom has come to be freedom from—freedom from oppression, freedom from discrimination, and freedom from each other. In sum, through the long, arduous struggle, where religion aided racial change, it has been unidirectional: like America itself, it has occasionally helped to free people, but has been unable to bring them together or overcome racialization. The abolitionist movement worked to end slavery and free slaves, not to unite Americans in a common community. Likewise, the Civil Rights movement worked to gain rights and freedoms. Although it used the rhetoric of togetherness in its efforts, it was, to the consternation of many, unsuccessful in its realization.

Much has transpired since 1964 in black–white relations. We turn now to an exploration of evangelical activity in race relations in the latter third of the twentieth century.

3

Becoming Active

Contemporary Involvement in the American Dilemma

"Gentlemen," the Promise Keeper speaker bellowed from the podium to a crowd of 60,000 largely evangelical men, "we have grieved our brothers and sisters of color. We have ignored their pain and isolation. We have allowed false divisions to separate us. We must reconcile our differences, and come together in the name of the Almighty God! Turn now to a brother of a different race, confess your sins and the sins of your fathers, and pledge to unite!" All across the expansive domed stadium, small groups formed around men of color. A great murmur of confession rose and reverberated off the stadium top, further amplifying the sounds. Soon, weeping could be heard, first only in pockets, then spreading like an uncontrollable wave, until the entire crowd was shedding tears of lament. "What we have witnessed here, men," the podium speaker said once the sounds began quieting down, "is the power of God's unity. You have tasted it. Now pursue it with a passion! Commit to forming a friendship with a brother of a different race. Be yokefellows, carry each other's burdens, and demonstrate true reconciliation!" [1]

Such evangelical events, commonplace in the 1990s, are a far cry from the 1950s and early 1960s, the period with which we concluded the previous chapter. The last third of the twentieth century marked a turning point for the evangelical movement on race issues. White evangelicals were more engaged with race relations than in the previous 100 years, and their recent swell of activity surrounding race relations may only be matched by the abolitionist period. We must understand what changed, and why it changed.

During this period, partly in reaction to the race-relations solutions that took precedence in the late 1960s and beyond, some evangelical leaders picked up a seemingly forgotten piece of Martin Luther King's vision—the need to reconcile races—and ran with it.[2] Over this period, they developed a formal theology of racial reconciliation. They devised principles and practices attempting to address a key issue pointed out at the close of Chapter Two: that blacks and whites probably knew less of each other in the late twentieth century than in previous times. This has been a vibrant period focusing on race relations for evangelicals. It began as a bud, developed and led by black evangelicals, and then flowered into fuller bloom, growing in influence, and increasingly involving more evangelicals, including whites. But something happened, we argue, in the translation from black evangelicals to a larger white evangelical audience. The popularized version for white evangelicals has emphasized mainly the individual-level components, leaving the larger racialized social structures, institutions, and culture intact.

The Beginnings of Modern Evangelical Reconciliation Thought and Activity

John Perkins, an African American reared in rural Mississippi in the 1930s and 1940s, was no stranger to racial and other difficulties. When he was just seven months old, his mother died; his father subsequently abandoned the family. Raised by his grandmother in the dire poverty of rural Mississippi, he left school after the third grade to help support the family. His opportunities were limited not only by his lack of education, but by the strict segregation of the South. In his teens, Perkins's brother was shot and killed by a policeman outside the black entrance to a movie theater. As he reflected in his autobiography,[3] he learned many hard racial lessons in his early years. The whites, he wrote, had the means of production (land, tools, and other assets); he had but his "wants and needs—and labor." The social system exploited him and fellow blacks. Further, the whites controlled the power. For him, the constant threat and actuality of violence were clear indicators of this power.

African Americans were most certainly at the bottom of this system, and the lowest of these, to Perkins, were black Christians. Their religion merely kept them "submissive to an oppressive structure," and they were "cowards and Uncle Toms." [4] White Christians were the dehumanizers, the destroyers of black people. Rejecting religion and the South, Perkins left Mississippi, vowing never to return.[5]

Far from the rural Mississippi of John Perkins, New York City was home to blood-lusting Harlem gang leader Tom Skinner, twelve years Perkins's junior. Convinced that the main purveyors of hate and black oppression were Bible-believing Christians, Skinner developed an acute and piercing hatred for both religion and whites. The teenage Skinner took his anger out on the people around him, namely other black gangs, and even those in his own gang. To gain the right to lead the Harlem Lords, he had to fight and defeat the current leader. He describes the fight in his autobiography: "I dodged his swing and drove my own knife into his side as I whirled. He dropped to his knees, holding his side in apparent disbelief. Blood was streaming through his fingers. ... he was finished. The Harlem Lords had a new leader!" [6] This was but the first of his stabbings. The twenty-seven notches on his knife handle marked how many bodies he had slashed and gored as leader of the Harlem Lords.[7] Skinner, like Perkins, lived in deep poverty. But his was an urban form, where "people paid outrageously high rents for places that were nothing more than rat traps. [One might] wake up in the middle of the night and hear the piercing scream of a mother as she discovered her two-month-old baby had been gnawed to death by a large rat." [8] Taking stock of his circumstances, Skinner "cursed the day that [he] was born black." [9]

Contemporaneously with Perkins and Skinner, in the Caribbean islands, lived a Jamaican named Samuel Hines. The son of a strict, legalistic minister, the young Hines rebelled against his upbringing, seeking "forbidden fruits." The last thing he ever intended to be was a minister. Yet at the age of sixteen he had a life-changing religious experience, and soon entered the ministry. But he encountered difficult times with his congregation. So difficult that he soon had had his fill of the church and ministry. It was then that he made his decision. He left his pastorate and Jamaica, and headed for England, intent on a new vocation and a new lifestyle.

Perkins, Skinner, Hines. Hardly candidates to be major "founding fathers" of an evangelical religious movement called reconciliation. Yet that is exactly what they became. Each, through different circumstances, was brought to a deep faith, and a deep need to see that faith lived out in practical ways in the United States. Specifically, they turned their attention to the divisions among blacks and whites, the poor and rich, the powerless and the powerful. For Perkins, this meant returning, after nearly fifteen years, to the people he had left in Mississippi, to live out reconciliation in the "war-torn" South of the 1960s. For Skinner, it meant traversing the country as an evangelist and "minister of reconciliation," focusing especially on the nation's youth. For Hines, it meant returning to the pastorate, coming to America, locating in the inner city of Washington, D.C., and preaching and practicing reconciliation. Interesting stories also can be told of the other original leaders, people like James Earl Massey, William Pannell, and E. V. Hill.

They shared some common characteristics. They were all black, all well versed—through experience—in the racialized United States, all willing to use the term *evangelical* and associate with white evangelicals, all influenced by Martin Luther King (some were personal friends of King), all committed to mentoring future leaders, and all completely sold on the idea that reconciliation was, in Samuel Hines terms, "God's one-item agenda."

What is this "reconciliation" to which these men devoted their lives? Reconciliation, as they proclaimed repeatedly, is the message of Christianity. The gospel story is about reconciling people to God and to other people. For example, they created a theology of racial reconciliation by using scriptures such as Ephesians 2:14–15, which says that Christ "has made the two one and has destroyed the barrier, the dividing wall of hostility ... to reconcile both of them to God through the cross, by which he put to death their hostility." [10]

According to this view, racial reconciliation is God's imperative. Conversely, racial division, hostility, and inequality are the result of sin. Christians' work is to show God's power by reconciling divided people. For true racial reconciliation, then, believers of different races must "admit, submit, and commit." [11] That is, they must admit that there are racial problems. They then must submit by recognizing the problems are spiritual and only solvable by surrendering to the will of God. They also must submit to each other by building loving relationships across racial barriers. Finally, they must commit to relationships, as in a marriage, and to overcoming division and injustice. As outlined by Perkins,[12] reconciliation is linked with two other Rs: relocation (moving to places of need) and redistribution (of talents, hopes, dreams, and materials). The end result, according to this model, is the reduction of racial division and inequality. In short, it is the ending of racialization.

According to Yancey,[13] these early leaders developed four major steps to achieve racial reconciliation. First, individuals of different races must develop primary relationships with each other. This is seen as imperative for reconciliation-minded evangelicals for both theological and social reasons. Theologically, they argued that God desires unity, and this is expressed at least in part through intimate associations such as close friendships and worshipping together. It is also rooted in reaction to the social context; this aspect of King's vision was largely abandoned in pursuit of political rights and economic opportunities. And finally, the development of mixed-race relationships has an important pragmatic function. Ideally it exposes whites, typically unable to understand or see the depths of racialized society, to a United States seen through the eyes of those experiencing its injustices.

The second major step demands recognizing social structures of inequality, and that all Christians must resist them together. These structures include, for example, unequal access to quality education and housing. The sin of "indifference" is noted by many of these early advocates of racial reconciliation. To sit on the sidelines while unequal and oppressive forces harm part of the Christian community is a grievous wrong. Whites must come alongside people of color in opposition to inequality. As Samuel Hines notes, "We need each other. Because of the interdependence of community, we all hold the key to other people's freedom. White people can't free themselves of their guilt, fears, and prejudices. Black people can't free themselves of the oppression and injustices. ... Racial divisions are robbing both sides." [14]

For the second step to occur, two other steps are necessary. The third step is that whites, as the main creators and benefactors of the racialized society, must repent of their personal, historical, and social sins. If historical and social sins are not confessed and overcome, they are passed on to future generations, perpetuating the racialized system, and perpetuating sin.

African Americans also have a responsibility. The fourth step states that they must be willing, when whites ask, to forgive them individually and corporately. Blacks must repent of their anger and whatever hatred they hold toward whites and the system.

The essence of the message of reconciliation, and the critique of evangelicalism that these African-American messengers began bringing in the mid-1960s, is concisely communicated by John Perkins: "Something is wrong at the root of American evangelicalism. I believe we have lost the gospel—God's reconciling power, which is unique to Christianity—and have substituted church growth. We have learned how to reproduce the church without the message." [15] These early African-American reconciliation advocates brought this message tirelessly to evangelicals through speaking, meetings, conferences, books, teaching, mentoring, invitations to observe their ministries, and crusades.

And it is a message that some white evangelicals and some of their institutions have heard, at least in part. Billy Graham was originally tentative on racial issues, separating such issues from the Christian faith. For example, recall that in 1952 he told a Jackson, Mississippi, newspaper: "We follow the existing social customs in whatever part of the country in which we minister. As far as I have been able to find in study of the Bible, it has nothing to say about segregation or nonsegregation. I came to Jackson only to preach the Bible and not to enter into local issues." [16]

To Perkins, Skinner, Hines, Pannell, Massey, Hill, and others who viewed the Bible as calling for the reconciliation of peoples, such a statement from a Christian was inconceivable, a complete misunderstanding of what the Bible says. Graham eventually came to agree, and by the mid- to late-1960s was advocating togetherness in visible ways. As we researched the articles dealing with racial issues in the flagship evangelical magazine *Christianity Today*, we saw this reflected in reports of his crusades. From crusades in Alabama in 1965, "the choir of 400 voices, about half Negro, sang with George Beverly Shea," and "almost 250 of both races stood shoulder to shoulder in front of the platform to register decisions for Jesus Christ." Leaders of both races in the state reportedly said: "We believe this will mark the beginning of a new day in our community." [17] And in his crusade in Montgomery, we see the first explicit mention of reconciliation, in the news report, "Billy Graham in Montgomery: A Stride Toward Reconciliation." [18] The report even claimed something rather radical for the time: "In a number of cases Negro Christians counseled whites who had responded to the invitation [to become Christians]." And of a 1972 crusade in Cleveland, *Christianity Today* reported that "black ministers and musicians were on the platform every night. Prominent black James E. Johnson, assistant secretary of the Navy, gave a testimony. ... Graham frequently touched on the note of reconciliation. ... he declared, 'Christianity is not a white man's religion. ... Jesus belongs to the whole world.'" Graham told the crusade crowd that the contemporary dilemma is that "the world has become a neighborhood but not a brotherhood." [19]

Christianity Today itself appeared to put more emphasis on racial issues. Even though the years 1957 through 1964 were a tumultuous and newsworthy period in U.S. race relations, during that time, the magazine had, on average, less than two reports or articles on race issues per year. But the rest of the 1960s saw significant growth to an average of seven articles or news reports per year. The growth was also evident in the number of pages devoted to race issues, from one page per year prior to 1965 to an average of twelve pages per year thereafter. Although the average numbers of articles and pages devoted to race issues declined somewhat in the 1970s, they remained far higher than the pre-1965 days. Some of these pages were devoted to interviews with, or citations of, reconciliation advocates like Tom Skinner, John Perkins, and William Pannell, helping to increase their visibility among white evangelicals.

An article in the form of a letter, illustrating that racial reconciliation was gaining some credence among some evangelicals, appeared in the January 1971 edition of *Christianity Today*:

DEAR WHITE PERSON:

Although we have known each other for centuries, we have not truly known each other. I, the black person, feel I know more about you because I had to. My will to survive forced me to learn about you. I was forced to learn your ways of doing things, forced to accept your concepts and values, and yet denied the right to share them. ... If I tell you that I have hostility and anger within me, how do you interpret those emotions? Do they make me a savage who will riot and burn your property? ... It seems to me that our society is presently paying for the many years of wrongs done to the black person. ... In my rational moments, I can understand that you are a product of your forefathers' teachings, and are not entirely to blame for your feelings toward me. But if you or I should pass feelings of racial hatred to our children, we stand condemned before God. ... Along with my feelings of anger and hostility, there is a strong sense of disappointment. This disappointment is felt most keenly toward those who had taught me of God's love for all mankind. ... I am still forbidden to attend some of your evangelical colleges and churches, and to be your neighbor. ... I have been referring to myself as the black person. But I still feel I have not been allowed to reach complete adulthood. You have made me doubt my ability to compete with you intellectually, and you keep stunting this area of my life with inferior school systems. ... I, the black person, suggest that you really get to know yourself. Evaluate your life experiences and see how they may have given you your views of the black person. ... If that happens, it will enable us to love and to live together and enjoy the blessing God intended us to share.

Your fellow human being and future friend,

THE BLACK PERSON[20]

Written by a black man, this plea contains all the components of reconciliation—from the need for cross-race relationships, to forgiveness and accepting forgiveness, to overcoming together the structures of inequality.

A white evangelical woman wrote a response to the letter, published in the March 1971 edition of *Christianity Today*:

DEAR BLACK PERSON:

Thank you for your wonderful letter. ... I cannot claim to speak for the whole white race as I write this letter. Although I am sure that many others feel as I do, I can only speak for myself. For many years I was guilty of ignorance. ... I did not know that black men were routinely but rudely questioned just for walking along the street, or that black homes were frequently invaded without benefit of warrant. Things like that never got into the news that reached me. ... I am guilty. I admit my guilt. But more importantly, I have repented. I have sought the forgiveness of the Christ-Savior of white and black and every person, and I am seeking to educate myself and others so that the gap of racial misunderstanding and abuse may yet be closed. ... I was especially

touched by this statement in your letter: "I am telling you these things because I want you to know me." I feel the same way about you: I am telling you
these things because I want you to know me. ... I want you to know that in
order to raise my level of awareness I have been sitting at the feet of black authors like ... William Pannell and Tom Skinner. ... I realize that [white]
evangelicals are not the only offenders. ... But we are offenders, God help us.
God forgive us. And please, Black Person, give us your forgiveness too. ... the
important goal to strive for in all my relationships is caring for other individuals as individuals. ... please judge me not by my color but by my individual
spirit. ... And please, when I reach out my hand in friendship to you, take it.

Your fellow human being,

A WHITE PERSON[21]

This response contains many of the aspects of reconciliation as well. She
confesses her sin, and she requests forgiveness. She is working to educate
herself by reading the works of reconciliation advocates. She clearly calls for
the development of interracial relationships.

But there are some perhaps subtle differences in her expression of reconciliation as compared to the black writer's letter. First, the letter from the
black writer uses the vehicle of a personal letter to communicate from one
race to another; the white writer, though, quickly individualizes the letter,
claiming that she cannot speak for other whites. She also asks to be seen as
an individual, not a member of a race, and says her goal is to treat individuals as individuals, regardless of color. This seems perfectly reasonable, but it
has an important effect. The need to work for social justice and social
equality between races is minimized, even dropped. If we are to focus on individuals only, then justice does not mean working against structures of inequality, but treating individuals as equals, regardless of the actual
economic and political facts. Equality is spiritually and individually based,
not temporally and socially based.

And this is the complaint that many black evangelicals had of white
evangelicals during this period. Some of the white elite evangelicals attempted reconciliation, but incompletely. The problem with whites' con-
ception of reconciliation, many claimed, was that they did not seek true
justice—that is, justice both individually and collectively. Without this
component, reconciliation was cheap, artificial, and mere words. It was
rather like a big brother shoving his little brother to the ground, apologiz-
ing, and then shoving him to the ground again.

DEVELOPING AND EXPANDING THE MESSAGE

The black advocates of reconciliation redoubled their efforts. The message
needed to be made clearer and audible to more people. Mentoring needed

time. In fact, the entire process needed time. And there were glimmers of hope. Some whites apparently grasped the message early on. These included people like Jim Wallis of the socially concerned Sojourners community and magazine in Washington, D.C.; Ronald Sider, co-founder of Evangelicals for Social Action and author of the controversial, best-selling book, *Rich Christians in an Age of Hunger*;[22] Ronald Behm, pastor of a southside Chicago church and coauthor with African-American Columbus Salley of another controversial book, *Your God Is Too White*;[23] and Tony Campolo, professor of sociology at Eastern University outside of Philadelphia.

Teaching, activism, and building networks moved forward, and more evangelicals—of all races and ethnicities—adopted the message of reconciliation and practiced its principles. The movement seemed to dissipate during Ronald Reagan's first presidency in the early 1980s, as evidenced by a dearth of publications on the topic and limited discussion in evangelical magazines like *Christianity Today*. But hindsight reveals that it was quietly gathering steam. The late 1980s and 1990s saw an explosion of new leaders. Out of the original few came new national and local racial reconciliation leaders such as Glandion Carney, Carey Casey, Curtiss DeYoung, Kathy Dudley, Joe Ehrmann (a former professional football player), Tony Evans, Leah Fitchue, Artis Fletcher, Wayne Gordon, Scottye Holloway, Craig Keener, Glen Kehrein, Bob Lupton, Michael Mata, Claudia May, Bill McCartney (the founder and head of Promise Keepers), Robin McDonald, Brenda Selter McNeil, Patrick Morley, Jesse Miranda, Cecil "Chip" Murray, Andrew Sung Park, Spencer Perkins (John Perkins' son), Ron Potter, Frank M. Reid, Chris Rice, Peggy Riley, Cheryl Sanders, Jody Miller Shearer, Barbara Skinner (Tom Skinner's wife), Glen Usry, Miroslav Volf, Raleigh Washington, and Dolphus Weary. Undoubtedly we have omitted more than we have named.

With this new generation the leaders were no longer all black. Of the list above, almost half are nonblack. For most of them, their thinking and involvement in racial reconciliation were shaped at least in part by the original reconciliation theologians. Dolphus Weary, for example, was one of the poor, young Mississippians to whom John Perkins returned. Under the tutelage of Perkins, Weary became the new head of John Perkins's original Mendenhall Ministries, and has since branched out to head a Mississippi reconciliation organization. Scottye Holloway also worked at Mendenhall Ministries and, in his words, "to stretch the arms of reconciliation and its message from the south end of the Mississippi to the north end," he established an interracial church centered on reconciliation in Minneapolis, teaches at a local evangelical college, and speaks to a wide variety of audiences about racial reconciliation.

A White Evangelical and Racial Reconciliation:
The Story of Curtiss DeYoung

Curtiss DeYoung is a white man who heads a multiracial reconciliation organization. He is the author of two books on reconciliation—*Coming Together: The Bible's Message in an Age of Diversity*[24] and *Reconciliation: Our
Greatest Challenge, Our Only Hope.*[25] A former pastor of an interracial
church, he now serves as a reconciliation consultant around the nation. He
has coined the term "artisans of reconciliation," meaning that Christians
must become skilled at the art of reconciliation and committed to excelling
in this skill. A graduate of the primarily black Howard University School of
Divinity, he lives in an interracial city neighborhood, attends an interracial
church, and is married to an African American. All of this is highly unusual
for a white American. We wanted to find out how he came to live this way
and to have a focus on reconciliation. He graciously agreed to a two-hour
interview.

Raised primarily in a suburb outside of Kalamazoo, Michigan, his social
networks were essentially all white. He lived in an all white neighborhood,
went to a white church, attended schools that were 99 percent white, and his
friends and relatives were white. About 1970, when he was just becoming a
teenager, he became fascinated with Martin Luther King. In his words,
"I began to read everything I could find written on Martin Luther King. I
was also intrigued by him as a preacher and speaker. If you track through
my junior high and high school years, I wrote a number of papers on Martin Luther King. If I had to do a research project, I would do it on Martin
Luther King. I just became intrigued with his life. That became my main
view into the issues of race."

After graduating from high school, he attended Anderson College, an
evangelical school in Indiana. On a class trip to New York City, he was
"awakened to the dynamics of class and poverty in our country. I just could-
n't believe it, that the United States could have a South Bronx. It looked like
a war zone." While at Anderson, he got to know the campus pastor and professor of biblical studies, James Earl Massey, one of the original advocates
for reconciliation. "We began what has become a twenty-year mentoring
relationship. It really developed during my time in college because he was
the college chaplain, and he was also teaching the Bible courses, so I took a
number of classes from him. And of course I was also intrigued because he
was a personal friend of Martin Luther King."

After graduating from college and serving a short stint as a youth pastor
back in Michigan, Curtiss DeYoung made a big decision. He would move to
Manhattan and work at a runaway shelter in Times Square. Most of the

youth he worked with were black, and a sizable percentage were Puerto Rican. Many of his coworkers were African American. Further, he was living at a Catholic house, and in the nation's largest city. The experience was overwhelming. As he recalled,

> I was completely out of my comfort zone the whole time in New York. I said to myself, I need at least an hour or two of comfort. I thought I could find a congregation of my own denomination, and there I would find people like me. I didn't know my way around the city, so I found a church in my denomination and simply went to the location, 154th St. and Amsterdam Avenue. I later found out this is the northern part of Harlem, but I didn't know it at the time. The subways and streets were fairly quiet on Sunday mornings, so there were not even visual clues as to where I was. And so I go into the church. As soon as I step into the church I realize that I am in an African-American church. I was greeted kindly with a "May I help you?" There probably had not been a white person visit to this church in years.

After telling them that he was from the same denomination (Church of God, Anderson) and that he had attended Anderson College, he was warmly greeted and invited to sit with some members. What happened next is extraordinary.

> I was escorted back to the pastor's office, who quickly discovered that I was there. He welcomed me, and wanted to find out more about me. He found out that I had gone to Anderson College, and in a colloquial way said, "Do you know my boy, Jim?" I didn't know who he was talking about. After a few times, he said, "You know, Jim Massey." He was asking if I knew James Earl Massey. I told him I was a student of his. And then I was "in," because I was a friend of James Massey. Then he asked me if I was a minister. I had been licensed as a minister while I was a youth minister, not ordained but licensed, so I told him that. He says, "Okay." He opens his schedule and asked me to preach for him two weeks from then. I'm blown away by the whole thing. I mean, it was like I was watching myself in a movie, not really part of what was happening. In shock, I naively said, "Okay."

Two weeks later, Curtiss DeYoung found himself preaching a sermon in a black church he had just visited for the first time. The response was warm and affirming. He came back the next week, and the next, and eventually made it his home church during his time in New York. The pastor, Rev. Levorn Aaron, took him under his wing and in the traditional black church style apprenticed DeYoung in the ways of pastoring and preaching. DeYoung preached, on average, once a month. As he said, "In that year I was really taught how to preach. I learned the need for me to slow down so that there could be the call and response. People were so supportive."

After a year, DeYoung made a decision to attend seminary:

James Massey came out to speak at an event that this church sponsored during my year there. After the event, he pulled me aside and he said, "When are
you coming back to Anderson?" This was his way of saying, "When are you
coming to seminary?" I wasn't planning on attending seminary, but his
words stuck with me. I went back, and by that time he was a seminary professor. I found, though, that Anderson School of Theology at that time didn't
have an urban ministry program. I stayed for a year and took every class that
James Massey offered. After a year, I transferred. I planned to go to Union
Theological Seminary in New York, and was accepted there. I was all set to go,
and decided to do a summer internship at the Third Street Church of God in
Washington, D.C. before I went. The pastor there was Samuel Hines. I spent
the summer there and in that summer I became much more fluent in the idea
of reconciliation because I discovered Samuel Hines and his congregation
understood urban ministry as reconciliation. He really dealt with class and
racial reconciliation there.

DeYoung attended the mostly African-American church during his
summerlong internship. He met a member of the congregation named Karen. Despite the strong national taboos against interracial dating, in the reconciling environment of the church, dating one another did not seem
outrageous. At the end of the summer, when it was time to head to New
York for seminary, Curtiss had a dilemma. He did not want to leave Karen.

The people of the church invited him to stay in Washington, D.C., telling
him they had a top-notch seminary he could attend—Howard University
School of Divinity. Persuaded to give it a try, he went to Howard to see if he
could gain acceptance. As fate would have it, the dean had previously been a
dean at the seminary in New York where DeYoung was currently accepted.
Finding out that DeYoung was accepted there, he told DeYoung he would
accept him at Howard. Within a month, DeYoung was a student at the
nearly all-black Howard University where, as he put it, "academically and
intellectually, as well as experientially, I was challenged around issues of
race and ways to look at things. What is more, I was in a predominately
African-American church where the pastor and congregation practiced
reconciliation regularly." Adding to his experience of reconciliation and
raising his awareness of life from an African-American perspective, Curtiss
and Karen married, and spent much time with her family.

The patient mentoring of the "old-line" reconcilers like Samuel Hines
and James Massey, and the density of his interracial experiences, help us understand how a white evangelical from a white world became a leader in the
reconciliation movement. Similar stories could be told for many other
"new-line" reconcilers. Tom Morley, another white evangelical reconciliation leader, tells of hearing Tom Skinner speaking and being deeply affected
by his message. They began a friendship, and a mentoring relationship:
"Tom poured hundreds of hours into discipling me around our dinner ta-

ble, after tennis, or in a car going somewhere. He never would give up on anyone; [he saw] the potential in everyone, even when others would write you off." [26] And he concluded in 1997: "I never would have been interested in reconciliation at all if it wasn't for Tom Skinner." [27]

THE CRUSADE FOR RACIAL RECONCILIATION

Since the late 1980s, the evangelical community has witnessed an explosion of racial-reconciliation conferences, books, study guides, videos, speeches, practices by organizations, formal apologies, and even mergers of once racially separate organizations. In 1997, the *Wall Street Journal* could refer to evangelicals as "the most energetic element of society addressing racial divisions."

This energy has led to a flurry of books published on the topic. Many books are coauthored by a black and white team, such as *More Than Equals: Racial Healing for the Sake of the Gospel*, by Spencer Perkins and Chris Rice; *Breaking Down the Walls: A Model for Reconciliation in an Age of Racial Strife*, by Raleigh Washington and Glen Kehrein; *Black Man's Religion*, by Glen Usry and Craig Keener; and *He's My Brother: Former Racial Foes Offer Strategies for Reconciliation*, by John Perkins and Thomas Tarrants.[28] Single-author volumes include: *The Coming Race Wars? A Cry for Reconciliation*, by William Pannell; books by Curtiss DeYoung; *Experiencing the Power*, by Samuel Hines; *Beyond Black and White: Reflections on Reconciliation*, by George Yancey; *Let's Get to Know Each Other*, by Tony Evans; *Racial Conflict and Healing*, by Andrew Sung Park; *Exclusion and Embrace*, by Miroslav Volf; and *I Ain't Coming Back*, by Dolphus Weary.[29]

Christianity Today published more on race since the mid-1980s than in any time in its history, and the growth continued to the end of the century. In the 1985–89 period, it published six articles per year and devoted fourteen pages per year to racial issues. In the 1990–94 period, it averaged eight articles and fifteen pages per year, and in the last half decade of the century it averaged eight and a half articles and sixteen pages per year. Since 1990, the great preponderance of articles and reports have focused on the reconciliation aspect of race issues. Other evangelical magazines, such as *Reconcilers*, *Sojourners*, and *New Man*, give many of their pages to reconciliation.

And evangelicals are going beyond merely publishing on the issue. A growing number of organizations and activities now emphasize racial reconciliation. A *Christianity Today* article "Racial Healing in the Land of Lynching" focuses on a reconciliation organization called Mission Mississippi, originally led by Tom Skinner and Tom Morley, and currently headed by Dolphus Weary. According to the report, "The movement is spreading remarkable impulse for reconciliation throughout the churches, businesses, and neighborhoods of the metropolitan area [of Jackson]." As part of Mission Mississippi, they have mass interracial rallies at local stadiums, and, according to the article, its participants practice "the kind of reconciliation that leads people from different races to eat in each other's houses and cry together on bent knees." [30]

The year 1994 saw another important event for racial reconciliation, "the Miracle of Memphis." The mostly white Pentecostal Fellowship of North America (PFNA) decided to seek reconciliation with black Pentecostal denominations. To demonstrate their change of heart, PFNA's board of directors dissolved their own organization. They then created the Pentecostal/Charismatic Churches of North America, an interracial organization, and elected Ithiel Clemmons, a bishop in a black denomination, the Church of God in Christ, as chairperson. [31]

And in 1995, the Southern Baptists formally apologized for their involvement in the sin of slavery and continuing sin. They asked for forgiveness and reconciliation. According to *Christianity Today* rankings, this was one of the top news stories of 1995 in the evangelical world.

Reconcilers Fellowship, an organization formerly headed by Spencer Perkins (son of John Perkins) and Chris Rice, sponsored a variety of reconciliation conferences. [32] For example, the Yokefellows conference brought together hundreds of interracial friendship pairs to discuss the difficulties and joys of such friendships, and to pledge to continue in their friendships and "spread the word."

The new generations of evangelical racial reconcilers includes those perhaps best placed to reach young people—music groups. Groups such as Take Six, Kirk Franklin, the Family, and DC Talk take the message of race and reconciliation around the nation. Beginning in 1994, Billy Graham began incorporating big-name Christian music groups in his crusades, having special "youth rally" nights. These events frequently draw the largest crowd of the week's crusade, often overflowing into seating outside the stadiums.

Billy Graham continues to use his influential position to draw attention to racial reconciliation. In a 1994 crusade in Atlanta, Andrew Young and Coretta Scott King appeared on the platform with Graham. Graham challenged Atlantans to worship and pray together regardless of skin color. "We've seen racial barriers broken down this week and expressions of love that have caused tears to roll down our cheeks. We call it the 'spirit of Atlanta,' when black and white will live together in peace." At a 1996 crusade in Minneapolis, he "commanded new converts to befriend members of other ethnic groups." [33] In a short article, "Racism and the Evangelical Church," Graham says that racial and ethnic hostility "threatens the very foundations of modern society." He points out that Christ came to bring reconciliation between people. Saying he shares in the blame, he writes that evangelical Christians "too often in the past ... turned a blind eye to racism." This must be no more. "Because racism is a sin, it is a moral and spiritual issue ... only the supernatural love of God can change our hearts in a lasting way and replace hatred and indifference with love and active compassion. No other force exists besides the church that can bring people together. ... Of all people, Christians should be the most active in reaching out to those of other races, instead of accepting the status quo of division and animosity."[34]

Many other evangelical organizations are devoted in whole or in part to racial reconciliation, including InterVarsity Christian Fellowship, Harambee Center, the Twin Cities Urban Reconciliaton Network, Chicago's Urban Reconciliation Enterprise, and the John M. Perkins Foundation for Reconciliation and Development, to name just a few. In terms of magnitude, visibility, and potential mass influence, however, the largest organization promoting racial reconciliation is Promise Keepers, the evangelical-based Christians men's movement led by former Colorado head football coach Bill McCartney. Promise Keepers commit to seven promises, one of which is "to reach across any racial and denominational barriers to demonstrate the power of biblical unity."

The Promise Keepers organization works hard to model racial reconciliation. Over 30 percent of its staff are persons of color, including people from all major racial groups.[35] From the beginning, McCartney has emphasized the need to integrate its stadium events. And he has done more than ask for it. Promise Keepers created a reconciliation division, appointing national strategic managers for each major racial group in the United States in hopes of reaching a greater diversity of men (and furthering the cause of reconciliation through education materials). African-American Raleigh Washington, an evangelical leader in the reconciliation movement and co-author of an influential book on reconciliation, was appointed head of the reconciliation division. McCartney himself has worked hard to integrate stadium events. He has flown to the cities where Promise Keeper stadium events are held and organized numerous meetings with local religious leaders of color, asking for their support and participation. He has also invited these leaders, at Promise Keepers expense, to Promise-Keepers' Colorado-based headquarters for meetings and discussion. Promise Keepers has also set up scholarships, available to anyone not able to afford the 50- to 60-dollar fee to participate in a stadium event. And in 1998, they took the radical step of dropping all fees, making the stadium events free to everyone.

In 1996, Promise Keepers made reconciliation its principal theme for the year. This included hosting in Atlanta what is believed to be one of the largest gatherings of clergy ever, with 39,024 attendees. McCartney planned the event to aid reconciliation: "Racism is an insidious monster," he told the assembled clergy. "You can't say you love God and not your brother." [36] In what was described as "perhaps the most moving event of the gathering, PK leaders invited men of color down to the Dome floor, while white ministers stood and cheered them." [37]

In its twenty-two stadium events in 1996, Promise Keepers presented the reconciliation message, the main theme of each conference, to over one million men. In 1997, Promise Keepers held a massive event in Washington, D.C., called "Stand in the Gap: A Sacred Assembly." According to the organization's own estimates, between 500,000 and one million men attended the event, which again emphasized reconciliation as one of its core themes. At all these events, participants could purchase materials to aid them in starting reconciliation groups and activities in their local churches and communities, and they were consistently encouraged to build bridges across dividing lines.

Clearly for evangelicals the 1990s witnessed a whirlwind of activity addressing issues surrounding race in the United States. This activity was rooted in the work of African-American religious leaders who developed a theology of reconciliation, creating a frame for others to understand racial issues and their faith.

SOMETHING LOST IN TRANSLATION

In 1995, Bill McCartney twice addressed the annual meeting at the National Black Evangelical Association, and spoke on the theme of reconciliation and Promise Keepers' commitment to overcoming racial division. That commitment was questioned by some at the conference: "What is Promise Keepers going to say about the anti-affirmative action atmosphere in this country? What are the men in the stadiums this summer going to hear about that?" [38] McCartney did not directly answer the questions, and the questioners were less than satisfied.

So too are some other black—and a few white—evangelical reconciliation leaders. Tony Evans, a reconciliation leader and head of the Urban Alternative in Dallas, said in an interview with *Christianity Today*, "The concerns of black Americans are not of dominant concern, by and large, to white evangelicals." [39] The article went on to claim that "Evans's opinion may sound extreme to many white Christians, but among black evangelicals, he is in the mainstream." [40] According to Tony Warner, Georgia area director for InterVarsity Christian Fellowship, "White evangelicals are more willing to pursue a white conservative political agenda than to be reconciled with their African-American brothers and sisters. It raises a fundamental question of their belief and commitment to the biblical gospel." [41] Curtiss DeYoung wrote that "systems of injustice in society and in the church exact a heavy cost on those outside the centers of power and effectively block reconciliation," and "declaring that we are equal without repairing the wrongs of the past is cheap reconciliation."[42] Carl Ellis, head of a Christian ministry called Project Joseph, attended both the Million Man March and Promise Keepers' Stand in the Gap meetings in Washington, D.C. He reflected on the method and focus of reconciliation among white evangelicals as he sees it: "Tears and hugs and saying I'm sorry is a good first step, but for me, the question is not one of changing the hearts of individuals as [much as] it is dealing with the systems and the structures that are devastating African-American people."[43]

Despite a near tidal wave of thought and activity focusing on racial issues by evangelicals along with a substantial broadening of the audience hearing about the importance of addressing race issues, apparently, not all is well. What agitates some within the black and other nonwhite evangelical communities?

As the message of reconciliation spread to a white audience, it was popularized. The racial reconciliation message given to the mass audience is individual reconciliation.[44] That is, individuals of different races should develop strong, committed relationships. There is also need to repent of individual prejudice. These are the means to reducing racial strife and division. Missing from this formula are the system-changing components of the original formulations. The more radical component of reconciliation espoused by the early black leaders and many of the current leaders—to challenge social systems of injustice and inequality, to confess social sin—is almost wholly absent in the popularized versions.

Thus, despite all the activity, at least some reconciliation leaders express frustration. As Cecil "Chip" Murray, senior pastor of the First African Methodist Episcopal Church in Los Angeles, wrote: "White evangelicals need an at-risk gospel. ... Calling sinners to repentance means also calling societies and structures to repentance—economic, social, educational, corporate, political, religious structures. ... The gospel at once works with individual and the individual's society: to change one, we of necessity must change the other."[45]

Something else seems to be lost in the translation. Promise Keepers' head McCartney, in his book *Sold Out*,[46] gives us an inside view. Seeing the many ways that American culture "inflicts pain, shame, and lack of opportunity on the minority communities," he went on a tour of churches across the nation, bringing the message of racial reconciliation. He shared his own experiences as a football coach, from the Bible, and in other ways, all designed to point to the necessity of racial reconciliation.

"But always," he writes, "when I finished there was no response— nothing. ... In city after city, in church after church, it was the same story—

wild enthusiasm while I was being introduced, followed by a morguelike chill as I stepped away from the microphone." Reflecting on the reactions, and the reactions to Promise Keepers' 1996 theme of reconciliation, he said: "To this day, the racial message remains a highly charged element of Promise Keepers' ministry," and "of the 1996 conference participants who had a complaint, nearly 40 percent reacted negatively to the reconciliation theme. I personally believe it was a major factor in the significant falloff in PK's 1997 attendance—it is simply a hard teaching for many."

Why these reactions? What is "hard" about the teaching? How do grassroots evangelicals think about issues of race, and how does understanding their thinking illuminate their placid responses to McCartney's message? In the next three chapters, we journey to a place little traveled: the minds and hearts of grassroots evangelicals as they discuss their views on "the race problem," racial inequality, and solutions to the American dilemma.

Color Blind

Evangelicals Speak on the "Race Problem"

By almost any definition, Debbie, white and twenty-seven years of age, is an evangelical. She holds firmly to the authority of Scriptures, is "born again," evangelizes with her words and actions, gives money for overseas missions, and is active in her church. She recently graduated from an evangelical Bible college and is now training to be minister of Christian education in her denomination. Growing up in the "wheat belt," she was sheltered from racial diversity. That changed somewhat when she attended a Bible college that was located downtown in a large city. However, she only saw this diversity from a distance, in passing; her schoolmates were nearly all white, and she spent most of her time with them.

We met for an interview in a restaurant on a Saturday morning. Throughout our discussion, she was very open and friendly, candidly stating her thoughts. When asked if she thought our country has a race problem, she matter-of-factly said: "I think we make it a problem." "How do we make it a problem?" we asked.

Well to me, people have problems. I mean, two white guys working together are gonna have arguments once in a while. Women are gonna have arguments. It happens between men and women, between two white guys and two white women. It's just people. People are gonna have arguments with people. I feel like once in a while, when an argument happens, say between a black guy and a white guy, instead of saying, "Hey, there's two guys having an argument," we say it's a race issue.

The only race problem Debbie sees is one of misinterpretation. In the normal course of interpersonal communication, conflicts arise. When this occurs between individuals of different races, it is incorrectly assumed to be a race issue. Did Debbie think there was a race problem beyond this? Yes, she said, there are times when problems genuinely occur between races, or actually between individuals of different races. To her, this happens when someone is "biased against a person solely for their race." This is due, in her view, to some people's ignorance, and is inexcusable for Christians.

Mary, a twenty-eight-year-old white and mother of two, is also strongly evangelical. Raised in a Christian family, she has been in a variety of churches and denominations over her life (usually due to moves to new areas), but has always been in an evangelical church. A college graduate, Mary is now a full-time homemaker and lives a comfortable middle-class life with her husband, a professional. Reared in Vermont, and now living in another Northeastern state, she has been relatively isolated from racial diversity. Her sister, however, to the dismay of their parents, married an African American.

Nestled in Mary's comfortable living room chairs, we turned to the subject of race relations. "Mary, do you think our country has a race problem?"

> I think so. This may sound really bad, but I think it is more going the other way. I mean we have tried for thirty years to become a unified nation and now it is a big black push to be separate again. You know, like the Million Man March was for separation. It is very frustrating. I am not racist and I don't notice my friend's color. But it is frustrating when "Oh, this is black heritage month, and this is Asian awareness and this is. . . ." Well when is there a basic white month? I think people end up going through school in Vermont—it's a white state, there are very few blacks—and they have repeated demonstrations on campus because there is not enough diversity. Well, if you have a chance to go to Boston where there is a big black population, why would you want to go to Vermont and be the only black student? But they were pushing affirmative action to increase the diversity. It's a frustration.

Mary went on to discuss her frustration with the individual-level prejudice she sees from a few whites—including her father, who did not speak to her sister for years after her marriage to an African American. But not supporting or engaging in such actions herself, she neither agrees with such people nor does she see such thoughts and actions as the center of the race problem. For her, the race problem is now primarily the results of "separatists" and a liberal emphasis on diversity programs. By emphasizing diversity and the race issue itself, she believes, we create deeper division, division that would lessen if left alone.

Debbie and Mary, like the large majority of white evangelicals we interviewed, only talked about race issues when we asked them directly about the race problem. For most white evangelicals, race was compartmentalized. They most certainly had thoughts about the race issue and, as we will argue, their thoughts are shaped at least in part by their faith, but the race issue in no way dominates their thinking. Race is not a focal point in their day-to-day lived experience.

Otis, an African-American evangelical in his early forties who attends a Pentecostal church, presents a strong contrast to Debbie and Mary. Otis began bringing race issues and race examples into the conversation very early in our interview. In fact, we actually never asked Otis any of our prepared race questions because he addressed them all in the course of answering other questions. We interviewed Otis, a friendly, soft-spoken man, at a local library and later continued the interview in his car as he responded to a call from work.

Toward the beginnings of the interview, we asked him a general question about Christian influence on society. For Otis, not enough Christians were living like Christians, at least outside their homes, and communities were not organized around Christian principles. We asked him what signs of this he saw in the community.

> I was in the military for twenty years. Then I came back. First, the housing I lived in, and the places I worked. Discrimination. ... What I am trying to say is the community is divided in many ways. It's divided by race. It's divided by income. And then you have people who like to scratch each other's backs. And they kind of form this net, and in this area they call it the good ol' boy system. They dominate like a monopoly. But is that really a Christian principle? And yet all of them go to church.

According to Otis, in his city in order to get a good job or a good promotion, the amount of formal education a person has is not nearly as important as being part of the good ol' boy system. He says he sees people and businesses take advantage of vulnerable people, such as single mothers, because they do not have enough clout. They are outside the network of power. He also sees racial segregation in many forms: "In this town the most segregated hour is eleven o'clock on Sunday morning. ... And not only that, even when five o'clock comes, the people leave their jobs, they pick up the same way of thinking. Like, go home to my little group, my little area, and I'm content in this area." He brought up a school debate going on in many communities nationwide. Should schools be integrated at the cost of busing long distances? Or should children go to local schools, even if that means segregation? Otis at first sounds like many white Americans in his response to the issue: "There has been a lot of controversy in the area about a return to segregation-type schools. I agree with that to a certain extent. I don't think a kid from one end of the county should be bused to the other. I'm sorry, I can't go along with that." But Otis's next words take a different direction:

> I can't go along with segregation either. For example, say on the west side of town scores are higher, so everyone wants to send their kids to that school. But because a kid is on that side, and the school is located on that side, the only way you can go to that school is because you live over there. But then it comes back to that dollar thing. You can't really afford to live in that neighborhood. Because you are held back ... there is no way you can live over there, so you can't attend school over there. To me, that's discrimination and segregation ... that's just the society we live in.

"What do you think committed Christians should do about these things?" we asked.

"The only way you're going to do it is through prayer. But we also have a moral obligation to speak out whenever possible. Let them know where you stand. And not be a part of it. Don't lend a hand to the situation."

We then asked if group struggles, division, and inequality were due to individuals within the groups. Otis responded, "You can't really say it's an individual. It's spiritual warfare going on. So quite naturally, people are going to come together in groups." Affecting all groups of people, spiritual warfare was, for Otis, the underlying explanation for the racialized society. Off tape, after the formal interview had ended, Otis recounted many serious incidents of discrimination he had experienced. He shared incidents from his youth, such as the things he saw done by the Ku Klux Klan. He talked about his difficult times in the army, where he was often treated viciously by superiors, made to do more work, not promoted, insulted and ridiculed more than others, and simply ignored. And he talked about his life since the army, where he sees and experiences segregation, discrimination, and inequality. Despite all the personal turmoil he has experienced on account of his race, he tells himself it is not individual people, but Satan warping systems and people to harm one another. His solution was and is to pray for help to endure and overcome suffering, to see the good that will come out of the bad. For Otis, because of its spiritual roots, racism is a poison passed on generation to generation, an evil spirit of racism, oppression, and injustice. People must stand together against the evil spirit with their faith.

Wilfred, an American Indian and a new Christian living in a large West Coast city, also has much to say about the race problem. We include his story in a book about black–white relations to help us illustrate the larger dynamics shaping people's assessments of race relations.

When we ask Wilfred if he thinks our country has a race problem, he laughs. The obviousness of the question strikes him as funny. A former drug dealer, he is currently homeless. Since his religious conversion, a true metamorphosis has occurred. Refusing to make money through criminal activity, having few marketable skills, and carrying a burden for his former "associates" and "clients," Wilfred spends many of his days walking the streets of the poor neighborhoods where he used to deal drugs. He works occasional day jobs and spends the rest of his time using whatever tactics he can to keep people from buying and selling drugs—including scaring young kids away, acting as a secret informant to the police, and "witnessing" to drug runners about the need to turn their lives around.

Nearly every day, he says, especially on the bus, he will hear, "Hey chief," meant as a slur on his heritage, often followed by "Go back to the rez." Sometimes this is the opening of a verbal or physical challenge. A few weeks before our interview, three young men accosted Wilfred while he was walking down the street. They called him chief and told him they had come to cut his pony tail. They then proceeded to beat him. At the time of the interview, Wilfred was still showing many of the bruises and a black eye from the pummeling. Being attacked by young, poor men, though certainly painful, is almost understandable to him. His other experiences based on race hurt more. More than once, after putting in a day's work, he has been offered alcohol as his pay (on one occasion, in the form of Listerine). Because he is American Indian, he says, it is assumed that alcohol is more than fair compensation for his day's labor.

Wilfred has also had rough experiences with the police. Walking late at night, he was stopped by the police and told to get in the squad car. He was then taken to an alley, commanded to get out and put his hands on the squad car, and interrogated about a crime he did not commit, complete with racial slurs. He then received a blow to the back of his head and was told to walk away without looking back.

But he sees these isolated events as simply part of a system. To be an American Indian, he said, is to be "on the bottom of the ladder" with blacks. The racial slurs, being offered alcohol in lieu of money, and being physically attacked are to him all just outward signs of this hierarchy. To be American Indian or an African American means a history of being dealt with harshly, being denied jobs, living in rural or urban ghettos, growing up (as he did) without parents, being poor, being expected to achieve little, and ultimately, he says, accepting and becoming what others expect of you. For him it also means, as he continues to struggle with it, seeing all white people as rich. The race problem is painfully real to him. It is complex, involving actions both by individuls and the larger community. It is people, it is policies, it is our society.

MAKING SENSE OF EVANGELICAL PERSPECTIVES

The responses of these four people embody much of what we heard from evangelicals on the race issue, with Debbie's and Mary's attitudes most common among whites. Debbie and Mary take a benign view of the race problem. From Debbie's perspective, much of what gets labeled "the race problem" merely represents inevitable disagreements between fallen human beings. Aside from this case of mistaken labeling, the true race problem, and it is relatively rare, is caused by individuals who view themselves as superior to others. Because Christians supposedly know that no one person is superior to any other person, the race problem exists mostly outside the church.

From Mary's perspective, the race problem would disappear if it were not for separatists dividing the nation. Although we will always have a few prejudiced people, the race problem and racism are essentially dead, living on only because of the activities of separatists and others who stand to gain from the existence of a race problem. These "race pundits" give artificial life support to a brain-dead patient. Pull the plug, and the problem will expire.

From the perspectives of Otis and Wilfred, the race problem is very much alive, permeating most aspects of society like the air they breathe, and it may never die. Both agree that behind the monster of racialization is Satan, who delights in division and oppression. Both also agree that Christians must combat the monster by uniting in prayer and action.

Why do we find these disparate perspectives? We focus first on the racial views of most white evangelicals. Much research points to the race problem as rooted in intergroup conflict over resources and ways of life, the institutionalization of race-based practices, inequality and stratification, and the defense of group position.[1] These are not the views of white evangelicals, however. For them, the race problem is one or more of three main types: (1) prejudiced individuals, resulting in bad relationships and sin, (2) other groups—usually African Americans—trying to make race problems a group issue when there is nothing more than individual problems, and (3) a fabrication of the self-interested—again often African Americans, but also the media, the government, or liberals.

The view that prejudiced individuals are the essence of the race problem of course reflects a focus on the individual as opposed to larger social units. As a Presbyterian man said: "I think our country has a perceived race relations problem. I think that we have individuals still that have race relation problems. I don't think that the county has in its current form a race relation problem." The idea that the United States had a perceived race problem, or that people try to make it a group-level problem was expressed by many of our respondents like Debbie at the beginning of this chapter. Although some try to characterize the race problem as a group-level issue, many white evangelicals strongly mistrusted this assessment and contradicted it. The problem is one of individuals and individuals only (or, as we will see, groups who or policies that say it is something else). Some found the whole idea of bad feelings toward a group difficult to comprehend. A Baptist woman said, "It's just very difficult for me to understand why someone would be against a group of people. You want to see them as individuals." And in some instances, respondents flat out said they did not like the questions about race because they seemed to be about groups of people rather than individuals. This became evident in an interview with a nondenominational evangelical man, so the interviewer asked about the objection:

Q: You don't like to make a distinction?

A: Yeah, it groups 'em and now you gotta think of 'em as a group and judge them as a group instead of individually. I prefer looking at individuals.

Common terms used to describe the race problem were prejudice, bigotry, anger, ignorance, lack of respect, fear of each other, poor communication, individuals hating or being angry at each other, and lacking Christlike love for one another. From this list we see that the problem is not only biased individuals, but poor interactions between individuals of different races. Bigotry, anger, ignorance, lack or respect, and so forth are not just wrong in and of themselves, but they make for poor, unhealthy interactions between people. This, in their minds, is one essence of the race problem. Christians are called to be in right relationship, individually, with God and with their fellow humans. Not to be is sin. This is much like evangelicals of the past who, even in the face of Jim Crow segregation, did not see such segregation as the key problem. Recall that during the Jim Crow era, "Most evangelicals, even in the North, did not think it their duty to oppose segregation; it was enough to treat blacks they knew personally with courtesy and fairness." [2] The racialized system itself is not directly challenged. What is challenged is the treatment of individuals within the system.

Individualism and defective personal relationships were constants in evangelicals' assessment of the race problem. We could marshal literally hundreds of quotes substantiating this. For many, the race problem, no matter how big or how small, ultimately came down not to a social issue, but to personal defects of some individuals in some groups as they attempted to relate to each other. To understand this assessment of the race problem, we need to introduce the concept of cultural tools.

Sociologist Ann Swidler argues that culture creates ways for individuals and groups to organize experiences and evaluate reality. It does so by providing a repertoire or "tool kit" of ideas, habits, skills, and styles.[3]

For many Americans, religion plays a key role in defining both their cultural tool kit and which tools are functionally most important to them. According to Ann Swidler, "As certain cultural resources become more central in a given life, and become more fully invested with meaning, they anchor the strategies" and realities that people develop.[4] For many religious Americans, their faith-based assumptions and beliefs are central to the formation of their other views. Sociologist William Sewell argues that a key feature of these guiding assumptions and beliefs is their transposability.[5] People not only employ their cultural tools in the context in which they were first learned, but transpose or extend them to new and diverse situations.[6] Thus, evangelicals, like others, use their religio-cultural tools not only in directly religious contexts, but in helping them make sense of issues like race relations. Accordingly, we must identify the core cultural tools of evangelicals to understand their accounts of the race problem. Because the United States is racialized, the religio-cultural tool kit varies by race. Historical and social contexts diverge radically by race, sharply shaping perceptions of reality. The ensuing discussion of cultural tools applies primarily to white evangelicals.

Religio-Cultural Tools in the White Evangelical Kit

The racially important cultural tools in the white evangelical tool kit are "accountable freewill individualism," "relationalism" (attaching central importance to interpersonal relationships), and antistructuralism (inability to perceive or unwillingness to accept social structural influences).

Individualism is very American, but the type of individualism and the ferocity with which it is held distinguishes white evangelicals from others. White evangelicals are certainly not what Hunter calls progressives.[7] Although for progressives, as for evangelicals, the individual is central, progressives believe morality to be the prerogative of each individual, and see individual happiness as perhaps the greatest goal. Most important for our present purposes, progressives view humans as essentially good, provided they are released from social arrangements that prevent people from living happily, productively, and equally—for example, racism, inequality, and lack of educational opportunity.[8] In this view, although individuals are pivotal, they are shaped in profound ways by social structures and institutions.

White conservative Protestants are accountable freewill individualists. Unlike progressives, for them individuals exist independent of structures and institutions, have freewill, and are individually accountable for their own actions. This view is directly rooted in *theological understanding*, as described (if somewhat overstated) by Stark and Glock:

> Underlying traditional Christian thought is an image of man as a free actor, as essentially unfettered by social circumstances, free to choose and thus free to effect his own salvation. This free-will conception of man has been central to the doctrines of sin and salvation. For only if man is totally free does it seem just to hold him responsible for his acts . . . . In short, Christian thought and thus Western civilization are permeated with the idea that men are individually in control of, and responsible for, their own destinies.[9]

Contemporary white American evangelicalism is perhaps the strongest carrier of this freewill-individualist tradition. The roots of this individualist tradition run deep, dating back to shortly after the sixteenth-century Reformation, extending to much of the Free Church tradition, flowering in America's frontier awakenings and revivals, and maturing in spiritual pietism and anti-Social Gospel fundamentalism. Although the larger American culture is itself highly individualistic,[10] the close connection between faith and freewill individualism to the exclusion of progressive thought renders white evangelicals even more individualistic than other white Americans.

But individuals do not simply have the freewill to make the choices they deem best. They are individually accountable to family, other people, and, most important, to God for their freely made choices. Quite unlike progressives, evangelicals believe there are right and wrong choices as determined by a divine lawgiver. Because evangelicals distrust basic human propensities (as the result of the doctrine of original sin), they view humans, if they are not rooted in proper interpersonal contexts, as tending to make wrong choices. For this reason, for evangelicals, relationalism moves to the forefront.

For evangelicals, relationalism (a strong emphasis on interpersonal relationships) derives from the view that human nature is fallen and that salvation and Christian maturity can only come through a "personal relationship with Christ." It is difficult to overemphasize the significance of this relationship for evangelicals. It is a bedrock, nonnegotiable belief. This importance was clear among the lay evangelicals we interviewed. When we asked evangelicals what it meant to be an evangelical Christian, a common element in their response was an emphasis on a personal relationship with Jesus Christ. According to one Baptist man, an evangelical is someone who acknowledges that "God has created individuals to be in a relationship with him. But because of our sinful nature we are set apart from that, and the way to have fellowship with God is through a personal relationship with Jesus Christ." *Transposing* the importance of this relationship, white evangelicals place strong emphasis on family relationships, friendships, church relationships, and other forms of interpersonal connections. Healthy relationships encourage people to make right choices. For this reason, white evangelicals, as we see, often view social problems as rooted in poor relationships or the negative influence of significant others.

Otis, at the beginning of the chapter, said that sin and the fallen nature of humans influence the race problem. But he did not limit these failings to individuals, as he explicitly stated when we asked him. For most white evangelicals, however, sin is limited to individuals. Thus, if race problems—poor relationships—result from sin, then race problems must largely be individually based. Certainly we heard white evangelicals communicate these themes. According to one Congregational man, race problems exist because "It is an issue of original sin." A Wesleyan man told us there was a race problem, and when we asked why, he responded: "It's human nature to be a sinner ... to be not as accepting of a black person." And another evangelical man, a member of a Missionary church, said, "We don't have a race problem, we have a sin problem." He explained that, as fallen beings, we do not want to take responsibility for our own actions. So we blame others, we fail to get along with others of a different race, and thus fail to accept them. In doing so, we express our sin problem. An evangelical woman who attends a nondenominational church told us the race problem "is in our hearts." For example, she said, when many whites see a black person walking down the street, they hesitate. When we asked why they hesitate, she said, "It probably originates with Satan keeping that difference in us." And a Baptist woman summarized the race problem for us in this way: "We don't love our neighbors as ourselves. That is the primary commandment of the Bible, to love our neighbor as ourself." The concept of individual sin lies behind many white evangelicals' accounts of the race problem. From this original sin, we fail to love our neighbors. These poor relationships are sin, antithetical to God's command.

Absent from their accounts is the idea that poor relationships might be shaped by social structures, such as laws, the ways institutions operate, or forms of segregation. Again, understanding evangelicals' cultural tools illuminates why this element is missing. White evangelicals not only interpret race issues by using accountable freewill individualism and relationalism, but they often find structural explanations irrelevant or even wrongheaded. The inability to see or unwillingness to accept alternatives not based on individuals is a corollary to accountable freewill individualism. This makes sense if we use the tool kit metaphor. As carpenters are limited to building with the tools in their kits (hammers encourage the use of nails, drills encourage the use of screws), so white evangelicals are severely constrained by their religio-cultural tools. Although much in Christian scripture and tradition points to the influence of social structures on individuals,[11] the stress on individualism has been so complete for such a long time in white American evangelical culture that such tools are nearly unavailable. What is more, white conservative Protestants believe that sinful humans typically deny their own personal sin by shifting blame somewhere else, such as on "the system." (Evangelicals are thus also antistructural because they believe that invoking social structures shifts guilt away from its root source—the accountable individual. However, evangelicals are selectively aware of social institutions—they see those that both impact them in their own social location and tend to undermine accountable freewill individualism.[12] For instance, they are aware of affirmative action because such programs can impact them in their social location, and they tend to oppose such programs because they go against evangelical understanding of accountable freewill individualism.)

Even when we explicitly asked about the possibility of systemic, institutionalized aspects of race problems, respondents had difficulty seeing anything other than an individual problem. For example, we asked this man attending a Moravian church:

Q: Is your perception that it mostly boils down to attitude or do you see it also in the legal system and job market? Kind of a more structural problem, as far as you know.

A: As far as I know I would have to say individual attitude. That would be my experience.

In some cases, respondents seemed to acknowledge institutional discrimination, but further questioning revealed something else, as expressed by this Presbyterian woman.

Q: Now do you view this as mostly an attitudinal thing or do you view prejudice and discrimination as having affected the legal system and housing patterns? Is it institutional or is it mostly just individual attitude?

A: I think it's individual attitude, but it affects larger areas.

Q: It affects the system?

A: I think it's within our government because our politicians are acting as individuals.

This woman saw prejudice and discrimination in institutions, but only insofar as they contained individual bigots. Even when respondents assented to the existence of systemic discrimination, they saw it as tangential, even superficial compared to the true problem of negative attitudes and unhealthy relationships. Ann Swidler argues that the cultural tool kit limits possibilities or, put another way, in providing a set of tools, it withholds others. For those we interviewed, the tools of individualism and personal relationships limited their ability either to recognize institutional problems or to acknowledge them as important.[13]

Yet this limitation on their vision was not complete. Many evangelicals did see an institutional aspect to the race problem. Like Mary in the opening of the chapter, they saw certain institutions as perpetuating a race problem that would disappear if left alone. To the extent that there is an institutional cause, therefore, it is that the institution portrays the race problem as something more then relational problems between a few sinful individuals. If these institutions would leave the race issue alone, the race problem would nearly disappear. For white evangelicals, the government is a major culprit in manufacturing a race problem. According to this Pentecostal man:

> I think that the majority of your white people would not have a problem with a black man or the black population if it were not for what the government has done in the social programs such as welfare and food stamps and things of that nature. It's not an incentive anymore to be something. ... So I think a lot of the whites have problems when you have two men who come for a job, in a government office especially, and the white man may be more qualified, but the black man gets it because of his color. It is now reverse discrimination and I think whites resent that. They don't resent that he is black, they resent what the government is doing because he is black. That is much of the race problem today.

And, in the words of this Presbyterian woman:

> I think you can blame our government for some of [the race problem]. A lot of politicians have used the welfare system to make a dependent class of people. The politicians abuse that class so they can stay in office.

Institutions and groups are seen to exist, but they are viewed as harmful. They use their power to undermine individualism and, in so doing, needlessly create and preserve a race problem. More culprits lurk, but before we go further, we need to explore the role of isolation from racial pluralism.

ISOLATION FROM RACIAL PLURALISM AND CULTURAL TOOLS

As interviewers, we were struck by how racially homogenous the social worlds of most evangelicals are, particularly those of white respondents. Other than an occasional acquaintance,[14] they had few interracial contacts. With a few notable exceptions, none lived in worlds that were not at least 90 percent white in their daily experience.[15] Many commented on this while answering the race questions. It was common for the respondents to speak of being sheltered, unexposed to racial diversity, insulated, in their own small world. As one Ohio woman from an independent church put it, "I live in my own little cubicle."

This isolation is important sociologically. Because the vast majority of white evangelicals do not directly witness individual-level prejudice (with the exception of some relatives who used the "N" word occasionally), the race problem simply cannot be as large an issue as some make it to be. Granted it was a problem in the past, and a residue may remain today because original sin remains, but the race problem is not severe. A number of respondents, as a result of their isolation and cultural tool kit, stated that the race problem was overblown, exaggerated by vested interests. A common theme was that the media exaggerated the race problem, as this Baptist man communicated:

Q: Do you think our country has a race relations problem?

A: Yes. Is it as bad as it is perceived or presented? No.

Q: Why do you suppose there is a perception that there is a bigger problem?

A: A lot of it's to sell newspapers and pump the ratings. It's visually graphic, it's exciting, it gets your attention. It brings in the ads, a lot of times. I mean newspapers and TV stations and radio are businesses first.

Another explanation, and quite common, was that people in other groups are the source of the problem. As one Presbyterian woman told us:

I see a little bit of a problem with a kind of reverse racism in the black community. We reached a point where a lot of whites want to accept blacks and give equal opportunity and so forth. I see some sort of a resistance to that in the black community.

Similarly, an evangelical woman attending a Nazarene church said:

[African Americans] have trouble getting out of that mindset [of oppression] and not seeing areas where progress has been made. They will attribute any problem to race where it may not be a racial issue at all. It may be a personal conflict and not have anything to do with race.

And another Presbyterian woman assessed the situation in much the same manner: "The problem is the black people. A lot of the black people do not want to see white people even working with them. ... It's not so much white against black, it's black against white."

One consequence of thoroughgoing evangelical individualism is a tendency to be ahistorical, to not grasp fully how history has an influence on the present. A variation of the other-group-is-to-blame position was to express frustration with people trying to reference the past to account for today. This nondenominational, evangelical man shared: "I believe there are blacks that hold a grudge about slavery still. None of us that are alive today, first of all, were alive then. So don't hold it against me for something that happened years and years ago." And for this Lutheran woman: "The black race, they need to let go of their roots that their great-great-great-great-grandfather was persecuted as a slave. So be it. That was wrong, but we're living now."

According to many white evangelicals, African Americans believe what they do in part because they are misled by black leaders, who either have an ax to grind, want to maintain the appearance of a problem because they make their living from it, or both. Because of their leaders, blacks are stuck in the past and are taught to mistrust whites. One Pentecostal man assessed the situation this way:

> You have, unfortunately for the blacks, a lot of leaders who want to keep them in this slavery stuff and make them think that the white man is trying to keep them down. I think they teach them this as a child. ... They won't forget it and leave it and move on. I never had slaves. Neither did my father. And I have no problem with a black man, but what I do have a problem with is a lot of their agenda, what is told to them.

The assessment was much the same for this Presbyterian woman:

> I think there is a leadership within the black community that has preached hate, so they'll remain in a high position. We need to forget the past; we can't undo it. We have to go forward. I think a lot of people are expecting restitution for something this society had nothing to do with.

A woman from a Christian and Missionary Alliance church put it this way:

> You have people like Jesse Jackson that started out in the 1960s doing a good thing by getting civil rights to people that deserved it, and abolishing racist views. Now he's turned into someone who has been doing this for thirty years, made a lot of money at it, and I think this is perpetuating a racist battle to keep the money flowing.

A nondenominational evangelical man conveyed this perspective in vivid terms: "Now you have all these 'religious leaders' like the Reverend Farrakhan who is just egging this stuff on! I mean, he's like just stoking the fire up, waiting for it to explode!"

Because our white respondents saw the playing field as essentially flat and the vast majority of people as unprejudiced, if they did encounter or heard stories of African Americans who were less than friendly toward white Americans, many felt it must be the blacks themselves who are to blame. Whether because they cannot forget the past, are overly sensitive, or incited by black leaders, blacks exaggerate the problem.

The issue here is not whether such analyses are correct, but that they are offered to the exclusion of other possible accounts of the race problem. Again, these views are rooted in the cultural tools evangelicals extend to race issues, and the application of these tools is shaped by the relative isolation of the respondents. For most white evangelicals, it is obvious that prejudice and discrimination are minimal, and if others realized this, the race problem would essentially disappear. As an evangelical pastor from Illinois put it, on the whole, "especially in the Christian community, I don't think there's that much division. … If we didn't give it so much attention, I think it would die of its own accord." [16]

THE RACE PROBLEM ACCORDING TO THE LESS ISOLATED

Understanding the cultural tools people use illuminates how people construct reality, including their racial reality. But, as we also claimed, knowing the cultural tool kit is not enough. We must examine the structural context within which these tools are applied. White Americans in particular are able to and often do live their everyday lives relatively isolated from other racial groups. In the previous section, we claimed that this isolation from racial pluralism allows white evangelicals to emphasize particular cultural tools. In this section, we extend that claim. When racial isolation is *reduced*, the tools are extended in a different fashion, and even at times abandoned (and new ones created).

Most nonwhites, because they are a smaller percentage of the population, are less isolated from pluralism. This is perhaps in part why Otis and Wilfred see things differently from most white evangelicals. This African-American Baptist man clearly expressed the role of exposure:

Q: Do you think our country has a race problem?

A: Does our country have a race problem?! (chuckles) We have a big one! Yeah, we got a big race problem.

Q: Why do you think we have a race problem?

A: Because I see it every day.

Like Wilfred, this man takes the answer to the question as so self-evident that it strikes him as funny (this was a common response among the non-isolated). Such a question is perhaps akin to asking evangelicals if they believe in God. The answer is so obvious that it is not really a question. Yet, if we wish to claim that the application of the tool kit is shaped by relative racial isolation, we must go further than cite answers from African Americans, who may very well respond differently for reasons other than their level of exposure.

When we examine the views of white respondents who are not as racially isolated, we see a new perspective. They view racial tensions and problems as real and significant. According to "contact theory,"[17] contact that does not meet certain conditions (such as equal status) typically leads to greater conflict and prejudice. This was substantiated by responses from relatively non-isolated respondents. A Lutheran woman in a small midwestern town described her feelings as her all-white town had become, in her estimation, about one-third nonwhite over the last decade. Asked whether there was a race problem, she said:

> It's hard in this neck of the woods because we've never really been exposed to it. Even as Christians we say, "Well, I don't have a problem with that." But all of a sudden, when your town is about a third other cultural groups, you find out that it's a little bit harder to mix than you thought that it was.

This woman went on to describe the perceived rising crime rate and uneasy, tense feelings between groups in the town. Part of the problem, she said, is that people are starting to see each other as groups, rather than individuals. If the townspeople viewed each other as individuals, the race problem, real as it currently is, could nearly dissolve. Relative non-isolation, then, appears to affect the way the cultural tool kit is applied, and thus the way reality is interpreted. For relatively non-isolated respondents, the race problem is neither a creation of the media nor does it persist only because some try to make it an issue. The race problem is real. Yet, the tool kit powerfully shapes the interpretation of the race problem such that it is still viewed primarily as individuals and poor relationships.

However, for those who have extensive and extended intergroup contact, whose social networks are interracial or largely nonwhite, the cultural tools are transposed in a different manner, and different interpretations become possible.

Carol, a former Lutheran who now attends a variety of neighborhood churches, is an example. Growing up isolated from blacks, she remembers feeling repulsed if she saw black people kissing or imagined herself kissing a black man. She recounted an incident in which she met a black girl in the park and for some reason ended up biting her. "I was overcome with the need to wash my mouth out, to spit, to try and get clean," she recalled.

But Carol's life has dramatically changed. She is now about as immersed in a nonwhite world as is possible. Married to an African-American man, she lives and works in an all-black community in a large midwestern city. She is so isolated from the white world she came from that she remembers it only vaguely and no longer has white friends. When asked if our country has a race problem, she responded quite differently from racially isolated white evangelicals:

Oh yeah, oh yeah, definitely, mmm-hmmm. ... The white people think they're superior, not all of 'em but some of 'em. They think they're better. Why? Because they got a better upbringing, better advantages? That doesn't mean there's something wrong with black people.

She went on to describe an experience based on race as further evidence that, from her perspective, race matters. In so doing, she revealed that she differs not only from most other white evangelicals, but from black evangelicals as well:

I went up to McDonald's one time right up here and I'm white in an all-black neighborhood, right? One black woman walked up to me and wanted a handout. I said, "I have no money" and she started cursing at me and telling me, "Well, what are you doin' in this neighborhood?!" I rushed to my car and got the heck out of there, you know. [The race problem] is real scary, it really is scary.

The interviewer followed up on this story, asking if she found it difficult to be white in her neighborhood or whether she was adjusting to it.

I'm adjusting to it. I think my daughter finds it hard because she's mixed. They call her cracker. Crackers are white. They call her Puerto Rican because she doesn't look like she's totally black, you know, and people resent her. But I do think that I'm probably better off in a black neighborhood. I'm more openly accepted than if my husband were to move in an all-white neighborhood. I think there'd be hell to pay there.

Whether or not her assessments are correct, the race problem is very real and tangible for Carol. It involves individuals and bad relationships to be sure. But she also suggests that it involves group issues, such as where mixed-marriage couples can and cannot acceptably live, the experiences of being a "mixed" child in our culture, and that race is associated with a sense of group position. Carol still thinks individualistically, but not solely so, as her perspective is nuanced by her structural reality. She realizes she is different from most whites, that these differences matter to people, and that the differences that matter are largely centered around race. From her perspective, then, it is difficult not to see how race plays a fundamental role in our society, even while her cultural tools of individualism and personal relationships continue to play a part in shaping her interpretation of reality. Because of her structural and thus social context, her individualistic perspective is modified to include aspects of a macro perspective.

Tim, an evangelical white man of lower-middle income in his early forties, is involved in some of the reconciliation activities we discussed in Chapter Three. He grew up in a large, diverse city on the West Coast, and then lived for nearly twenty years in Hawaii, the one U.S. state where whites are not the majority of the population. Tim sees the race problem as a sin problem, but as he expounded on this, he talked differently from most white evangelicals. Like Otis, sin was not only individual, but social as well. According to Tim, our nation is going against "spiritual laws that are just as applicable as gravity. When you break them they eventually break you. So our society is breaking down because we are not following unseen guidelines, boundaries that we are stepping over."

"What spiritual laws, with regard to race issues, are we shunning?" we asked.

> Ultimately, one is that Jesus said He is our peace, he has torn down the wall of division. ... Even from the foundation of this country, even though we were a nation of immigrants, we have always been divided. There has never been unity. We are a melting pot but we have never become one color. ... Every country or situation has some kind of walls of racial or economic distinctions. And again I think it is just one of those issues where if we want to align ourselves with God, He says we are all one, we are either all one in sin, or all one in grace.

Tim, having the same historic faith and equipped with the same cultural tools as other white evangelicals, transposes them differently, even adapting and revising them to his social location. He did talk about individual sin, and the need for people to take personal responsibility, but, as we see, he has come to view at least race as a group issue. God says the dividing walls between people have been torn down, yet racial division is clearly evident. From Tim's perspective, people must therefore all be involved in corporate sin. For most white evangelicals, isolated from racial pluralism, their cultural tools do not direct them to reason in this way. They diverge from Tim in three ways. The race problem does not typically include racial group division, as it does for Tim; it is not as severe as it is in Tim's assessment; and the race problem is seen as the result of individual sin or the artificial creation of self-interested others.

WHAT ARE SOME CONCRETE EXAMPLES OF "RACISM"?

Although the form of racism changes with the form of racialization, its constant function is to justify the racialized system. We did not expect our respondents to view racism in this way, but we wanted to grasp how important racism was to them, what it meant to them, and what specific, concrete examples they would cite to illustrate it.

In our national survey of over 2,500 Americans, 80 percent of white evangelicals said racism is a "very important" issue for Christians to address. But such survey questions do not ask people to rank priorities. So how important is racism really? The results of our interviews are suggestive. When we asked people to name the top issues Christians should be concerned with, only 4 percent of white Protestants named racism as an issue. In contrast, a third of African-American Protestants cited racism, with one-quarter naming it as the single most important issue for Christians to address. Further, as we have noted, outside of the specific section of the interview devoted to race questions, our white respondents rarely mentioned the issue of race. The race issue may be of some importance to ordinary evangelicals, then, but other issues—such as moral decline, family breakup, crime, and children's education—are more important.

Racism, individual-level prejudice, and individual-level discrimination all appear to have the same meaning for our respondents because they used these terms interchangeably. Just as important, when asked for concrete examples of racism, our respondents struggled to provide an answer. Many gave vague generalities, such as not liking a person because of skin color, name calling, putting people down, seeing a group rather than individuals, or not trusting other people. When we pressed further, asking again for specific examples, real or made up, respondents were often at a loss. Some would cite historical examples that used to happen but no longer do (e.g., separate drinking fountains). A few cited contemporary issues in the news, such as black church burnings, or hate groups like the Ku Klux Klan or Skinheads. Some cited examples of reverse racism, such as affirmative action, blacks not liking whites, a relative being looked at angrily by a black man, and other such accounts.

A substantial number of respondents simply could not cite specific examples. They would either change the subject, continue to talk in vague generalities, or simply plead ignorance on the issue. For example, this evangelical Covenant woman said: "I don't know, I don't see ... I don't see blacks being discriminated against. I think it's very subtle in [my state]. It's more obvious I think probably in other parts of the country." This Episcopalian woman gave much the same response: "Um, I don't know how to answer that, I really don't. You know, discrimination I think is a problem in certain areas. See, we're so sheltered from that, I, you know, I'm trying to think of what I read and that's not even fair because that's more of a biased opinion."

After realizing that respondents were not giving specific examples, we attempted to press them further. Even when we probed, we often could not get specific, concrete examples, as this exchange with a Pentecostal woman illustrates:

Q: So would you say there's racism in the country?

A: Oh, yes, sure.

Q: And what are concrete examples of that? What does that look like?

A: What does it look like? What do you mean?

Q: Well, where is the racism? What exactly is it?

A: We don't have racism here. I think it's in your big cities.

Q: So what exactly is the racism in these big cities? What exactly do you mean?

A: Well I mean the whites don't like the blacks and got all kinds of things against them and vice versa. It just isn't whites against blacks. Blacks do not like white people.

In summary, most respondents assented to the existence of racism, as this is one expression of imperfect human nature, a result of original sin. Not surprisingly, racism was interpreted as individual-level prejudice or discrimination and nothing else. More surprisingly to us was that when white evangelicals were asked to provide concrete examples, a substantial number could not. Our respondents acknowledged racism not because they were actually aware of any specific instances, but because, given their understanding of humans as fallen beings, isolated occurrences of individual-level discrimination are always possible. As far as they knew, they themselves had never engaged in racism. Moreover, they did not believe America's institutions to be racist.

Conversely, our nonwhite respondents had no trouble producing specific examples of racism, nor did the relatively racially non-isolated whites, usually both at the individual- and institutional-levels. As many race scholars note, not having to know the details or extent of racialization is an advantage afforded to most white Americans.

All this helps us understand why two-thirds of white Americans (and evangelicals) believe conditions for blacks are improving, while just one-third of African Americans believe that. It also helps us understand why African Americans are nearly three times as likely as white Americans to feel conditions for blacks are deteriorating.[18] Whites and blacks are widely divergent both in their interpretation of the actual state of race relations and of what causes the problems. After hundreds of years of efforts, far from being brought closer together, white and black evangelicals, and Americans in general, are widely separated, perceiving and experiencing the world in very different ways.

LINKING VIEWS OF THE RACE PROBLEM AND RACISM TO RACIALIZATION

From interviews conducted back in the late 1960s, Wellman concluded that many white respondents believed "agitators cause racial problems; white America does not," and "America proclaims that all people are equal and there is no reason to believe otherwise."[19] The same holds true among contemporary white evangelicals. Although some individuals may be prejudiced, they think, America is not racialized. We have tried to show why they hold these beliefs. In the process, we moved beyond the simplistic explanation that white evangelicals, to protect their advantages, simply lie or distort the truth. We cannot conclude that their expressed views are merely smoke screens to divert attention from what they know to be true. Instead, we have argued, the cultural tools and intergroup isolation of evangelicals lead them to construct reality so as to individualize and minimize the problem. They do so honestly and with good intentions, if somewhat one-sidedly.

On careful reflection, we can see that it is a necessity for evangelicals to interpret the problem at the individual level. To do otherwise would challenge the very basis of their world, both their faith and the American way of life. They accept and support individualism, relationalism, and anti-structuralism. Suggesting social causes of the race problem challenges the cultural elements with which they construct their lives. This is the radical limitation of the white evangelical tool kit. This is why anyone, any group, or any program that challenges their accountable freewill individualist perspective comes itself to be seen as a cause of the race problem. Again, white evangelicals make this assessment with the best of intentions. As Wellman noted, most white Americans honestly desire a color-blind society, and often oppose the color-conscious for that reason.[20]

What is more, because most white evangelicals perceive racism as individual-level prejudice and discrimination, and do not view themselves as prejudiced people, they wonder why they must be challenged with problems they did not and do not cause. As they communicated to us over and over, they do not have much interracial contact, but when they do, they are friendly toward people they do meet from other races, and some even claim healthy interracial friendships.

From the isolated, individualistic perspective of most white evangelicals and many other Americans, there really is no race problem other than bad interpersonal relationships (or people or programs trying to make it something more than this). And it truly is hard even to think of examples of racism, other than a general sense of bad interpersonal relationships, and occasionally what is heard from the media (if the media can be trusted). The white evangelicals we interviewed do not want a race problem. They want to see people get along, and want people to have equal opportunity. They see these as essential to living out their faith. In short, they yearn for color-blind people. This is the contemporary white American evangelical perspective.

But white evangelicals' cultural tools and racial isolation curtail their ability to fully assess why people of different races do not get along, the lack of equal opportunity, and the extent to which race matters in America. Although honest and well intentioned, their perspective is a powerful means to reproduce contemporary racialization. Because reality is socially constructed, a highly effective way to ensure the perpetuation of a racialized system is simply to deny its existence. Contemporaries are not doing this out of some old form of Jim Crow racism, but based on their cultural tools and relative isolation—themselves partially the products of racialization. With no apparent intent, the result—the maintenance of a racialized United States—is the same.

This perspective misses the racialized patterns that transcend and encompass individuals, and are therefore often institutional and systemic. It misses that whites can move to most any neighborhood, eat at most any restaurant, walk down most any street, or shop at most any store without having to worry or find out that they are not wanted, whereas African Americans often cannot.[21] This perspective misses that white Americans can be almost certain that when stopped by the police, it has nothing to do with race, whereas African Americans cannot.[22] This perspective misses that whites are assumed to be middle class unless proven otherwise, are not expected to speak for their race, can remain ignorant of other cultures without penalty, and do not have to ask every time something goes wrong if it is due to race, whereas African Americans cannot. This perspective misses that white Americans are far more likely than black Americans to get a solid education, avoid being a victim of crime, and have family and friends with money to help when extra cash is needed for college, a car, or a house. This perspective misses that white Americans are far more likely to have networks and connections that lead to good jobs than are black Americans. This perspective misses that white Americans are more likely to get fair treatment in the court system than are African Americans. And this perspective ultimately misses the truth revealed by Joe Feagin's and Melvin Sikes's exhaustive study of black middle-class Americans: "Today blatant, subtle, and covert discrimination against African Americans persists in virtually all aspects of their public life. ... Racial discrimination is pervasive, and cumulative and costly in its impact." [23] The individualistic perspective encourages people to dismiss such evidence as liberal, wrongheaded, overblown, or as isolated incidents. Such a perspective, then, fails to see or acknowledge, as Cornel West puts it in *Race Matters*, "The sheer absurdity that confronts human beings of African descent in this country—the incessant assaults on black intelligence, beauty, character, and possibility." [24]

Ultimately, such a perspective effectively reproduces racialization. Because its existence is not recognized, action is not taken to overcome it. Attempts at corrective action, perhaps by black Christians, may be countered by white evangelicals because such action simply seems wrong from their vantage point. To the extent that overcoming racialization depends in part on social programs and policies, evangelicals' general opposition to such programs and policies perhaps serves to heighten racialization. But the influence of reproducing racialization may go even further.

The individualistic perspective is much less likely to miss racial issues when the person affected is oneself. So white evangelicals can recount times they have felt discriminated against, ranging from hearing a snide remark from someone, to feeling a sense of unfriendliness from someone at a restaurant, to driving through a black neighborhood and feeling uncomfortable, to blacks as a whole having a chip on their shoulder, to programs and laws designed for the benefit of one race only. Thus, the individualist perspective does not eliminate the ability to see socially structured issues. What it does do, in the context of a racialized society, is eliminate the ability to see advantage, therefore creating a society where all compete for something akin to Bakhtin's most favored victim status.[25]

We stand at a divide. White evangelicals' cultural tools and racial isolation direct them to see the world individualistically and as a series of discrete incidents. They also direct them to desire a color-blind society. Black evangelicals tend to see the racial world very differently. Ironically, evangelicalism's cultural tools lead people in different social and geographical realities to assess the race problem in divergent and nonreconciliatory ways. This large gulf in understanding is perhaps part of the race problem's core, and most certainly contributes to the entrenchment of the racialized society.

Controlling One's Own Destiny

Explaining Economic Inequality Between Blacks and Whites

Christian thought and thus Western civilization are permeated with the idea that [people] are individually in control of, and responsible for, their own destinies.

Rodney Stark and Charles Glock

God helps those who help themselves.

Ben Franklin, *Poor Richard's Almanack*

Television, national magazines, and major newspapers excel in communicating through pictures. Pictures of ghettos, substandard housing, and poverty on the one hand, and pictures of exclusive suburban neighborhoods, multi-million-dollar homes, and wealth on the other hand, vividly, if inadvertently, communicate the vast economic inequality between blacks and whites. How do these pictures communicate this reality? Almost invariably, when the media wishes to communicate the depths in American poverty, they show African Americans. Likewise, to communicate the extremes of wealth of America, they feature a Bill Gates, or gated communities populated principally by wealthy whites. African Americans fall below the poverty line more than three times as frequently as non-Hispanic whites, are substantially less likely to own homes than are white Americans, and their median household wealth is only 8 percent that of Anglos.[1] Even middle-class African Americans, we saw, are on shaky footing. For example, the median net assets for college-educated whites are nearly 20,000 dollars. But for college-educated blacks, median net assets are a miniscule 175 dollars.

For white evangelicals, the race problem does not include economic inequality. Although most evangelicals are aware of the inequality, often through the visual images presented by the media, inequality is a separate issue from the race problem. Yet, because racial inequality is central to what is meant by a racialized society, we must explore how white evangelicals explain this reality. How people explain racial inequality shapes how they vote, what policies they support, and the solutions they advocate.[2] For this reason, the way evangelicals explain racial inequality helps us assess evangelicalism's influence on black–white relations.

EXPLAINING RACIAL ECONOMIC INEQUALITY:
THE VIEWS FROM A NATIONAL SURVEY

How do evangelicals explain racial inequality? Do they differ in their explanations from other Americans? A comparison to other Americans can be done with national survey data. We use the General Social Survey for this purpose. This annual survey, conducted by the National Opinion Research Center in Chicago, is nationally representative and asks questions on a variety of issues. Because we found no differences on questions about racial inequality between those who called themselves evangelicals and those who called themselves fundamentalists, we combined them into one group we call conservative Protestants.[3] This gives us a large enough sample to make generalizations. To be conservative Protestant, people must say their primary religious identity is evangelical or fundamentalist, and they must assent to two primary hallmarks of these groups: belief in the afterlife and belief that the Bible is the literal or inspired word of God.

The key set of questions on how Americans explain racial inequality begins: "On average blacks have worse jobs, income, and housing than white people. Do you think these differences are . . ." People are then asked to respond "yes" or "no" to each of four possible explanations, and they can respond affirmatively to more than one or negatively to all. The four possible explanations in the survey are:

1. Because most blacks have less inborn ability to learn?

2. Because most blacks just don't have the motivation or will-power to pull themselves up out of poverty?

3. Because most blacks don't have the chance for education that it takes to rise out of poverty?

4. Mainly due to discrimination?

Considering these four, we see that two—ability and motivation—are largely individualistic explanations. That is, the problem lies with black individuals. The other two—education and discrimination—are largely structural explanations. That is, the problem lies outside black individuals.

Because white evangelicals and other white Americans historically shared similar cultural tools, we expect that both these groups are more likely to cite individual reasons than structural reasons. But, because these cultural tools are indigenous to the conservative Protestant subculture, affirmed in the subculture, and held with characteristic evangelical vigor, we expect conservative Protestants to differ from other Americans in degree. In short, we expect them to be even more individualistic and less structural than other white Americans. Specifically, based on their cultural tools of accountable freewill individualism and antistructuralism, we expect the following:

1. Compared to other whites, white conservative Protestants are more supportive of explanations that affirm individualism.

2. Compared to other whites, white conservative Protestants avoid acknowledging contemporary social structures, unless the social structures hinder individual determination.

But one individual-level explanation—lacking inborn ability—poses a problem. It is an "old-time" biological explanation that has been socially unacceptable for decades,[4] and also denies the importance of individual determination. We expect very few Americans, regardless of religious identity, to adopt this explanation.

The survey confirms this expectation. Explaining the black–white socioeconomic gap in terms of inferior inborn ability is easily the least cited explanation. Only about one in ten Americans views this as an explanation, and conservative Protestants do not differ from other white Americans. (See Table A-1 in Appendix A.)

Also as expected, the rank order of explanations is similar for both white conservative Protestants and other whites. Both groups are most likely to cite lack of motivation by blacks as the number one reason for black–white inequality. This reason is followed by lack of access to quality education. Discrimination is the least cited explanation. But, as expected, the similarities end here.

White conservative Protestants blame blacks more—or hold them more accountable—than other whites do. Nearly two-thirds of white conservative Protestants say that blacks are poor because they lack sufficient motivation, compared to half of other white Americans. White conservative Protestants clearly are more likely to see inequality as rooted in black individuals than are other whites.

In contrast, white conservative Protestants are significantly less likely to explain racial inequality in structural terms. Although almost half of other white Americans cite lack of access to quality education as an explanation, only one-third of white conservative Protestants do. With respect to the discrimination explanation, conservative Protestants differ again. Just one-quarter of white conservative Protestants, compared to slightly over a third of other Americans, agree that discrimination explains the racial disparity.[5]

White conservative Protestants, it appears, are more individualistic and less structural in their explanations of black–white inequality than other whites. We can see this disparity best by comparing the ratio of individual to structural responses. Here is how. Take the percentage of those citing motivation, and subtract the percentage of those citing discrimination. Doing so, we find that the conservative Protestant disparity of 35 percentage points is *more than twice* the 15-percentage-point disparity for other Americans. For the motivation/education difference, the conservative Protestant disparity of 30-percentage points is *six times* as large as the 5-percentage-point gap for other whites. The stronger emphases placed on individual causes and the weaker emphases placed on structural causes by conservative Protestants, when combined, lead to an impressive deviation from other whites. And this white conservative Protestant difference remains even when we account for other differences between these groups, such as age and region of residence. Further, the white conservative Protestant effect remains strong even after controlling for individuals' levels of traditional prejudice. (This analysis is in Table A-2 of Appendix A.)

Religiously-based cultural tools matter in how people explain racial inequality. Because white theologically liberal and conservative Protestants possess divergent sets of religiously based cultural tools,[6] their explanations should diverge even more widely from each other than do the explanations of white conservative Protestants and other whites. We define theologically liberal Protestants as those Protestants who claim that "theologically liberal" is their primary religious identity and who do not interpret the Bible literally.

Although we find no differences for the ability explanation of racial inequality, the similarities again end here. While 62 percent of white conservative Protestants choose the individual-level explanation of lack of motivation, only 40 percent of white theologically liberal Protestants do.

For the structural explanation of lack of access to education, the comparative percentages are 32 percent for the conservatives and 58 percent for the liberals; for discrimination, the comparative percentages are 27 percent and 43 percent (see Table A-3 in Appendix A). Not only are the percentage differences large, but the explanations' rank orders differ as well. Among white conservative Protestants, motivation is the most frequently cited reason, followed by education and discrimination. Among theologically liberal Protestants, education is the most frequently cited reason, followed by discrimination, and, finally, motivation. Cultural tools matter.

And race matters too. Black Americans, like white theologically liberal Protestants, rate lack of ability and motivation as the least likely explanations of racial inequality; also like white theologically liberal Protestants, over half cite lack of equal access to education. But unlike white theologically-liberal Protestants, the number one reason cited for racial inequality—by two-thirds of African Americans—is discrimination. This leads us to ask: Does religious identity influence black Americans' explanations of racial inequality?

Yes. (See Table A-4 in Appendix A.) Black conservative Protestants differ from other black Americans; but the conservative Protestant effect runs in the *opposite direction* of white Americans. Black conservative Protestants, compared to other blacks, are *less* individualistic and *more* structural in their explanations of racial inequality. Black conservative Protestants are less likely to cite lack of motivation as an explanation of racial inequality than are other black Americans. Conversely, they are more likely to cite discrimination than are other black Americans.

The opposing effects of black and white conservative Protestantism on explanations of racial inequality are important. This means that the divide in how whites and blacks explain racial inequality is actually greater for religious conservatives than for other Americans. Although Chapter Three explored the strong efforts black and white evangelicals have made to reconcile racial differences and unite, at least in how they explain racial inequality, they are farther apart in their views than other Americans. In accounting for economic inequality, it appears that *conservative religion intensifies the different values and experiences of each racial group, sharpening and increasing the divide between black and white Americans.*

Based on survey data, white conservative Protestants differ in their explanations of racial inequality from other whites, from theologically liberal white Protestants, from African Americans, and most dramatically from black conservative Protestants. A key reason why these disparities exist, we argue, is that white conservative Protestants use their religiously based cultural tools, forged in the crucible of race relations in America, to account for racial inequality. Although the survey results are consistent with this argument, the survey does not allow us to know if the cultural tools that we hypothesize as distinctive are truly being used. In-depth interviews allow us to address this question.

EXPLAINING RACIAL ECONOMIC INEQUALITY: THE VIEWS FROM OUR INTERVIEWS

In the personal, in-depth interviews with evangelicals,[7] we asked essentially the same question used in the General Social Survey: "Studies show that on average blacks have worse jobs, income, and housing than white people." However, rather than offer closed-ended options, we then simply asked, "Why do you think this is?" The responses from this method gave us much richer information than mere survey data.

We found that a pivotal and dearly held assumption for a large majority of white evangelicals is that all Americans have equal opportunity. According to one Presbyterian woman in her mid-sixties, for example, "They [blacks] have all the opportunities we [whites] have." Another woman, in her mid-twenties and a member of a nondenominational church, confidently put it this way: "If they want to achieve the same level as a white person, they can."

The concept of equal opportunity both derives from and maintains accountable freewill individualism. Much of conservative Protestant theological thought views humans as free actors who are personally responsible for and in control of their own destinies.[8] It takes but a limited extension of this freewill individualist perspective to arrive at equal opportunity. Further, freewill individualism requires a belief in equal opportunity, or the world would be grossly unfair and God unjust.

And it is here that we see how the cultural tool kit limits possible explanations. The equal opportunity assumption, combined with the concept that we are equally created, sets the equation used to solve the "Why do we have a racial socioeconomic gap" question:

Equally Created + Equal Opportunity + X = Unequal Outcome

In the face of this equation, the possible range of explanations is curtailed. Assuming people seek consistency between their assumptions and reality, one cannot solve for X with an explanation such as unequal access to education or structural discrimination, for example.[9] The cultural tools have limited the possible solutions. Only a few main explanations are now available.

Which predominate? The explanations and the percentage of white evangelicals citing each are reported in Table 5-1.[10] We collapsed three miscellaneous types of explanations—lack of ability, lack of information for blacks to take advantage of available opportunities, and black spiritual weakness—into one category (Other). We did this because few evangelicals cited these explanations. Even in combining them, they were mentioned by just 8 percent of white evangelicals. As with the General Social Survey data, God-ordained differences are rarely cited, even among conservative Protestants. If they are not God ordained or the result of spiritual weakness, then what explains the vast inequities?

Table 5-1

Explanations for Black–White Socioeconomic Gap, White Evangelicals[a]

Explanation	Percent Citing
Black Culture	52
Lack Motivation/Initiative	48
Culture, Motivation, or Both[b]	72
History	29
Welfare	21
Discrimination	21
Education	16
No Inequality	14
Other	8

N=117

[a]Totals add to more than 100% because respondents could cite more than one explanation

[b]Total is not the sum of culture and motivation because many respondents cited both

Source: Pew Evangelical Interviews, 1996

Given their tools, the large majority of white evangelicals solved the equation with the explanation of lack of motivation and, as we will see, closely related "cultural" arguments. Nearly three-quarters of the respondents cited these reasons. If there is one overarching theme that most white evangelicals shared in using these explanations, it was that black Americans lack hope and vision. They lack the ability to see what is truly possible. Representative of this perspective was Thomas, a member of a nondenominational church, and an economically successful graduate of an elite undergraduate evangelical college and elite MBA program. Thomas pensively reflected on this issue, solving the equation with "culture" and lack of motivation:

> I am wondering if there is a vision that a person can see or can capture. I think often times there is not. A vision of the world in which people are going to need to function. I probably kept myself going, not knowing exactly what I wanted to do down the road. But just knowing that I wanted to get good grades to keep the doors open. And fortunately I had just enough discipline to get myself through. ... If [African Americans] have a chance to catch a vision it would help people stay focused enough to get themselves there [to economic success]. Everyone wants to be the pro athlete born with natural skills. But it takes effort to get there. Maybe they just don't have quite the drive or courage and don't know what it's going to take to be on the other side. It takes initiative and it takes an extended family. I think it's tough for people who don't have that extended family to catch the vision.

Thomas was reflexive, building an understanding of racial inequality with his cultural tools. From the viewpoint of Thomas, he had "succeeded" because of what he did, and, except for family, independent of any social structures. He had enough vision to direct himself. Conversely, the inability of African Americans to "catch the vision" was central for him, and failure results from lack of individual initiative and from cultural deficiencies (really, dysfunctional relationalism) such as family breakdown. This lack-of-vision explanation was repeated over and over, and serves to show the optimism in the conservative Christian American way.

Thomas, like the majority of respondents, pointed to what we call "cultural" reasons, a category not even included in the General Social Survey list of explanations for racial inequality. But what is meant by culture? For our respondents, culture amounts to either aggregated accountable freewill individualism or relationalism. Because evangelicals are aggregationists (they see social groups and society not as something unique, but as the sum of individuals), their use of "cultural" accounts often meant projecting an individual problem (bad choices) across many individuals. Having too many children is one example. As this nondenominational woman from Ohio somewhat roughly put it: "So many black people have beaucoup [large numbers of] kids. I only had two because I feel as though that's what I can afford. And, I mean, sometimes I think they just don't use the brains God gave them." Failing to know God properly is another example, as expressed by this Pentecostal woman: "I know myself that when people find God, one of the first things they do is clean up and get a job." Another commonly cited reason was that blacks choose not to speak "mainstream" [white] English. According to one southern Presbyterian man, "The blacks are not willing to accept that to learn correct English is a major step toward advancing in society." In their use of these cultural reasons, white conservative Protestants do not mean patterns of behavior rooted in values (e.g., blacks have many children because they highly value large families), but rather that blacks are making poor choices (e.g., black individuals do not exercise responsibility in child-bearing, faith, or speech). In this sense, the only difference between the black motivation category (they lack initiative) and the black culture category (they have too many babies, they do not speak correctly) is that the culture category does not reference motivation specifically.

A second dimension of the black culture category, intertwined with the first, draws on evangelicals' cultural tool of relationalism. Respondents use their understanding that people make wrong choices if they are not in proper relational contexts with others. As a result, black individuals are seen as doing poorly economically because their families lack strong bonds, or because significant others do not steer them to make right choices. As one Congregational woman told us, "I see the breakup of the family as being the key to the whole thing, just the nonblessedness of the people. [For those who are not poor] I think it's because they have been in Christian families." Even in these cases, however, the onus for achievement remains on the individual, who is the ultimate accountable entity, as this young Baptist man illustrates: "They have really dropped the ball when it comes to family responsibility for raising their children. I hate that the kids have to suffer for that, but the kid's responsibility is to say, 'I'm not going to let that happen [to me].'"

In short, for most white evangelicals, blacks suffer from relational dysfunction and a lack of responsibility. And these deficiencies are debilitating in the American system, as this Missionary-church man from the Midwest communicated: "I don't know if our society really allows laid-back people to succeed. You have to be an achiever in this country to succeed. You can't just do whatever."

We have not yet mentioned the irritation this question raised for a number of white conservative Protestants. Our respondents appeared to be friendly, open, committed, caring people. But many did not like it when asked this race question. Either they did not agree with the premise of the question (those who denied there was inequality), or they were irritated by blacks themselves (or the seemingly implicit suggestion that whites might somehow be at fault). A sub-explanation contained within the motivational and cultural explanations was the "lazy-butt account." When this account was offered, it was almost in conjunction with anger or irritation. One Baptist man, for example, said:

> There are a lot of people just sitting back on their butts, saying because of circumstances in the past you owe me this and you owe me that. There's a lot of resentment in the white community because of that and we just kind of need to get over all of that and move forward. Everybody is responsible for their own actions. Life is not the circumstances; life is how you deal with the circumstances and how it makes you better and how you move forward.

A Wesleyan woman remarked:

> A lot of them don't care. They don't want to work. ... You go downtown and you see some of these apartments, low-income housing. It's trash. I mean, they don't care and then they complain. Well, get off your duffer and do something. Make a better life for yourself. Clean up your house, pick up your trash, get some kind of job.

And a nondenominational man has this to say:

> I think they chose to live like that because it is an easier way out. I am a firm believer in this: God said he would provide for our needs, and he does. But if you want out of a gutter, you're going to have to work to get out of a gutter.

The lazy-butt account and other responses of irritation were offered by respondents from their twenties through their eighties, across denominations and income levels, and in all parts of the country. Although we want to stress that many white evangelicals did not use this account, we also want to be clear that many did find our question offensive. What is it about inequality and black Americans that arouse such responses? After all, the respondents talked much about love for their neighbors, particularly those in the Christian family. African Americans are by and large Christian—a larger percent self-identify as Christian than in white America—so they should be particularly exempt from such responses. What then is so offensive?

African Americans, despite their Christian association, violate key tenets of white conservative Christianity. African Americans, in their eyes, are not true accountable freewill individualists, are relationally dysfunctional, and sin both by relying on programs rather than themselves, and by shifting blame to structurally based reasons for inequality. Although African Americans may be Christians, they are not good white American Christians. African Americans violate and challenge much of what is core to white American conservative Christianity. At first glance, the question about why racial inequality exists is not a religious question. Yet, because of the close historical and present-day connection between faith and the American way of life, at least for white conservative Protestants, it is a religious question.

Racial inequality challenges their world understanding, and it challenges their faith in God and America. And insofar as it does, it is capable of arousing impassioned responses, for they are now dealing not just in mundane policy matters, but with issues of cosmic significance. To these respondents, race, especially the black race, is one of America's thorns in the side. If only blacks would "catch the vision," change their habits, stop trying to shift blame, and apply themselves responsibly—in short, act more Christian, as they define it—racial inequality would be but a memory.

The remaining cited explanations were offered much less often. About one in five people cited welfare, by which they meant Aid to Families with Dependent Children [AFDC], food stamps, and related programs for the poor. Because welfare is most certainly structural, we must examine what white evangelicals mean when they cite welfare.

White evangelicals used this explanation in one of two distinct ways. For one group, welfare undermined accountable freewill individualism and relationalism, and it was African Americans who were to blame for accepting welfare. These respondents almost always also combined welfare with the black culture or motivation explanations. This Baptist woman from a northern state, as was common, linked welfare to family dissolution:

> I think ultimately it goes back to the fact that they have a lot of single-parent homes. [Any idea why they have a lot of single-parent homes?] Well, in a lot of instances there was no family to start with. [What do you mean?] I mean the AFDC payments. A woman gets money for each child she has and there is never a husband involved. In this area it is very common for a black girl in her late teens to be having her third or fourth baby, unmarried. My daughter works in OB (obstetrics), that is how I know. Very common, because they get their AFDC payments.

Welfare does not just break down the family, it leads to individual sin. Further, it is blacks who, perhaps because they are seen having less initiative or moral fortitude, are more likely to receive welfare. It was also common to link welfare directly to the demise of individual initiative and responsibility among African Americans. This blue-collar man from the Northeast related a personal story to illustrate his point:

> I was standing in line at a McDonalds for lunch one day. There was a young black girl that walked up to the counter next to me and there was a black girl working behind the counter, and they knew each other. They had a "Help Wanted" sign out. The girl behind the counter said "Let me get you an application." And the girl on my side said, "How much do they pay?" She told her $5.25 an hour, and she said, "Well I can make that much on welfare. Why should I come to work?" So I think that through the welfare system they have grown dependent on it and to count on that rather than count on themselves.

Welfare is clearly seen as violating the Protestant work ethic, either caus-
ing people to lack individual motivation and responsibility, or catering to
the human tendency to look for the easy road.

But respondents did not always view blacks as directly to blame in citing
welfare. A second meaning in citing welfare, employed in about half the
welfare references, was that the government was to blame. By trying to solve
individual-level problems with social programs, the government is not only
foolish, but as one Presbyterian woman put it, creating a system "no different from slavery." Another woman, a member of an Assembly of God
church, was not shy in implicating the government, even while making
welfare recipients seem less than admirable: "It has to be blamed on the
government. The government makes it easier for somebody to sit home and
collect welfare and have baby after baby."

The theological understanding of social structure as co-opting freewill
individualism (antistructuralism) clearly plays a role here. Because systems
and programs are viewed as *obviating personal responsibility and not
changing the hearts of individuals*, they are ultimately destructive. A woman
who attends a Free Church said this about the welfare system: "It's just
bondage, you know, and Jesus wants to be our source and he wants to set
us free from bondage." Because it is bondage, only one answer remains.
A married Christian Reformed Church mother of two communicated this.
After implicating the welfare system as a system in which "We have paid
their mothers to have their fathers stay away from home," she was asked
what Christians should do about the welfare system. She replied, "They
should get involved in politics and get rid of the welfare system. [Do away
with it entirely?] Yeah." Welfare is seen as both terribly misguided and
sinful, running counter to most things American and, in their understanding, most things Christian. It is far better, according to this Assembly of God
woman, to "give them the basics of God and teach them about Jesus. That's
going to bring them a whole lot more out of poverty than it is to give them a
welfare check."

After culture or motivation, "history" was the most commonly
cited explanation, by 29 percent of the respondents. For three-quarters
of those citing history, it appeared a creative way of holding firmly to the
conservative Protestant schema and the current-day equal opportunity
assumption without placing direct culpability on the present society.
About one in seven evangelicals simply denied that there was any inequality, such as this Church of Christ man: "I'd have to see this to believe it.
I don't believe that." In fact, we were sometimes told we were asking the
wrong question. This well-to-do Congregational man, for example,
replied: "I think a better question is: Why is there a substantial growing
percentage of economically wealthy blacks in this country? How did

they achieve that? This is what we ought to be studying."

Lack of access to education and discrimination were the only given contemporary structural explanations not charged with undermining accountable individualism. But even here, their use was mixed. Half of the respondents citing discrimination or education also named culture or motivation, and the ordering of these varied. Some clearly favored structural explanations, others an individual responsibility or relational explanation, even while recognizing the existence of discrimination. This Michigan man, after saying blacks are trapped in urban centers and being asked why, responded:

> One way is through the banking history and not approving mortgages. Another way is not allowing people to buy homes. But let's not confuse tactic with result. It may be and I would probably agree that it is more difficult for a black you to succeed in life than a light you to succeed in life. So be it. If you want to succeed, you are going to go out and do. That is the kind of possibility thinking that needs to occur in this country.

This man clearly grasped structural constraints, but here we can perhaps see the white evangelical cultural tools operating most powerfully. His central religious tools of antistructuralism and accountable freewill individualism render structural issues secondary to the belief that obstacles, with individual drive, can be overcome. Individual initiative conquers all.

With a few exceptions, respondents solved for X using the equation we introduced earlier: *Equally Created + Equal Opportunity + X = Unequal Outcome*, where X is equal to individual, relational, historical, or governmental deficiency. The religious cultural tools of conservative Protestants clearly appear to be used in explaining black–white inequality.

One further test of our argument is available. At the conclusion of each interview, interviewers ranked the evangelical respondents on an "evangelical scale," based on their adherence to theologically evangelical hallmarks, their strength of connection with evangelical institutions (churches, colleges, para-church ministries), and strength of identity as an evangelical. These subjective rankings ranged from one—evangelical in name only— to ten—strong "card-carrying" evangelicals. About half the interviewed evangelicals were classified as strong evangelicals (eight or higher), and the other half as weak to moderate (one to seven). After finding no differences on sociodemographic indicators, except that strong evangelicals were about five years younger on average, we compared these two groups by broad explanation categories. (These are reported in Table A-5 of Appendix A).[11]

Although we must limit our interpretations to the sample, the differences between these two relatively homogenous groups impressively illustrates the centrality of the religious factor. White evangelicals steeped most deeply in the institutional subculture and theology of conservative Protestantism accentuate the general evangelical patterns. They are more likely to cite black culture or lack of motivation than other evangelicals. Whereas two-thirds of moderate evangelicals cite black culture or motivation, more than 80 percent of strong evangelicals do—a full 15-percentage-point difference. If we also include the antistructural rationales of history and welfare, the gap between weak-to-moderate and strong evangelicals widens to 20 percentage points. Although 75 percent of weak-to-moderate evangelicals cited one or more of these reasons, an amazing *95 percent* of strong evangelicals did so.

Identical percentages of weak-to-moderate and strong evangelicals cite education and discrimination—about one-third of each group. Alone, this suggests no religious effect. But this is a misleading conclusion. If we consider the percentage of people citing *only* such individualism-inhibiting structural rationales, one in five weak-to-moderate evangelicals is found in this category. For strong evangelicals, the comparable figure is only one in twenty. Moreover, of the weak-to-moderate evangelicals who cite these structural reasons, only 41 percent also cite antistructural reasons. For strong evangelicals who mention such structural reasons, however, *84 percent* also give antistructural reasons.

In sum, the interviews reveal how thoroughly individually accountable, relationalist, and antistructuralist respondents were in their explanations, even when giving ostensibly social structural accounts. This pattern was accentuated for strong evangelicals.

THE EFFECT OF INCREASED CONTACT WITH AFRICAN AMERICANS

White evangelicals' explanations for racial inequality derive in part from the cultural tools they extend to race issues. But these tools are always applied within a structural context—namely, the degree of intergroup isolation. Contact theory says that under the right conditions, having contact with people from other groups can reduce prejudice. But does intergroup exposure change how people explain racial inequality? For an answer, we turn back to the General Social Survey.

To measure the level of white contact with blacks, we combine answers to two questions: (1) Are there any blacks living in this neighborhood now? and (2) During the last few years, has anyone in your family brought a friend who was black home for dinner? Because these questions are asked of only a small (but random) percentage of respondents each year, we combined surveys from 1972 to 1994. This measure of racial contact is far from perfect. Yet, if we find effects from this minimal level of contact, it suggests the strength of the relationship between contact with black Americans and explanations of inequality.

We classify white conservative Protestants into two groups: a high interracial contact group—those who say African Americans live in their neighborhood and that someone in their family has had an African American over for dinner in the last few years, and a low contact group—all other white conservative Protestants. [12] Despite the limitations of our interracial contact measure, we find significant changes for all four explanations offered by the survey (detailed in Table A-6 of Appendix A). Those in the "high contact" category are less individualistic and more structural in their explanations of racial inequality than other conservative Protestants. Individually, explanations decline by 15 percentage points or more, and the structural reasons increase by 10 percentage points, substantially reducing the gap between individual and structural reasons. For the low contact group, motivation is cited by 73 percent of the people, while education is cited by 42 percent, a gap of 31 percentage points. For the high contact group, however, that gap shrinks to just 4 percentage points (56 and 52 percent, respectively). Even with our weak measure of contact (or reduced isolation), we find important differences in how white conservative Protestants explain the racial gap. [13] Our survey data do not tell us, however, the causal direction of the relationship.

Our interviews with evangelicals help with the causality question. The higher the contact with black Americans, the less likely our respondents attribute primacy to individual-level explanations of the racial gap, and the more likely they are to attribute primacy to structural-level explanations. This appears to result from increased contact. When we asked Pat, a member of an Evangelical Covenant church, why there was economic inequality between blacks and whites, she said without hesitation, "They've been discriminated against." Rarely hearing this response, we asked her why she thought this was the reason. She responded, "I have a black brother-in-law. I've heard some of his stories, know some of his experiences, and other family members of his." Her long-term contact with her brother-in-law and his family members, she told us, is the reason she believes discrimination accounts for the racial gap.

But does this mean that knowing one or two African Americans leads to the same explanation as offered by this Covenant woman? No. It is important to highlight that at this limited level of contact (an individual or two rather than a network), the effect is sporadic. Factors that affect it include the depth of the relationship, what the African American believes and shares, and in what social context the person is known (with the job context having the least impact). As sociologists Mary Jackman and Marie Crane found in their study, [14] having a black friend or two seems to serve for whites as "a license to believe whatever they wish to" about blacks, and, because they have a friend, to be quite certain in their beliefs. An example is this West Coast evangelical man we interviewed:

> That is the way they are brought up, with their mom waiting for the check from welfare. There is not a strong work ethic. Now I have some black friends and they have raised themselves above that. They work hard and they don't have much use for their own people that are still acting like that.

Jackman and Crane found that for whites' contact with blacks to have a consistent effect on support for government aid to blacks (the issue their study focused on), a much higher level of contact was needed. It appears whites need networks of contacts with blacks, such as in neighborhoods, places of worship, work, and school because this significantly reduces their interracial isolation.

Beth is one such person we interviewed. On moving to a new metropolitan area and searching for a place to worship, some initial contacts led her and her husband to an interracial city church. With some trepidation, this eventually led them to move to the neighborhood of the church, which is nearly all African American. She has now become rather involved in the church and working with her neighbors. She plans for her two preschool-aged children to attend public schools in the neighborhood, and so has also been involved with the local schools. When we turned to the subject of racial inequality, Beth had much to say. In her explanation, we see her draw from the evangelical toolbox, but she uses modified tools, tools that better capture her social context:

> First, I don't not think it has anything to do with being inherently less able to do well. Some groups have experienced more discrimination than others. When the Bible gives us a remedy to limit great extremes of wealth and poverty from developing, it's because God knows that if you have less you're gonna be able to get less. That's basically what happens. You don't see groups catching up; you see the gap growing wider. ... Some people want to point to things like certain groups having a greater level of single-parent families and other morality problems. But are they poor because they have those morality issues, or do they have those morality issues because they are poor?

This is not the response Beth would have given five years ago. Her extensive network of black contacts—that is, her radical reduction in interracial isolation—changed the way she employs her cultural tools to explain racial inequality. Individually based explanations recede, structural explanations emerge. She, like many evangelicals, interprets the Bible literally. But she draws on different passages and gives a different emphasis. Rather than stressing passages emphasizing personal responsibility solely, she draws on more communal concepts, such as the Year of Jubilee, where God commanded the Israelites to "start over" every seven years as a means of avoiding radical discrepancies in economic resources.

At this point, some might believe that extensive black contact makes Beth, and others like her, more accurate in their explanation of racial inequality. Others might believe that Beth's change is the result of being overly and incorrectly influenced by black Americans. Regardless of how one interprets the change, we have shown that a significant reduction in intergroup isolation alters how cultural tools are extended to explain the racial gap.

THE CONNECTION BETWEEN EXPLANATIONS OF BLACK–WHITE INEQUALITY AND RACIALIZATION

Access to economic resources strongly shapes life experience, life chances, and the ability to maximize children's life chances. The racial gap in occupational status, income, employment rates, labor force rates, and wealth is substantial. In this chapter we described and explained white evangelicals' explanations for the black–white economic gap. As heirs of traditional values that make the United States distinct, white evangelicals overwhelming hold both that the United States offers equal opportunity to all and that inequality results from lack of individual initiative and noncompetitive practices, such as accepting single-parent homes, having too many children, not stressing education, being too willing to receive welfare, and being unable to move beyond the past. White Americans favor individualistic explanations over structural ones.[15] White American evangelicals are even more inclined to this pattern.

None of the white evangelicals we interviewed, with the exception of the few non-isolated whites such as Beth, spoke of inequality in other ways available to them from the Bible and Christian tradition. For example, they did not mention biblical principles and references calling for economic justice and equality.[16]

Comparing this chapter and Chapter Two, contemporary evangelicals' explanations for racial inequality, then, are essentially unchanged from a century ago (with the exception of the demise of the "inherently inferior" account). Now, as then, the racial gap is not explained by unequal opportunity or discrimination or shortcomings of the society as a whole, but rather by the shortcomings of blacks. Now, as then, the types of explanations given have important implications for how the inequality is addressed.

Those who employ individualistic explanations are more receptive to aiding black Americans whom they perceive as trying hard, and to removing laws that create artificial barriers preventing economic success.[17] They are also more likely to oppose government assistance of any type to blacks.[18] For example, according to researcher Martin Gilens,[19] the factors that are the strongest predictors of opposition to welfare are, in order of strength, (a) blaming blacks for racial inequality, (b) an individualistic perspective, and (c) blaming the poor for their poverty. Apart from undoing bad laws and government programs, those offering individualistic explanations, when asked what the government or businesses or labor should do about racial inequality, respond that they should do nothing.[20] The contemporary evangelical perspective, like that of its ancestors, is one that strongly supports laissez-faire capitalism. Individuals should be free to pursue their own ends, and rewards should be distributed based on effort. A meritocracy is both a goal and what America already is. As a result, "Most Americans believe that opportunity for economic advancement is widely available, that economic outcomes are determined by individuals' efforts and talents (or their lack) and that in general economic inequality is fair."[21]

This helps us understand why our respondents, apart from being irritated at the racial inequality question, were not at all bothered by the racial inequality itself. Except for a few people, inequality in no way troubled, moved, or animated our respondents. It was matter of fact, par for the course, as acceptable as a Sunday-afternoon nap. And for this reason, "We have reached an era of stable, comfortable acceptance by whites of the black–white gap."[22] Given that white evangelicals—and Americans in general it appears—are both comfortable with the black–white gap and inclined to do nothing about it, we do not think it too risky to conclude that evangelicals will make little contribution toward reducing the black–white gap. But we wish to extend our argument further to say that evangelicals, despite not wanting to, actually reproduce and contribute to racial inequality.

A PARABLE

Allow us to illustrate with a parable. Both Maridel and Parker were overweight, to the point of being unhealthy. They decided it was the time to do something drastic. Responding to an ad for a Fat-Away program, they drove to a rural area in their state, where they were taken to separate areas of the woods. For six weeks, they would be locked into these "compounds," as they were called. In each compound, according to the ad, were the perfect ingredients needed to lose weight. Their goal was to each lose forty pounds. What they did not know is that the less-than-ethical Fat-Away organization was really a research laboratory studying the effects of various diets, exercise programs, and weight-loss expectations on people's weight change. Without a word to Maridel and Parker, they placed Maridel in a compound designed to help her lose weight, but they placed Parker in a compound designed for Parker to gain weight.

In Maridel's compound were running trails, a swimming pool, state-of-the-art exercise equipment, a basketball court, and a sauna. In her cabin were magazines on proper nutrition, instructional videos on how to lose weight, an abundance of natural, healthy, low-fat, low-calorie foods, and no sweets. Each day she was greeted early by fit and trim people who asked Maridel to go on a run with them, talked about how much they loved being thin, and encouraged her that she too can be thin—wonderful conditions for losing weight.

In Parker's compound was only a tiny cabin. No exercise equipment was available whatsoever, but there were plenty of videos and movies that showed high-calorie foods looking sumptuous, more high-calorie goodies than even a sumo wrestler could desire, and just a few fruits and vegetables. The only other people Parker saw were also obese, and though they talked about losing weight, they seemed not to really care about their weight—not good conditions for losing weight.

The program called for each participant to weigh in at the start, and then every two weeks thereafter. At the end of two weeks, with neither aware of what was inside the other's compound, Maridel and Parker were taken to the weighing room. They each took their turn on the scale. Maridel stepped on the scale first. She had lost nineteen pounds! Parker's turn produced far less excitement. He actually gained two pounds.

Maridel, who assumed that both she and Parker had the same type of compound, was irritated with Parker. "We paid good money to be here, Parker. How can you waste it? You have to exercise, you have to eat right!" Parker tried to make his case, but it only made Maridel more irritated. Maridel told Parker he needed to try harder. Parker, though he was depressed about his weight gain and the difficulty in exercising adequately and eating right, resolved to do so.

But try as he may, Parker kept eating too many bad foods. And he exercised very little. He became depressed, and his depression only made him eat more and exercise less. After another two weeks, back he and Maridel went to the scales. Maridel, with wonderful weight-loss opportunities, and taking full advantage of them, lost another fifteen pounds. Parker, however, actually gained more weight then he had the first two weeks. Maridel could not believe what Parker was doing to himself. "Don't you know why we are here? Parker, this place is designed for us to lose weight. If you can't do it here, where can you?"

"I don't think this is all that great a place to lose weight," Parker sniped. "The food here is fatty, and exercising is next to impossible." Maridel was taken aback. Finally she replied, "It wouldn't matter if that were true,

Parker. When we get home, the food can be fatty and exercise difficult, but you must learn to eat and exercise right, regardless." Parker, increasingly frustrated by Maridel's comments, retorted, "No way is it as easy as you're making it seem. I think that Fat-Away is treating me unfairly. I'm not even sure I want to lose weight."

With that Maridel was dumbfounded. If Parker was not even going to try, if he was going to blame others, perhaps he deserved to be obese. But she also thought that if only Parker could have a vision of what he could look like, he would take advantage of Fat-Away and lose weight. She encouraged Parker to imagine being thin, toned, and healthy. "Wouldn't it be wonderful, Parker? If only you would try."

Back they went for another two weeks. At the final weigh-in, with the predictable result of Parker not having lost weight, Maridel simply resigned herself to the idea that Parker wanted to be overweight. Why Parker would want this, she was not sure, but of one thing she was sure—until Parker decided he wanted to lose weight, he would not.

Maridel is partially correct in her final assessment. Parker will not lose weight unless he tries. His "attitude" will have to improve. He needs a vision, a goal, and the motivation to get there.

But she misses the vast difference in environments that render the correlation between individual initiative and outcome far less than perfect. Due to structural differences, only a very few with incredible willpower could possibly lose weight in an environment like Parker's. And likewise, in an environment like Maridel's, only a very few could possibly gain weight.

In this example, the white evangelical tool kit would direct evangelicals only to look at Parker's effort and personal responsibility, or to render them supreme. But missing the structural conditions that both constrain and shape Parker would actually serve to maintain Parker's weight. By not recognizing the structure that impacts Parker, the weight-gain compound is allowed to continue enticing and constraining him. Further, to tell him that his effort alone determines his weight does little more than frustrate Parker and might even, in his frustration, make him less able to lose weight. This is not the intent, but it is the result.

The same holds true with racial inequality. By not seeing the structures that impact on individual initiative—such as unequal access to quality education, segregated neighborhoods that concentrate the already higher black poverty rate and lead to further social problems, and other forms of discrimination—the structures are allowed to continue unimpeded.[23] Cornel West, a Harvard scholar, writes that "to engage in a serious discussion of race in America, we must begin not with the problems of black people, but with the flaws of American society—flaws rooted in historic inequalities and longstanding cultural stereotypes." And we must "acknowledge that structures and behavior are inseparable, that institutions and values go hand in hand."[24]

Not seeing the structures that both affect and create individuals also contributes to low self-esteem. As Harvard sociologist William Julius Wilson found, residents of poor inner-city neighborhoods strongly believe in the need for individual initiative, but this belief, in the face of limited opportunities, wears people down.[25] "Sometimes you can try and then you say 'I'm tired of trying,'" responded one thirty-five-year-old welfare mother of three. "You try so hard it seems as if when you just about to get up, something happen to knock you back down and you just forget it, then." Cornel West writes that those with the individualistic perspective "rarely, if ever, examine the innumerable cases in which black people do act on the Protestant ethic and still remain at the bottom of the social ladder." Because of this, they continue to champion effort and, in so doing, "inadvertently contribute" to racialization.[26]

For the reasons discussed in this section, evangelicals' application of their cultural tool kit, in the context of intergroup isolation, unwittingly contributes to the reproduction of racial inequality.

Let's Be Friends

Exploring Solutions to the Race Problem

If you want a better WORLD, Composed of better NATIONS,
Inhabited by better STATES, Filled with better COUNTIES,
Made up of better CITIES, Comprised of better NEIGHBORHOODS,
Illuminated by better CHURCHES, Populated with better FAMILIES,
Then you have to start by becoming a better PERSON

Book advertisement, back cover of *Christianity Today*

Calling people you do not know and asking them if you can interview them for two hours is an interesting experience. The people you call are always surprised that you want to talk to them, and often somewhat suspicious. But what is most amazing is that the people we called almost always said yes. Despite knowing little about us, they not only agreed to meet, but more often than not invited us to their homes.

Such was the case with Hal, a sixty-year-old Southern Baptist man who lives in a suburb of a large southern city. When we called him to tell him about our project, and to ask if we could meet, he first asked a few questions about our purposes. How did we get his name? We work for a university, not a marketing agency? We are not trying to sell anything? After his concerns, all quite reasonable, had been addressed, he graciously agreed to an interview. He invited us to his home, and gave us careful directions from the airport where we would be arriving.

As we drove to his home some thirty miles from the airport, we passed through a variety of areas, some poor, some wealthy, some racially mixed, but most occupied primarily by one racial group or another. Hal's suburb was neither the poorest nor the wealthiest we saw on our drive, although it was probably closer to the wealthy end. It was primarily white—according to the 1990 census data on Hal's suburb, about 94 percent white. Hal's home was tucked away on a curved road that ended in a cul-de-sac.

After parking the car, we walked to his door. Before we could knock, Hal and his wife came to the door to greet us and invite us in. They asked if we wanted some iced tea. After a few introductions, we sat down and began the interview. As in most interviews, we did not turn to our questions on race until nearly an hour into our discussion. Talking about other issues for this long is an effective way to learn about the people and to see if they answer the race questions in ways consistent with how they responded to other inquiries. By the time we got to the race questions, we often could anticipate how they would answer.

We asked Hal if Christians had specific solutions to the problems of race relations. By that time, we could have guessed the general direction of his answer. As in his other responses, he easily tied in his faith to his answer, and he employed his main cultural tools. With little hesitation, he shared his response: As people become Christians, the race problem dissipates. "How so?" we asked.

> There's a top-down approach. At the top is our personal experience of love and forgiveness. Then we combine that with Jesus' commands: love God with all your heart, soul, and mind, and love your neighbor as yourself. So, as we experience His love and forgiveness firsthand, we respond back to Him in praise and thankfulness, allowing his love and respect for us to flow. That love and respect then overflows into our love and respect for our neighbors. When that outpouring is experienced at a personal level and applied to others, then that's of great benefit, and it is the great problem solver. It's at a one-on-one, friendship level. As a Christian, if it circumvents the personal level, then it's missed the mark, the Christian mark.

Hal's response displays every major component of what white evangelicals across the country told us is the Christian solution to the race problem. To place their responses in the appropriate context, we must draw on what we learned in the preceding two chapters. For white evangelicals, the "race problem" is not racial inequality, and it is not systematic, institutional injustice. Rather, white evangelicals view the race problem as (1) prejudiced individuals, resulting in poor relationships and sin, (2) others trying to make it a group or systemic issue when it is not, or (3) a fabrication of the self-interested.

Given that issues of inequality, systematic injustice, and group conflict are not part of their assessment, we did not expect to hear these addressed as part of the solution. And we rarely did. What we did hear from many was what others have called the "miracle motif." [1] The miracle motif is the theologically rooted idea that as more individuals become Christians, social and personal problems will be solved automatically. What is the solution to violent crime? Convert people to Christianity, because Christians do not commit violent crimes. What is the solution to divorce? Convert people to Christianity, because Christians are less likely to get divorced. What is the solution to the problems of race? Our grassroots evangelicals told us. According to a nondenominational woman from the Midwest, "Christianity has the answers to everything if individuals become Christians. [How this applies to the race issue] is that we see each other as God's children. How can we look down upon anybody that He created?" A women from the Northeast who is a member of a Congregational church said, "If you're a Christian, you're going to accept other people. Never mind what color or race, you're going to accept them as equal." And this Church of Christ member from the Midwest responded, "If everybody was a Christian, there wouldn't be a race problem. We'd all be the same."

Derived in part from the cultural tools of freewill accountable individualism and relationalism, the miracle motif holds, like the quotation opening this chapter, that society is improved by improving individuals. Hal calls this the top-down approach, but most would call it the bottom-up approach. Because society is viewed as merely the aggregation of individuals, social change is achieved by personal change and renewal—most important, by people becoming Christians. Part of this belief in the miracle motif, at least for race relations, is rooted in what sociologist Stephen Hart calls the Christian building block of universalism.[2] As Hart says, this principle is "encapsulated in St. Paul's formula that 'there is no longer Jew or Greek, there is no longer slave or free, there is no longer male or female; for all of you are one in Christ Jesus' (Galatians 3:28)." The focus of this principle, he writes, is that every human being is a child of God, loved and respected, and thus we owe and want to give the same to others. We are fundamentally equal.

The principle of universalism is clearly applied in Hal's solution to race issues, and helps us understand why he and most white evangelicals believe that the race problem dissolves when enough people become Christians. Hal told us that when people become Christians, they are overwhelmed by the love, respect, and dignity given to them by God. And this overflows such that Christians inevitably impart that to others. Given white evangelicals' understanding of the race problem, and the principle of universalism—with its emphasis on equality before God, and equal love, respect, and dignity—we see why the miracle motif makes logical sense to most evangelicals.

We heard the universalism themes of equality, love, and respect repeatedly. We need merely to listen to the words of evangelicals to see their application of the universalism principle to solving race problems. An Evangelical Free church woman from the Midwest said, "The Bible says in Christ there is no Jew, no Greek—which were races. There is no male or female. There is no slave or free. We are all one in Christ. So we should look at each other as equal." Similarly, a Presbyterian woman from the South told us that "all people are created equal and we are all equal in God's image. No one is inferior or superior. ... I think if people just understood that one basic truth, there wouldn't be a lot of the [race] problems we have." A charismatic evangelical from a nondenominational church confidently answered our query about a Christian solution to the race problems: "Oh definitely. To me, it's so basic—love one another. You know, God says love one another as I have loved you. So to me, that's the whole Christianity in a nutshell. It's loving people." And a young evangelical woman from the West Coast replied: "Love your neighbor as yourself. The Samaritan, he was a different culture, different everything. Yet, he took care of somebody from a different culture and religion than he was. I think that is the solution for the problems of race—you love them."

And how should one love them? How is equality expressed? Using their cultural tools, evangelicals apply universalism *interpersonally*, to the exclusion of other strategies, such as working for more just laws. The solution to the race problem in the United States—and the solution to most any social problem anywhere in the world—is through the personal influence strategy, which derives from the cultural tools of accountable freewill individualism and relationalism. This is the one-on-one, friendship, personal level that Hal says must be present in the Christian approach if it is not to miss the mark. As one evangelical woman put it, the problems of race will only be solved "by talking one on one. One person talking to one person, showing they care. The Berlin wall came down one chip at a time. It starts one stone at a time." Some evangelicals—both men and women—said that Promise Keepers had influenced their thinking about the race problem solution, as this Christian and Missionary Alliance church man communicated: "I learned this response from Promise Keepers. One man getting to know another across racial lines, establishing an honest friendship."

What the white evangelical solutions rarely entailed were solutions beyond the individual and interpersonal levels. In fact, employing their cultural tool of antistructuralism, any alternative solutions, from their perspective, simply were doomed to failure. Another Promise Keeper evangelical man told us that the "only ultimate solution" to the race problem is people turning to Christianity, maturing in their faith, and loving their brothers and sisters. A major reason the United States still has race issues is "because we're dealin' up here [holding his hand above his head] on the superficial level with programs and laws. It's only with Christianity that you can change people's hearts. You'll see people of all kinds of colors at Promise Keepers hugging and praying for each other. That's the only way to a solution." Anything beyond the interpersonal level is "superficial" and, ultimately, not a solution. It is individuals who must change, not the institutions, laws, or programs that may shape individuals.

Another man, a well-to-do member of a Congregational church from the Midwest, engaged us in an extensive discussion as to why the interpersonal level is the correct level for a solution. After telling us that the resolution to race problems was to "love your neighbor as yourself," he continued: "But you don't legislate that. It is incredible to me that the federal government thinks it has so much influence over you and me that they can legislate racism away. Government is not going to affect in any significant form racism in this country." He had earlier discussed the process called redlining, whereby banks and mortgage companies allegedly "draw a red line" around areas they deem as too risky to make loans, and these are typically nonwhite areas. Recalling this, we followed up our present discussion by asking, "Should redlining be addressed one-on-one, changing the hearts of loan officers, or is that an area where the government should be involved?" He replied:

> The government already outlawed it. Why is it still occurring? You answered your own question. When the mortgage officers say that I, as an individual, am not going to do that, and when he withstands the persecution that God guarantees us as Christians, such as his boss firing him, that is the way change happens. That is the way change occurs.

Thus, as we have seen in previous chapters, the cultural tools of individualism, relationalism, and antistructuralism are used consistently, and powerfully shape white evangelicals' worldview.

Solutions to "Racism": The Views from Our Survey

But are white evangelicals' solutions any different from those of other white Americans? To get an answer, we conducted a national telephone survey of 2,591 randomly selected adult Americans. Our survey has some advantages over the General Social Survey we used in the last chapter. Our survey asked many more questions about religious identity and doctrine, allowing us to create a more sophisticated and refined measure of evangelicals. We also asked a series of specific questions on solutions to racism. In Chapter One, we discussed a unique perspective on racism: it is the collective misuse of power that harms another racial group, it is rational, and it includes the justifications provided for racialization. But from our readings and preliminary interviews, we knew that Americans view racism differently. So for our survey we used racism according to its narrower interpretation as racial prejudice and discrimination.

We asked the people in our survey a series of solution-to-racism questions. Before we did this, however, we first asked this question: "Do you think that racism is a top priority that Christians (if they had earlier identified themselves as Christian)/ people (all others) should be working to overcome, or not?" Just under 80 percent said yes, it should be a top priority. It is these people only who we asked how racism should be addressed. We said to them: "[Christians/people] disagree about the best way to work against racism. For each of the following possible ways, please tell me if you think it's a very important way that [Christians/people] should work against racism." We then offered four alternatives, in rotating order:

1. Try to get to know people of another race

2. Work against discrimination in the job market and legal system

3. Work to racially integrate congregations

4. Work to racially integrate residential neighborhoods

We anticipated that, for white evangelicals, their support for the racism-reducing alternative would decline as we moved from alternative one to alternative four. That is, based on their cultural tools, the universalism principle, and the wording of our question, we expected white evangelicals to give highest support for getting to know people of another race, followed by working against discrimination, then integrating congregations, and finally, integrating neighborhoods.

The reason we expected the highest support for getting to know people of another race is straightforward: it best captures the personal influence strategy, the interpersonal, one-on-one approach of evangelicals. We also expected the work-against-discrimination alternative to garner considerable support from evangelicals because it invokes the equality and freedom of opportunity aspects of universalism and because it clearly resonates with the American values of equality, fairness, and opportunity. We expected the least support for integrating neighborhoods, because this solution suggests changing the very structure of metropolitan America, moving whole groups of people rather than individuals, and moving people against their will. This may only be achievable through government policies. This alternative violates nearly all tools and principles that evangelicals use to arrive at a solution. What is more, given their assessment of the race problem and the causes of racism, for them, macro-level changes like working against residential segregation do not get at the root problems—people's hearts and poor relationships.

For integrating congregations, arriving at an expectation was more complicated. One the one hand, integrating congregations connotes structural change, moving whole groups rather than individuals, and perhaps moving people against their will. For these reasons we expect a level of support comparable to the level of support expected for integrating residential neighborhoods. But on the other hand, congregations are the extended families of evangelicals (and others of course). They thus represent a more micro, relational scale than do residential neighborhoods. Further, they are separate from the state, so integrating them suggests less movement against people's will than residential integration. Because congregations are viewed more on an interpersonal rather than a large-scale level, and because integration of congregations suggests a greater degree of volunterism than does residential integration, we expect a relatively high level of support for this alternative by evangelicals. Given the factors for and against evangelical support of this alternative, we expect support to be less than getting to know others and working against discrimination, but more than integrating residential neighborhoods.

To measure evangelicalism, we followed the extensive work of political scientists Lymon Kellstedt and Corwin Smidt.[3] Individuals who are strongly evangelical are those who say they are evangelical and display the doctrinal hallmarks: claim Christ is their Savior and Lord, say Jesus is the only way to salvation, view the Bible is true in all ways, and actively evangelize or give money for evangelizing. We measure strength of evangelical identity with the following categories: (1) those who did not chose an evangelical identity, (2) those who chose evangelical as one of their religious identities but not their main one, (3) those for whom evangelical was their main religious identity, but not their only one, and (4) those for whom evangelical was their only chosen religious identity. We created an index of evangelical strength by summing the responses to this religious identity variable and the four doctrinal questions. For ease of reporting, we classified people into three groups: (1) "not evangelical"—those who did not assent to any of the doctrinal hallmarks and did not call themselves evangelical; (2) "strong evangelical"—those who assented to all the hallmarks and said their main or only religious identity was evangelical; and (3) "moderate evangelical"—all others.

The survey confirms our expectations for white "strong" evangelicals (detailed in Table B-1 of Appendix B). The most frequently cited very important way to address racism—by nine out of every ten strong evangelicals—is getting to know people of another race. Following closely behind that response is working against discrimination in jobs and the legal system, making sure all get a fair chance and equal opportunity (83 percent). From our interviews, we know that evangelicals supported this alternative not because they advocated institutional, systemic changes to end discrimination, but because they wanted people to be treated fairly by other individuals within these structures. Integrating congregations, though receiving substantially less support as a way to address racism than the first two alternatives (58 percent), receives much more support than integrating residential neighborhoods (38 percent). Our in-depth interviews shed light on evangelicals' thinking about these alternatives.

In some interviews, we asked evangelicals whether they thought integrating congregations and integrating neighborhoods were reasonable ways to address racism and race relations problems. The responses to integrating congregations helped us understand why about 60 percent of strong evangelicals in our survey thought it is a very important method to address racism, and why another 40 percent did not. Those who supported the idea of more racially mixed congregations did so because they saw it as a better reflection of how the true Church should look. They saw it as a way to address racism because it would show openness and allow friendships to form between Christians across race. Thus, those who supported integrating congregations did so as an extension of the getting-to-know-people alternative.

But there is another aspect to their support. When white evangelicals spoke of integrating congregations, they meant that their specific congregation is or ought to be open to all people. They did not mean they should consider going to a mixed or nonwhite congregation. No one spoke about this possibility. Further, no one spoke of the need for the congregation to adapt or diversify the way it does things to become racially mixed. This means that it must be other people, not them, who would have to make the change. In this light, although they may support congregational integration, it is difficult to conceive of it actually happening on any large scale as a result of that support.

Those who did not support the mixed race congregations idea were fairly pragmatic in their reasons. Comfort and enjoyment were common themes. In the words of one Christian Reformed man, "I think the whole concept of blacks and whites worshipping together is great, but how can you do that when you feel so uncomfortable?"

Our interviews revealed almost complete opposition to residential integration as a way to address racism—making us wonder how 38 percent in the survey could have said it was a very important method. Again comfort was cited, such as with this evangelical woman from the Midwest:

> Well, you can try it, but I think people are comfortable in their own neigh-
> borhoods. That is their center, where they are. Once in a while, they should
> reach out and cross over for some special things. That would be helpful. But I
> do think that it's important to keep a nucleus within.

But the most common objection was that neighborhood integration im-
plied force against people's will. When we asked this Evangelical Free
church woman if integrating neighborhoods would be a way to address
race problems, she replied, "I don't think you can force anybody to do anything." We followed up her response by asking, "So overall you would say
neighborhood integration would not help?" To which she reiterated her position: "I wouldn't force neighborhoods to be integrated." Although the
question did not say how integration was to be achieved, it was usually assumed to imply force, a violation of freewill, and because it implies macro-
change, to be a solution at the wrong level. One evangelical man, expressing
concern that his church and neighborhood were 99 percent white, said it
would be nice to have more racial mix. The interviewer then asked him if
integrated neighborhoods might help reduce race problems. His response,
said in a gentle tone, conveyed these concerns:

> Any solution that doesn't come naturally [from the heart rather than from a
> government policy] is gonna cause a problem. No one, I don't care, no one
> wants to be told where to live, Christians or non-Christians. No one wants to
> be told by government or some other authority who to associate with, so I
> don't think that forced issues are going to fundamentally solve the problem.
> The solution is going to come, if it ever does come, through the natural work-
> ings of people getting to know each other and finding a way to get to know
> each other. It's got to happen one-on-one.

A classic statement of the evangelical position, this response seems to
overlook the possibility that integrated neighborhoods might be one means
for "finding a way to get to know each other."

To examine what solutions are advocated by evangelicalism's flagship
magazine, *Christianity Today*, we studied all issues published from 1994
through 1998. We classified any articles and shorter news pieces dealing
with solutions to racism into the four alternatives given in our survey.
Those that did not fit these four alternatives we omitted.[4] The alternative
most commonly advocated is getting to know people of other races, cited
two and half times more often than any other alternative (see Table B-2 in
Appendix B). As the subtitle of one article clearly summarizes it: "How
24,000 Mississippi Christians Are Beating Racism One Friendship at a
Time."

The second most advocated solution is integrating congregations or, as was often suggested, advocating the establishment of sister churches. That is, in an extension of the friendship theme, *Christianity Today* often advocates or reports on churches of different races getting together periodically to worship, work on projects, and establish relationships.

The remaining two alternatives—working against discrimination and integrating neighborhoods, not viewed as unique to or perhaps compatible with Christians or the Christian perspective—are almost never discussed or advocated.

COMPARING RESPONSES TO THE SOLUTIONS-TO-RACISM ALTERNATIVES BY EVANGELICAL TYPE AND RACE

Does being evangelical influence responses to the solutions-to-racism alternatives? We suspect it does, but only for those alternatives seen as unique to Christians by the evangelical community. Based on our survey, we see a similar pattern to what we have noted in previous chapters. On race issues, white evangelicals are, in kind, similar to other white Americans. Where they differ, when they do, is in degree (detailed in Table B-3 of Appendix B).

Stronger evangelicals are more likely to cite getting to know people of other races. Whereas 68 percent of non-evangelicals cited this as a very important way to address racism, that figure climbs to 79 percent for moderate evangelicals, and 89 percent for strong evangelicals. No significant differences exist by evangelical type for the work-against-discrimination alternative, as both evangelicals and other Americans draw on similar values to support the principle of no discrimination. We again see support for integrating congregations increasing according to evangelical type (from 39 percent for non-evangelicals to 58 percent for strong evangelicals). This is probably in part due to congregations being more important to evangelicals, who thus are more likely to feel that activities within congregations are worthy ways for them to address racism; and congregational integration is often viewed as an extension of the friendship model. Finally, we find no differences in support for integrating neighborhoods. About two-thirds of whites, regardless of evangelical type, do not view integrating neighborhoods as a very important means to address racism. Although we do not know from our research the reasons why non-evangelicals tend to oppose residential integration as a way to address racism, we suspect it is for reasons similar to evangelicals—it is a non-individualistic solution, implies governmental involvement and force, and implies discomfort. Thus, evangelicals differ from other Americans in the solutions they tend to stress. For the solutions they do not emphasize, they are similar to others in their responses.

How do black evangelicals compare to white evangelicals on these solution-to-racism alternatives? We expect black evangelicals to be similar to white evangelicals for the first two alternatives because they share a common core of values and cultural tools that lead to responses on these alternatives. But for the integration options, we expect black evangelicals to be more supportive than white evangelicals. Conservative black churches have traditionally served as a refuge from the impacts of race in the United States, and a place where institutionalized, systemic factors are discussed and critiqued. As one example, consider that the Civil Rights movement, which worked to change the system and bring about greater systematic justice, was centered in the black church and largely led by the black clergy.[5]

Our expectations are confirmed (see Table B-4 in Appendix B). For the getting-to-know option, we find an identical level of support for strong evangelicals, regardless of race (90 percent). Also, evangelical type has a similar impact across race: for both whites and blacks, there is a twenty-one-percentage-point increase for strong evangelicals over non-evangelicals in the level of support for this option. Similarly, for the work-against-discrimination option, we find no significant effect of evangelicalism and no differences by race.

The integration options tell a different story. About one-third of white and black non-evangelicals and half of white and black moderate evangelicals view integrating congregations as a very important way to address racism. But strong evangelicals differ by race. Whereas 58 percent of white strong evangelicals cite this reason, that figure swells to 87 percent for black strong evangelicals.

For neighborhood integration, African Americans, regardless of evangelical type, are more supportive. Whereas about one-third of whites view this alternative as a very important way to address racism, half of black nonstrong evangelicals do. For black strong evangelicals, support rises to nearly two-thirds. As in the last chapter, white and black strong evangelicals appear even more racially divided than other Americans. This seems to be particularly so with respect to structural factors, whether explanations for racial inequality or solution-to-racism alternatives.[6] Evangelicals believe their faith ought to be a powerful impetus for bringing people together across race. Ironically, their faiths seem to drive them further apart.

SOLUTIONS TO RACISM FROM THE PERSPECTIVE OF THE LESS RACIALLY ISOLATED

White evangelicals' cultural tools, and their strategies for social change, help us understand the solutions to racism they propose and support. But knowing the cultural tool kit is not enough. We must examine the structural context within which these tools are applied. Certainly the structural context is part of the reason why black and white evangelicals differ from each other in their understanding of race issues. As the survey and interview data show, evangelical African Americans support individual-level solutions to racism, but they are much more likely than their white counterparts to support structural solutions.

Representative of this pattern is LaRetta, an African-American evangelical woman from an area of a midwestern city that was originally home to Irish, German, and Jewish immigrants, but is now over 90 percent African American. When we asked her about solutions to race problems and racism, she responded with the familiar language of needing to love one another. But she extended her Christian understandings further. She talked about the role of the social environment on people's attitudes, and then she cited an issue white evangelicals did not mention or see as a problem, even if asked: "If you never dusted that table and just keep it in order, it's gonna get dirty. The same with the racism thing. If we are just gonna keep movin' out, puttin' a 'For Sale' sign up, it's not gonna get better." Then she specifically addressed Christians and the maintenance of residential segregation: "A lot of people in the church got their 'For Sale' sign up, so we're not dealin' with it, we're not dealin' with the problem."

Viewing the race issue from a different structural position than most whites, she modifies the application of her cultural tools. She still views the love of Christ as the answer, but this love extends beyond personal relationships to the social environment and housing arrangements. Moreover, from her structural context, LaRetta, who had used the "miracle motif" to respond to other questions in the interview, did not select this to respond to the race questions. Although she used the familiar language of needing to love one another, she did not agree that simply by becoming a Christian such love would naturally occur.

As always, though, our best evidence for the argument that the degree of isolation from black Americans matters is the responses of nonracially isolated whites. Although we have but few in our sample, we find that they give responses similar to black evangelicals. For example, one Nazarine woman, who attends a multiethnic church, had this to say about the Christian solution to racism: "Christianity is not just reconciliation to God but reconciliation with people. You start out at the personal level and you see people as people. We also address systemic injustice, looking for ways to help either advocate for people who don't have a voice or help make the playing ground a little more equal." Interpersonal relationships are a must, she says, but reconciliation and love are expressed by also working against structural causes of racial inequities.

Another example is the solution given by Beth, whom we met in the last chapter. She has an extensive network of black relationships, and because she lives in a nearly all-black community and attends an interracial church, she views life differently than she did a few years ago, including her perspective on solutions to racism:[7]

> If you really want true healing, you have to have forgiveness, and I think that maybe that's the unique part that Christianity brings. Yet, we could do all that, but racism would still be there. That doesn't mean that we should throw up our hands and not do anything. John Perkins uses an excellent illustration. You're in the seventh inning, and one team is up twenty to nothing. Then we find out that the winning team has been cheating all along. And then they say, "Okay, okay, okay, we're sorry. Let's go back out and finish the game." Obviously, they're already twenty runs up, so that's one reason why I'm uncomfortable with kind of "Let's just go to a relationship but not really address the [structural] issues" approach. The legacy is there. So it's not a "I forgive you" and it's done. It's just too complex for that. It's gotta be a lifetime process.

Again, Beth transposes here cultural tools, starting off very much like most evangelicals. But then she goes further. Her non-isolation seems to create a nuanced view of the solution, a recognition of the complex issues involved. Like the African-American woman cited earlier, she does not invoke the miracle motif. She also sees the issue and solution as more than individuals becoming friends. Non-isolated white evangelicals, it appears, employ their tools in a different way, modifying them to make sense of their social structural context.

What Is Racial Reconciliation to White Grassroots Evangelicals?

In Chapter Three, we explored the contemporary history of racial reconciliation thought and action among evangelicals. This theology and sociology—to establish primary relationships across race, challenge social systems of injustice and inequality, confess historical, social, and personal sin, and accept apologies and move past bitterness—is offered as the solution to racialization. But we argued that as the message of racial reconciliation spread from black evangelicals to white grassroots evangelicals, the message was popularized and individualized, coming to mean only that one should express forgiveness and make a friend across racial lines.

To understand what racial reconciliation means to white evangelicals, we asked them. Our findings surprised us. Despite the tidal wave of efforts to communicate the message of racial reconciliation, more than 60 percent of the white evangelicals we interviewed had not heard of racial reconciliation or did not know what it meant. That organizations like Promise Keepers do

have an impact, though, is evident in two ways. First, strong evangelicals—
those most integrated into the subculture—are more likely to know about
racial reconciliation than other evangelicals—51 percent compared to 26
percent. Second, among strong evangelicals, men, at 61 percent, are much
more likely to know about racial reconciliation then women, at 43 percent.
In contrast, for weak to moderate evangelicals, there is no gender difference—about 25 percent of both groups know about racial reconciliation.
Thus, the message of racial reconciliation brought by evangelical organizations is doing a better job at reaching strong evangelicals. And, since the
largest organization bringing the message—Promise Keepers—is for men
only, strong evangelical men are much more likely to have heard the message than are strong evangelical women.

And what message are they hearing? In our in-depth interviews we asked
those who had heard of racial reconciliation what it means and how it is
achieved. Thomas, whom we met last chapter, is a strong evangelical and is
familiar with racial reconciliation. When we asked him what racial reconciliation means and how it should be achieved, he responded:

> I have words with you, I have done something that's been troublesome for
> you, if it comes to my attention, if I am convicted of it, I can come back to you
> and address it. I guess I think about those things more individually. I would
> individually deal with any individual situation. There are an awful lot of indi-
> vidual acts in this, a lot of individual pieces. To categorize this [as a race prob-
> lem] nearly makes it sound like all Caucasian males think the same way, and
> so as a group they must reconcile themselves with all African-American
> males. That is such an oversimplification.

Thomas takes the message of reconciliation he has heard, already popularized by removing components that require addressing social inequalities, and, apparently using his cultural tools, further individualizes it. He
simply rejects any talk of group issues and the need for groups to seek and
accept forgiveness as "oversimplifications." The correct view, in his opinion,
is that if two people disagree or are in conflict, and they are of different colors, then seeking individual forgiveness for the individual act is what con-
stitutes racial reconciliation.

And this should be expressed by getting to know people of another race.
As this Covenant church woman from the West communicated, "Think
about your own attitudes, then start to make friends with another race.
Then a lot has happened." A Presbyterian man from the Northeast said racial reconciliation is "Tolerance for people that are different from you, and
reaching out with an apology" by developing a relationship across race. And
a Christian and Missionary Alliance woman from the Midwest told us that
racial reconciliation is when "any person could go anywhere and be friends
with anybody no matter what they look like."

Clearly, racial reconciliation here is radically individualized. Although occasionally broadened to mean a white congregation meeting with a black congregation, this too was seen as valuable only insofar as it could lead to individual friendships. When we asked whether supraindividual factors are part of racial reconciliation, we got a decisive "no." One woman, a member of a charismatic nondenominational church, was representative. When asked if racial reconciliation could be aided through laws, she was adamant: "We're not going to do it by laws. It will never be done by laws, never, never." When we asked a nondenominational man whether integrated neighborhoods could contribute to the mission of racial reconciliation, he turned the discussion to individuals and their preferences: "It takes one person at a time. . . . You have two different kinds of people from two different kinds of neighborhoods. A black from inner-city Chicago is uncomfortable in this neighborhood. And a white from here is uncomfortable in inner-city Chicago," so integrated neighborhoods are simply not realistic.

Other considerations lead people not to consider integrated neighborhoods as part of racial reconciliation for them personally, even if they thought it might be a good idea in principle. One woman, whose husband was heavily involved in Promise Keepers, was, along with her husband, attempting to live out racial reconciliation, which she views as "an acceptance of people of different races, forgiveness extended toward each other, and then an interaction with each other." To those ends, she and her husband have attended cross-race "confession" services, have gone out to dinner with a black couple, have gotten together with black families, and have attended seminars on reconciliation. One of those seminars was led by John Perkins, an original proponent of racial reconciliation, and his team. She had this to say about the seminar:

> They actually believe that you go and live in neighborhoods with each other. [What do you think of Perkins's idea of actually changing, reshaping housing patterns, residential patterns?] I think it's a great idea if you're supposed to do it. [If you are supposed to do it?]. You know, its like home schooling. I don't feel called to do it. I can still think it's a great idea. I am just crusty enough to say that Perkins's idea, it's going to affect real estate value. So you've got to be willing to pay financially for it as well.

Despite being quite involved in racial reconciliation, that involvement is limited to her definition and her methods. It should not involve actual financial sacrifice or the possibility thereof, unless one is specifically called by God to make such a sacrifice. Apparently, racial reconciliation—the evangelical solution to racism and race problems—is quite limited in scope and content for ordinary evangelicals due to their worldview and the personal cost of alternatives.

EVANGELICAL SOLUTIONS TO THE RACE PROBLEM AND RACIALIZATION

Two factors are most striking about evangelical solutions to racial problems. First, they are profoundly individualistic and interpersonal: become a Christian, love your individual neighbors, establish a cross-race friendship, give individuals the right to pursue jobs and individual justice without discrimination by other individuals, and ask forgiveness of individuals one has wronged. Second, although several evangelicals discuss the personal sacrifice necessary to form friendships across race, their solutions do not require financial or cultural sacrifice. They do not advocate or support changes that might cause extensive discomfort or change their economic and cultural lives. In short, they maintain what is for them the noncostly status quo.

We thus have a common problem. White evangelicals want to see an end to race problems because both their Christian faith and their faith in the American creed call for it. But they are constrained by at least two forces. First, their cultural tools point them only to one dimension of the problem. As Stokely Carmichael and others have noted, when problems are at least in part structural, they must be addressed at least in part by structural solutions. If a building is on the verge of collapse due to an inadequate design, improving the quality of the bricks without improving the design is not a solution. Evangelicals, for all their recent energy directed at dealing with race problems, are attempting to improve the bricks, even having bricks better cemented to other bricks, but they are not doing anything about the faulty structural design. If their focus continues to be only on making better bricks, their expenditure of energy will largely be in vain.

Second, some white evangelicals appear to avoid changing the design not only because they lack the cultural tools, but also because changing the design would be costly. When people are comfortable with their lives, even in the face of design flaws, it seems reasonable that they would prefer improving the quality of bricks as the solution over rearranging the bricks, for this risks their own comfortable positions. Like many other white Americans, at least some white evangelicals do not want and are not willing to substantially rearrange their own lives to reduce the race problem. Although their faith directs them in many powerful ways, white American evangelicals, unless burdened by an individual "calling," assume that faith does not ask them to change the material aspects of their lives for this cause. Given their aversion to discomfort (a universal human trait) and cultural tools, they offer "Christian" solutions such as asking forgiveness, converting people to Christ, and forming cross-race friendships.

The problem with these solutions is that, by themselves, they do not work. Consider the idea that race problems will dissipate if people convert to Christianity. As evangelical historian Lee Nash noted a quarter of a century ago, the miracle motif, while holding much appeal and "not a little Christian truth," is a major hindrance to the fulfillment of Christian responsibility.[8] The miracle motif perspective allows Christians to avoid working with non-Christian reformers, and overlooks that people do not automatically become mature Christians on conversion. More fundamentally, it also mistakenly presumes that multilevel problems can be solved by unilevel solutions. What is more, it directs the church to become so focused on evangelizing that new converts are taught that Christian maturity consists of preparing for and actually evangelizing, to the exclusion of taking on social responsibility.

Or consider the making-friends solution. Sociologists Mary Jackman and Marie Crane carefully examined the effect of having an intimate cross-race friendship on whites' racial attitudes, preferences, and support for the government ensuring integrated schools, equal housing opportunity, and equal job opportunity. Their conclusions? Having a close, cross-race friendship—or even two—has only minimal effects, and only on three of the ten factors they examined. Similar to our findings that changes in racial perspectives occur mainly in the context of interracial *networks* rather than by merely having an intimate friendship, they found that intimacy is less important than having a variety of contacts, such as also having black acquaintances and living in mixed neighborhoods. They did find certain conditions under which cross-race friendships have significant, consistent independent effects on more positive racial beliefs, feelings, social dispositions, and policy views. Those are: (1) having an African-American friend while at the same time living in a neighborhood with African Americans and having African-American acquaintances; (2) Having an African-American friend of *equal, and especially higher, socioeconomic status*. Thus, cross-race friendships produce the result expected by white evangelicals, but only under the conditions of relative integration and socioeconomic equality.[9]

But even if these conditions were not necessary for the cross-race friendship approach to work, the massive extent of residential, congregational, and other forms of segregation and racial inequality (all of which are structurally maintained) continually mitigates against the successful formation of friendships and precludes the opportunity of enough people ever forming enough friendships to make a difference. Friendships are formed primarily under two conditions—similarity and proximity. The structures of racial segregation and inequality render similarity and proximity far more unlikely than under conditions of integration and equality. So, although evangelicals work to establish friendships, structural conditions work to limit both the number and success of cross-race friendships.

White evangelical solutions to racialization are thus limited and, by themselves, ultimately doomed to failure. Although laudable for bringing in necessary components missing from most policy-oriented, structural solutions—personal responsibility, repentance and forgiveness, interpersonal interaction, the acknowledgment of what Myrdal labeled as the moral and spiritual aspects of the problem—the white evangelical prescriptions do not address major issues of racialization. They do not solve such structural issues as inequality in health care, economic inequality, police mistreatment, unequal access to educational opportunities, racially imbalanced environmental degradation, unequal political power, residential segregation, job discrimination, or even congregational segregation. White evangelical solutions do not challenge or change the U.S. society that "allocates differential economic, political, social, and even psychological rewards" to racial groups. In short, their prescriptions fail to render race inconsequential for life opportunities.

The result, as we saw in the last two chapters, is that white evangelicals, without any necessary intent, help to buttress the racialized society. Like their forebears during Jim Crow segregation, who prescribed kindness toward people of other races and getting to know people across races, but did not challenge the Jim Crow system, present-day white evangelicals attempt to solve the race problem without shaking the foundations on which racialization is built. As long as they do not see or acknowledge the structures of racialization, they inadvertently contribute to them. And, insofar as they continue to give solutions that do not challenge racialization, they allow racial inequality and division to continue unabated.

A SUBSTANTIAL SHIFT IN FOCUS: THINKING MORE BROADLY

The last three chapters revealed two important findings: (1) The cultural tools of white evangelicals led them to minimize the race problem and racial inequality, and thus propose limited solutions. All these help reproduce racialization. (2) But in each chapter we found exceptions. Under the condition of extensive cross-race networks, white evangelicals modified the use of their cultural tools and their racial understandings, so much so that their understandings began to resemble those of African Americans. This suggests an important possibility. If white evangelicals were less racially isolated, they might assess race problems differently and, working in unison with others, apply their evangelical vigor to broader-based solutions.

But it is of course no accident that the vast majority of white evangelicals—and other whites as well—are racially isolated. As long as the white American population is larger than the black American population, by mathematical law, whites will be more isolated from blacks than vice versa.

And unfortunately, housing and other forms of segregation by race and class are institutionalized features of the American landscape.

But one form of segregation carries particular importance in isolating evangelicals by race: congregational segregation. According to our survey, evangelicals are more likely to attend church overall, attend more frequently, and spend more time in congregational activities than are people in any other major American Christian tradition.[10] Thus, for example, we examined the percentage of survey respondents by tradition who participate in church activities in addition to Sunday worship services, once a week or more. This high level of activity characterized a full 60 percent of evangelicals, compared to 38 percent of mainline Protestants, 28 percent of liberal Protestants, and 19 percent of Catholics. Evangelicals are also more likely to have close friends from the same denomination than are people in other traditions.[11] Thus, the congregations that evangelicals attend not only shape their theological views, but are where they spend a great deal of time, compared to people in other major Christian traditions. Racially segregated congregations therefore have important implications for the racial isolation of evangelicals.

In our next chapters, we broaden our perspective beyond our strict focus on evangelicals, considering the larger processes within American religion that shape in part what we found in the preceding chapters. The nature of our task moves us beyond our data on evangelicals, toward much more theoretical and abstract arguments. In the next chapter, we explore the processes that generate racial division between congregations. This is essential for understanding evangelicals and race relations.

7

The Organization of Religion and Internally Similar Congregations

"Because of our cultural backgrounds," said Nancy, a white Presbyterian woman, blacks and whites "might not enjoy the same kinds of worship. The way we express our worship to God is different. And so if I choose to worship the way I enjoy worshipping, and my black brothers and sisters want to worship in another fashion, that should be okay." Nancy's thoughts are echoed by many people in the United States. For many, although it is perhaps not the ideal case, there is certainly nothing wrong with attending racially distinct congregations, as long as the motivation is not prejudice. People are comfortable with different worship styles, want to be with familiar people, and have different expectations about congregations. For these reasons, if congregations end up being racially homogenous, it is acceptable, if not preferable. Some we interviewed, however, were clearly bothered by racially separate congregations, and frustrated that their congregations were not integrated. Still others were indifferent, appearing not to have thought much about the issue prior to being asked.

Some lament congregational segregation, some find no problem with it, and others are indifferent, but almost no one denies that congregations are racially divided. According to the 1998 National Congregations Study, about 90 percent of American congregations are made up of at least 90 per-cent of people of the same race.[1] Why is this so, given the vast diversity in ra-cial and ethnic groups in the United States? How does this continue to be the case, despite many groups' theologies, official statements, sincere desires, and efforts for more diverse congregations? No longer does it seem plausible to say that this high degree of homogeneity is principally due to white prejudice. African Americans with options to attend "white" churches far more often attend African-American congregations, even if they have to travel farther to get there. Korean Americans, even those in the second and third generation, primarily attend Korean congregations, even if they must pass white and black congregations to get to such a congregation.

Rather than attributing this congregational homogeneity to white preju-dice, or even to the need of minority groups to create places of refuge from the dominant society, we argue that in the face of social and religious plu-ralism, the organization of American religion powerfully drives religious groups toward internal similarity.[2] Our argument provides theoretical in-sight and elaboration to the basic position communicated by Nancy at the beginning of this chapter—that to the extent that people can choose, they chose to be with people like themselves. But much more is operating than pure personal choice, and these factors lead people to internally similar congregations. To make our case, we explore factors on a variety of levels, from the seemingly autonomous individual, to subcultures, to the working of entire social systems. These are all connected of course, but by looking at each of them in turn, we gain a fuller understanding of the overwhelming push toward internal homogeneity. We see how congregations end up in-ternally homogenous, without being comprised of prejudiced people, and even despite the desire of some for mixed-race congregations. We also note how evangelicalism has unwittingly contributed to, supported, and used arrangements and methods that propel congregational racial separation.

In support of these concrete claims, we must introduce more abstract reasoning than in previous chapters. We begin by briefly outlining the orga-nization of American religion, which may be roughly represented by the metaphor of a religious marketplace. We show how this marketplace devel-oped—beginning with the separation of church and state, and leading to religious pluralism, increased competition, and a growing emphasis on personal choice. These factors mean that religious congregations need to specialize and market their services to survive and grow. But we argue that these processes strongly encourage homogeneity *within* congregations.

Why? To answer this question, we must examine why people are in reli-gious groups at all. We find that such groups help provide people with meaning and belonging. How do religious groups most effectively provide, and individuals find, meaning and belonging? In exploring the factors that aid meaning and belonging, we see that they all favor similarity within congregations. Thus, the very organization of American religion drives toward the separation of peoples.

This is most important, for, in the next chapter, we use our understanding of internal similarity and the religious marketplace to examine how the organization of American religion contributes to racialization far beyond the mere racial division of congregations.

BECOMING A "RELIGIOUS MARKETPLACE"

What is our business? Who are our customers? What do they value?

> A sign said to hang over the desk of Rev. Bill Hybels, pastor of the 15,000-member evangelical Willow Creek Church in Chicago and head of the national Willow Creek Association.

Americans love shopping malls, replete with stores of all kinds and for all tastes. A wonderful example is the Mall of America in Bloomington, Minnesota. With over 400 stores, fifteen movie theaters, dozens of restaurants, a Camp Snoopy amusement park, an "underwater world," and much more, the choices are bewildering. But the amazing variety of choices is also its strength. It is what draws millions of visitors each year from around the world to frequently cold and snowy Minnesota. The "mega-mall," as it is often called, is currently a crowning achievement of the modern-day marketplace, a consumer bazaar.

One story of America is the continuous expansion of this marketplace into areas not traditionally driven by market principles. Religion is a prime example. Classical theorists of the nineteenth century[3] repeatedly pointed out that in preindustrial societies, religion was not chosen. One's religion was ascribed, given at birth, shared by the whole social group. One's religion was not only the religion of one's parents, but also the religion of one's relatives, neighbors, and community members. Moreover, the local institutions, laws, norms, and values all supported the same religion. Religion was so "given," so essential to individual and corporate identity, so intertwined with all other spheres of life, that the concept of religion as a separate entity often did not exist. In fact, whole tribes and societies, such as the present day Yanamamo of South America, did and do not even have a word for religion. What is more, religious missionaries to faraway lands speak of converting whole villages and tribes rather than individuals.[4] In such circumstances, converting individuals one at a time is unworkable.

Despite exceptions, which we will explore, this has changed drastically in the United States and many other places. Others have described, conceptualized, and theorized about these changes in detail.[5] We merely summarize these changes because they are foundational for our argument. To do so, we use the metaphor of the religious marketplace.[6] Akin to the shopping mall, Americans have a bewildering variety of religious forms from which to choose. Necessary conditions for any marketplace are suppliers, consumers, and some degree of freedom to choose (even though that choice occurs within a social context). American religion provides all these.

For a religious marketplace to exist, a society cannot have state-established, supported, and regulated churches. For example, in medieval Europe the Catholic church was the officially recognized and supported religion. If one was born in Europe during this time, one was Catholic by ascription, and essentially by law. To be otherwise carried great personal cost and peril. Further, to be otherwise probably did not even occur to most people, as it does not occur to most Americans to become Confucian. Catholicism was the established church, so government and religion were not separated. In fact, "the idea of a civilization in which state and church would work together ... was so firmly rooted that for most Europeans it was difficult to imagine that anything else could be."[7] This obviously prevented the operation of a religious marketplace.

Early colonial America was hardly different with respect to the institutional, social pervasiveness of religion. As Louis B. Wright wrote, when modern Americans try to project themselves "into the period of [their] colonial ancestors, one of [their] greatest difficulties is a comprehension of the pervasiveness of religion and its universal influence upon men, women, and children of the earlier age."[8] An important reason for this social pervasiveness was the establishment of the church by the state. Religion was simply not left to individual choice, nor was it often imagined that it could be so.[9]

The Enlightenment, a general rationalistic movement of thought, eventually altered the landscape of Western culture. Enlightenment thinkers believed that the truth about God and the world were discoverable by using their rational faculties. One consequence of this seminal change in world understanding was the questioning of the religious establishment—that is, state support of a religion. The well-known Virginia Bill for Establishing Religious Freedom (1785), which called for the disestablishment of religion—ending state support of a religion—and was strongly influenced by Enlightenment thinker Thomas Jefferson, is one example of how the Enlightenment contributed to the demise of the established church order.

But it was not only the Enlightenment that contributed to disestablishment. From the 1720s through the 1740s, the Great Awakening of the early evangelicals, according to Handy, also played a pivotal role. During this time, mass meetings stressing emotionalism and pietism were popularized.

The Great Awakening's main impact also undercut church establishment. The awakenings polarized established churches and led to divisions and greater pluralism. They also resulted in churches becoming increasingly dependent on "winning voluntary support" if they were to survive and thrive. "The awakening spirit placed the emphasis on the inner religious experience of the individual Christian rather than on the traditional theologies and establishment securities." [10] Further, "many of the awakened felt that God was doing his work through the revival and the churches that absorbed its spirit much more than through the older forms and established churches." [11]

Enlightenment principles and the Great Awakening ideals of evangelicals reached their high point in the American revolutionary period. Although attempts were made to maintain the established church, "the combination of Enlightenment leadership and disestablished masses was too great, and Jefferson's Bill for Establishing Religious Freedom was the result." Not only Jefferson's bill, but also the passing of the First Amendment to the Constitution, which reads, "Congress shall make no law respecting an establishment of religion, or prohibiting the free exercise thereof." With the passage of the First Amendment, disestablishment at the national level was firmly in place, and this was followed, over time, by disestablishment at the state level. Disestablishment meant that religious groups could no longer depend on the state for their survival. This met with hearty support from many evangelicals of the time. Some evangelical groups, such as Baptists, had labored for disestablishment and, according to historian Mark DeWolfe Howe, many evangelicals welcomed disestablishement "because of the deep conviction that the realm of spirit lay beyond the reach of government." [12]

As religion scholars such as historian Nathan Hatch[13] and sociologists Roger Finke and Rodney Stark[14] note, when religion becomes disestablished, it opens the doors for creative religious entrepreneurs to market their alternative faiths to religious consumers. The general public, likewise, is freed—at least in the ideal—to choose among options. Disestablishment in the context of a new, pluralistic nation led to a religious marketplace. With only slight exaggeration, the United States can be characterized as the "mega-mall" of religious consumerism.

Take the real-life case of Al and Sue Jamison. They had recently moved to a new metropolitan area when we interviewed them. We were interested in how they found a place of worship, with over 3,000 options possible in their new location. They told us that having moved due to job transfers many times over the past ten years, they had, through trial and error, decided exactly what form of worship and doctrine they preferred. They had also determined that a loosely connected association of churches, all organized around the same guiding principles—the Willow Creek Association—came closest to their preferences. So the Jamisons called the local association in their new state. Of the over sixty such churches in the state, they determined that twenty-five were within acceptable driving distance. The Jamisons then began an "initial screen," conducting a short telephone interview with a representative from each of these churches. Based on these initial interviews, they decided that five churches met their criteria most closely. They then spent the next month visiting each. From their first round of visits, they narrowed the list of five churches to three. Representatives from each of the three churches were then invited to the Jamison's home, on successive nights, to provide more information about the congregations. When Al and Sue finished their in-home interviews and visited each of the three churches a second time, they selected the church that they concluded best matched their preferences. After two months, their church shopping was complete, and they were satisfied customers.

Undoubtedly, this is an extreme example of church shopping. Yet it illustrates the way in which American religion is indeed a marketplace. Many will not go to this extreme to select a place of worship—just as many will not go to this extreme to buy a car—but the point is not how detailed and thorough people are in their searches. Rather, the point is that people select among options to satisfy personal preferences. As consumers, although they are influenced by forces outside themselves, such as the subcultures in which they live, the final decision is usually theirs, not society's or that of some other entity.

Wherever one finds a marketplace, full of consumers looking to make choices and purchases, one finds competition. If consumers are free to choose among alternatives, and survival of the suppliers is contingent on consumers, then suppliers must compete for consumers. The religious marketplace is thus shaped in part by competition. Because survival of religious organizations in the United States depends primarily on the religious consumer, not on state support, and a vast number of religious and nonreligious alternatives exist, religious groups compete for adherents. Part of how they do this is to appeal to particular market segments of the population.

At the mega-mall, one does not find 400 stores selling the same products. Rather, stores often survive by specializing—for example, selling only socks or memorabilia or Japanese noodles. Not everyone will want to buy Japanese noodles, to be sure, but by specializing in them, the owners of the Japanese noodle store create a stable market niche. Their store is the place to go for consumers demanding Japanese noodles, whether they demand such products because of ethnicity/cultural background, natural affinity for such noodles, or advertising-driven tastes. According to theorists of the religious economies model,[15] people have particular demands for religious expressions—like Al and Sue Jamison—and entrepreneurs create niches by catering to those demands—in the Jamisons' case, the Willow Creek Association.

Clearly, one consequence of the religious mega-mall is increased product variety—that is, religious pluralism.[16] If people have divergent religious demands, an effective way to compete is to specialize to meet the demands of one submarket. This leaves others' needs unmet, but those are filled by other suppliers.

A reasonable question is why religious organizations do not compete using the department store approach, trying to offer something for everyone? Although reasons abound, one obvious reason is that some tastes necessarily negate others, rendering the department-store approach ultimately impossible for single religious organizations. As examples, some people demand "high church"—solemn hymns; learned, impersonal teachings; tradition; ritual. Other people demand "low church"—uptempo, "contemporary" music; flamboyant, emotional preaching; emphasis on experiencing the supernatural through emotion. Some prefer an education hour in addition to worship, and others do not. For those who prefer an education hour, some prefer it before worship, others after. Some prefer a worship service that is predictable and timed, others prefer unpredictability and emphasize the event of worship over its length. Among Christians, some prefer communion on the last weekend of each month, and others on the first weekend of each month, others on each weekend of the month, others every time a religious service is conducted. And the list goes on. The point is that all options simply cannot be offered when one option precludes another. Nor can all options successfully be offered without ending in chaos.[17] Some congregations and denominations do try to generalize rather than specialize, and the result is often the same: loss of membership, commitment, and group solidarity. By not creating a distinctive identity and giving distinctive meaning, the department store approach—in the religious sphere, often indicated by dominant values such as tolerance, diversity, openness—fails. To understand why this is so, we must first understand why people become part of religious groups.

WHY CONGREGATIONS ARE INTERNALLY SIMILAR

"People meet together for worship within the basic sociological groupings into which they are born."[18] Religious disestablishment leads to pluralism, increased competition, and individual choice. These in turn are associated with specialization and niche marketing—that is, marketing specifically to a certain segment of the population. And these processes lead to something else, something of tremendous importance for understanding evangelicals and race relations. In the process of competing, of developing niches and assuring internal strength, congregations come to be made up of highly similar people. Individual congregations tend to be made up of people from similar geographic locations, similar socioeconomic statuses, similar ethnicities, and, perhaps first and foremost, predominately the same race. From the perspective of race relations, evangelicals and religious groups in general are in a quandary. The processes that generate church growth, internal strength, and vitality in a religious marketplace also internally homogenize and externally divide people. Conversely, the processes intended to promote the inclusion of different peoples also tend to weaken the internal identity, strength, and vitality of volunteer organizations. Let us explore this further.

Why Are People in Religious Groups?

As we noted in another work,[19] it is a basic sociological principle that the human drives for meaning and belonging are necessarily realized through interaction with others, primarily in social groups. It is within the context of groups, especially religious groups, that one answers questions such as, "Who am I?," "Why do I exist?," "How should I relate to others?," and "How do I understand tragedy?" A primary way that social groups provide members with answers to these questions, and thereby provide identity and meaning, is by imparting a normative and moral orientation toward life and others. And humans must have such orientations. Their understanding is formed not just by what is, but what ought to be. No one can opt out of commitment to some fundamental moral orientation or take a normative view "from nowhere." Given this, people find and maintain their moral orientations in social groups, in actual relational networks. Religion is, by its very nature, a central source of the types of morally orienting collective identities that provide people with meaning and belonging.

The more satisfactorily a religious group provides meaning and belonging, the stronger that religious group is. But how is this accomplished? Sociology of religion scholar Peter Berger says that this is always an achievement, precarious to be sure.[20] The answers to this question—explored in the following sections—provide clues as to why congregations are internally similar.

Groups Need Boundaries and Social Solidarity

Two important ways that groups provide meaning and belonging are by establishing group boundaries and social solidarity. In the context of a pluralistic society, social groups construct and maintain collective identities by forming symbolic boundaries. These boundaries create distinctions between them and other groups. A group is a group, in part, by virtue of its difference from other groups; put another way, by virtue of its internal similarity. Groups must symbolize and utilize symbolic boundaries to both create and give substance to shared values and identities.[21] In many respects, we know who we are by knowing who we are not. Thus, an ingroup always has at least one outgroup by which it creates identity. Blacks are not whites, Lutherans are not Presbyterians, evangelicals are not mainline Christians, Carolina Tar Heels are not Duke Blue Devils. Of course, symbolic boundaries are created, and thus can be altered. The point is not so much which boundaries are created or whether they can be altered, but that boundaries are necessary for identity. The more permeable and fuzzy the boundaries, the less effective is the group in providing meaning and belonging, weakening the group.

Pluralism, competition, and niche marketing influence the formation of group identity by providing comparison groups, often sharpening boundaries. Groups that stress tolerance, openness to diversity, and inclusiveness typically lack the ability to have strong comparison groups by which to define their boundaries (with the exception that they may compare themselves to groups that do draw distinct boundaries). Their boundaries are fuzzy, and they thus find it more difficult to provide meaning and belonging. In sum, groups that are more capable of constructing distinct identity boundaries, short of becoming genuinely countercultural, produce stronger collective identities. As a consequence, they often maintain or grow in size and strength. This is the essence both of our subcultural theory of religious strength[22] and the religious economies view of religious strength.[23]

But there is more to social group strength and internal similarity than simply drawing distinct symbolic boundaries. "A house divided cannot stand." Our translation? Any group that lacks social solidarity eventually fails. A group typically is said to have solidarity if its members are cohesive, working for a common purpose, and closely knit. Sociologist Michael Hechter offers a novel and important way to assess group solidarity.[24] For him, social solidarity increases as members' private resources contributed to group ends increase. These resources include money, time, social ties, skills, knowledge, and allegiance. We may use marriage as an example. A married couple, the smallest group possible, forms to provide certain collective benefits. An individual is a "good" family person if she or he gives to, spends time with, and is dedicated to the marriage. When someone spends too much time away from or gives too little resources to the marriage, their partner is upset, the marriage is "on the rocks," and, if this pattern continues, dissolution is often the result. If a marriage is to survive and be strong, it must have internal solidarity. The same is true of any group.

Hechter says that high levels of solidarity exist principally in groups whose rationale is creating social benefits *that members themselves desire to consume.* Because they desire certain benefits, they are willing to contribute to the group to produce them. As we explore below, religious groups arise out of human desire for meaning and belonging. Each group's main focus, as Hechter notes, is thus first and foremost internally directed. If a group is to achieve solidarity, necessary for the survival of a volunteer group, its primary purpose cannot be to do something outside the group, but rather to create something within the group, as in the case of married couples.

But cannot groups' social goods be used for serving others, bringing different parts of society together, overcoming inequality and discrimination? Yes, but only insofar as internal solidarity is achieved, group identity defined, and meaning and belonging provided. Given the energy needed to achieve these, too great a focus outside the group often means inattention to the group's needs, which weakens the group. Seminary professor C. Peter Wagner, in his analysis of religious groups that attempt to focus outwardly, reiterates the work of Kelley:[25] "As churches constitute themselves agents to produce social change, they are likely to lose, rather than gain, social strength." [26] Social solidarity is sacrificed, and the group loses its energy and strength.

Internally Similar Congregations Are Less Costly

Viewed sociologically, religious groups exist to supply members with meaning, belonging, and security (often including eternal salvation). Most people want to satisfy their needs with minimal cost. "But," writes Michael Hechter, a socially generated benefit "can be attained only if members comply with various rules designed to assure its production." [27] If members do not attend worship service, it is difficult to produce the experience of collective worship. If members do not contribute time and money, it is difficult to run a congregation. Given our assumption that meaning, belonging, and security are all necessarily social, members must to some degree participate. They must sacrifice for the group in return for the fulfillment of essential needs.

So how can people be motivated to participate? One way is to pay them. Compensation is possible only in firms that produce marketable goods or services for those outside the group, because the compensation itself must be produced. Congregations often pay head clergy and perhaps a few others, but the majority of participants are not monetarily compensated. If they are not compensated, and members choose to be part of the group, they must be receiving satisfaction of basic needs. And indeed this is the other method of motivating people to contribute to the collective good—because it is necessary to meet their needs.

Why do groups vary in what they demand to create collective benefits? The higher the cost of producing a social benefit, the higher the obligations.

Hechter gives this example. If community security is more costly than entertainment pleasure from a poker game, we should expect community security to require greater obligations.

In a pluralistic market, and given that most people seek the greatest gain for the least cost, *internally diverse* congregations are typically at a disadvantage. The key generalization is this: the cost of producing meaning, belonging, and security in internally diverse congregations is usually much greater—because of the increased complexity of demands, needs, and backgrounds, the increased effort necessary to create social solidarity and group identity, and the greater potential for internal conflict. Thus, *internally homogenous congregations more often provide what draws people to religious groups for a lower cost than do internally diverse congregations.*[28] This is another reason why congregations tend toward internal homogeneity.

Social Psychological Reasons

The findings of social psychologists also help us understand how meaning and belonging are provided, and why congregations tend toward internal similarity. People generally prefer to be with people like themselves, says a basic social psychological principle, and so say the people we interviewed. Studies find that status similarity among friends is high, especially for characteristics like race, sex, and age.[29] Verbrugge also found high similarity by religious preference. One reason for these similarities is that social associations between like people are more stable. And stability enables the creation of meaning and belonging, the very reasons people seek and need social associations and groups.[30] Moreover, as a variant to the adage we have already cited, "a house divided cannot stand," Verbrugge notes that similarity allows people and groups to establish consensus, again aiding in the creation of meaning and belonging. So the attraction of people to similar persons and groups has much to do with fulfilling basic human needs.

It does not matter that there is little or no biological basis for the perception that people are racially similar. If a society attaches importance to some characteristic, that society will come to see people with that characteristic as similar. Individuals then use those categories when choosing groups and other social associations. Because we do not categorize people by ear size, even though people differ significantly in this characteristic, we find no cultural similarity among people with similar ears. But such categories could conceivably be socially constructed. If ear size came to be an important social dividing line, we would begin to find big-eared congregations and little-eared congregations. Prejudice is not needed for this to occur. Rather, real cultural differences would develop by ear size and interactions with like-eared people would become easier, smoother, and ultimately more satisfying.

But more is at work here. If the big-eared/little-eared distinction existed in the past, it would be likely, by the simple law of inertia, to continue in the present. Given the choice, people tend to choose what they already have. Cognitive psychologists call this the status-quo bias.[31] The status-quo bias is the tendency of people to stick with what they have, even if gains could be made by selecting an alternative. That is, the choices people make vary depending on where they make them.[32] Researchers attribute this tendency to "loss aversion."[33] Loss aversion means that, given a person's reference point, the prospect of losses weighs more heavily than that of foregone gains.

Sociologist Mark Chaves and economist James Montgomery conducted an interesting experiment to examine loss aversion and the status quo bias at work in religious choices.[34] They first had respondents rate, on a scale of one to ten, the importance of various religious options, such as congregational friendliness and travel time. After this, they gave respondents a reference point. This was done by randomly distributing a scenario according to which, for instance, respondents currently attended either a nearby congregation of below average friendliness, or a very friendly congregation over an hour away. Assigned these scenarios, respondents then were asked if, in real life, they would prefer a congregation of average friendliness and a twenty-minute drive away, or a very friendly congregation but a sixty-minute drive away.

What did Chaves and Montgomery find? Regardless of how people had initially ranked the importance of relative religious options, they were now far more likely to prefer the congregation that most closely matched their randomly assigned reference point. For example, even if people had ranked minimal travel time as more important than friendliness, they were more likely to chose a very friendly church far from their home once they had been given that scenario as their reference point.

People's choices are shaped by preferences, perceived similarity, and the degree to which meaning and belonging are met. But these, cognitive psychologists tell us, are shaped by their histories (their reference points). This helps us understand why parents' religion and denomination are excellent predictors of an individual's own religion and denomination.[35] The status-quo bias, among other factors, operates powerfully. Given that U.S. congregations since the Civil War have been overwhelmingly racially homogenous, the status-quo bias tells us, other things equal, that they will remain so.

Macro Sociological Reasons

There are still other, larger reasons that congregations end up internally similar. Sociologist Peter Blau notes that because social association depends on opportunities for contact, social relations are more common between persons in proximate rather than distant positions.[36] That social relations tend to form between people of similar sociodemographic characteristics is known as the "homophily principle."[37] Because religious groups recruit adherents through the networks of its members,[38] the homophily principle suggests that homogenous groups remain homogenous.

Should we assume that all groups are homogenous? If a group is originally mixed, although the homophily principle strongly suggests it will not be, presumably it would continue to be mixed. Further, mere chance "mutations" or concerted efforts of a group to diversify could result in heterogeneity. But in a pluralistic, competitive, choice-driven market such as the United States, this is highly unlikely. Heterogeneous volunteer groups, such as congregations, are inherently unstable.

The experiences of one congregation we will call First Church help us understand the instability of racially heterogeneous volunteer groups. A newly ordained African-American evangelical pastor set out in Seattle, with the support of his denomination and the sense of following God's will, to establish an interracial church. Knowing that congregations recruit adherents through the networks of their members, and that members' networks tend to be racially homogenous, he determined that the new church would need to be racially mixed from the start. So he began visiting white and black churches in the area, telling the congregations of the vision to establish a mixed-race church, and asking for volunteers to be charter members. After a year of preparation, the first public service was held, and the congregation was almost evenly split between blacks and whites (no other racial groups were represented). The same was true of the music team. From the musicians to the singers, the composition was nearly fifty–fifty.

But, as the church grew, something happened to its mixed-race nature— it disappeared, and the congregation became nearly all-African American. Perhaps because the pastor was black and thus practiced a nonwhite style of preaching and leadership, perhaps because white Americans are accustomed to being the majority, a pattern developed in who visited and who became members. More blacks than whites visited, and even more blacks than whites became regular attendees and members. As this happened, the church had fewer and fewer white visitors.

And another significant development occurred in this process. Some white members began expressing concerns, primarily to other white members, that their spiritual needs were not being met, that the service now catered more to the black members. They expressed less than complete comfort with the type of music, the length of the service, the style of preaching, the types of programs, and the way that people related to each other. But more than this, some of the white members began feeling like outsiders, as if their voices did not carry as much influence as the voices of the black congregants. Some even questioned the church's commitment to having a mixed-race membership. After about a year, one of the charter member white families decided to leave. Shortly thereafter, another of the original white families left. A downward spiral effect took over. Even fewer whites visited the congregation, and the white members, many of whom originally did not share the concerns some whites had been expressing, now themselves began to feel like outsiders, as if they were somehow on the fringe. They felt this way despite the best intentions and efforts of the pastor and black leaders in the church to let them know they were as important as anyone else in the congregation. Soon another white family left, and another, and another. Within three years after the founding of this mixed-race church, fewer than ten whites remained. And in interviews, nearly all the remaining whites said they were contemplating leaving, even the few that were in mixed-race marriages.

As we interviewed those whites who had left First Church, all spoke of feeling as if their needs, and their family's needs, were not being met at the church. It felt, they said, as if the church was going in a different direction than was needed by their family. All were adamant that their leaving had nothing to do with race, but rather that the church was simply not meeting their needs. And all said that although they were now part of nearly all-white congregations, they did not choose their new churches based on race, but fit, comfort, and felt need.

Are these people lying, merely trying to put an acceptable face on their racial prejudice? Unlikely, given that they voluntarily became members of a mixed-race church. While we can debate whether the whites who left were prejudiced but unaware of this bias until they became part of First Church, we do not need to know this. Whether they were prejudiced or not most likely would not have altered the fate of this church. How can we make such a claim?

As groups compete and form distinct identities—which, as we saw, they must do to remain viable—they carve out a unique position or niche in social space. According to sociologists Pamala Popielarz and J. Miller McPherson, voluntary organizations such as First Church lose members who are atypical of the group—described as those who are at the edge of the niche rather than the core—faster than other members.[39] They term this *the niche edge effect.* Because social network ties influence membership duration in voluntary groups,[40] "Members at the edge of the organization's niche will have higher turnover than members at the center of the organization's niche, as a result of their higher proportion of extraorganizational ties and their lower proportion of intraorganizational ties."[41] This is in part why a white family or two leaving First Church led to a spiral effect of more whites leaving and less whites visiting. Given the historical division in social networks along racial lines, with fewer whites in the church, there were fewer within-church social network ties to keep whites there and recruit new white members. Whites leaving also meant an increasingly greater number of social ties outside the church for the remaining whites, making the church less central for them, and making them feel increasingly like outsiders, and that their needs were not being met.

Given that people have options, the niche edge effect is partly why colleges, businesses, or, in our case, religious organizations, have a higher dropout rate of people with atypical sociodemographic characteristics. Because the United States is racialized, both historically and currently, race is a quintessential example of what Peter Blau calls a "consolidated characteristic." [42] By this term he means that several characteristics—such as race, education, income, wealth, family background, and cultural practices—tend to vary together. According to empirical tests in U.S. metropolitan areas, race is the single most consolidated characteristic of all.[43] And, as the percentage of blacks in the metro area rises, the more closely related are race, education, income, and other variables. Because race, socially defined, is a longterm, highly visible indicator of other differences, it is along this characteristic that we find the homophily principle (friendships forming between similar people) and the niche edge effect (organizations losing nonsimilar members faster than other members) operating most powerfully. In the case of First Church, as the percentage of African Americans in the church rose, we can expect that the whites in the church really did become divergent from the average member, not just racially, but—because of the principle of consolidation—culturally, educationally, and more.

In addition to network ties, Popielarz and McPherson show that intergroup competition, which they term the *niche overlap effect*, also operates to create homogenous groups. When the niches of groups partially overlap, they recruit some same-kind members. For example, First Church recruits white members, but so too do "white" churches. For the members simultaneously being recruited by multiple groups—again, those on the edge and thus most dissimilar—the result is less stability of membership in any one group, due to finite access to time and other resources. Thus, atypical group members are not only more likely to leave a group due to a lack of intraorganizational ties, but because competition for them to join other groups is more intense than it is for core group members.

Our interviews with the white members who left First Church illustrate this niche overlap effect. Due to their abundant ties with people in other churches very different from most people of First Church, but similar to the whites formerly of First Church, they were frequently invited to come to churches of friends and acquaintances. This "competition" was particularly intense once the white First Church members started feeling like outsiders at First Church. Other churches that they were aware of through network ties seemed more and more attractive—so much so that, in the best interests of their families, they felt it only made sense to switch.

In the deregulated religious marketplace of the United States, the niche overlap effect implies that competition between religious groups drives them to be what they often do not want to be—homogenous.[44] This is because they must focus limited resources on a relatively unique niche and, as we have seen, because atypical members do not generally remain members. Therefore, because individual congregations are situated within a marketplace of competing congregations, attempts at pluralism are often overridden by the homogenizing structural factors of the niche edge and overlap effects. And this is in part why stated ideology or religious values regarding race often make little difference in the actual level of within-group heterogeneity.[45]

FROM THE ABSTRACT BACK TO THE CONCRETE: RELIGIOUS ORGANIZATIONS AND THE HOMOGENOUS UNITS PRINCIPLE

In the United States the denominations and congregations that grow typically apply the understanding of similarity and niche marketing, whether explicitly or not. The clearest argument for having homogenous congregations probably is made by evangelical seminary professor C. Peter Wagner.[46] In his book, *Our Kind of People*, he pulls together evidence from a variety of sources and experiences to, as the back cover of the book says, transform "the statement that '11 a.m. on Sunday is the most segregated hour in America' from a millstone around Christian necks into a dynamic tool for assuring Christian growth."

Wagner's argument is quite simple. Undoubtedly, congregations are extremely homogenous. Although people often lament this fact, he argues that they should not. First, ethnic and racial groups, in and of themselves, are amoral. Second, people prefer to worship in their own cultural groups. Third, denominations and congregations that use the "homogenous units principle," which means that volunteer organizations function best when composed of just one cultural group, grow and are more vital. For example, the nation's largest Protestant denomination—the Southern Baptist Convention—which starts at least one new church per day on average, uses the "homogenous units principle." Southern Baptists regularly start white churches, black churches, Chinese churches, Korean churches, Mexican churches, Haitian churches, and so on. And fourth, because Wagner views the primary mission of Christianity to evangelize—much like evangelicals before him—not only are homogenous congregations acceptable, but the homogenous units principle is an essential tool for Christian growth. As he summarizes, "For optimum conditions of growth, the composition of a congregation should be compatible with the needs for social companionship felt by the unchurched people in the community." [47] And, "the local congregation in a given community should be only as integrated as are the families and other primary social groups in the community." [48]

Wagner takes social structures and conventions as given—from how groups of people are defined and classified, to giving ultimacy to individual preference. Religious institutions should not try to change these—as it makes them ineffective and weakens their internal strength, he argues—but rather should determine the best way to grow, given the socially constructed realities. The "best way" is directly in line with social scientific knowledge of why groups form and what makes them strong. To provide meaning and belonging, groups must create unique collective identities sought by the members, and this becomes far more difficult and is less satisfying in heterogeneous groupings. Thus, atypical members do not stay members, and if the group has no "typical" members, it dissolves as members are recruited into other, more homogenous groups.

A FINAL WORD

The organization of American religion is characterized by disestablishement, pluralism, competition, and consumer choice. This organization is partly shaped and often capitalized on by evangelicals. [49] And as a consequence of sociological and social psychological principles at work, congregations become and remain highly racially homogenous. Although racially homogenous churches certainly can result from individual and group racial prejudice, the principles discussed in this chapter indicate that, given U.S. history, merely eliminating racial prejudice would not end racially divided churches. The need for symbolic boundaries and social solidarity, the similarity and homophily principles, the status quo bias, and the niche edge and niche overlap effects all push congregations, and volunteer organizations in general, continually toward internal similarity.

We have shown that the organization of American religion leads to racially separate congregations. We are now ready, in the next chapter, to explore the implications of religion's organization and internally similar congregations for producing and maintaining racialization.

Structurally Speaking

Religion and Racialization

"Religious faith ... is as much a particularizing force as a generalizing one."
Clifford Geertz, 1968

Religion has tremendous potential for mitigating racial division and inequality. Most religions teach love, respect, and equality of all peoples. They often teach of the errors inherent in racial prejudice and discrimination. They frequently proclaim the need to embrace all people. They speak of the need for fairness and justice. They often teach that selfishness and acting in self-interested ways are counter to the will of the divine.

In the United States, where Christianity continues to be the dominant religion, faith motivated the fight against slavery. It played a central role in the Civil Rights movement. It is currently motivating at least some evangelicals to form cross-race friendships, establish sister churches with congregations of another race, have interracial prayer breakfasts, and more. It directs others to value and desire openness, tolerance, and diversity. It guides some people to vote in ways that reduce racial division and inequality. It motivates some people to volunteer in groups working against racial hate and discrimination. For others, it motivates them to form organizations intent on reducing inequality and strengthening justice. Yet others are guided to donate money to such organizations. Some employers who are religious might be directed by their faith to set up some kind of "affirmative action" hiring policy. Others might be motivated to make sure their organization treats employees of different backgrounds fairly.

Stories of the positive actions of religious people and organizations to combat racial division and inequality abound. While we could continue our list, we wish only to illustrate that religion—its people and its institutions—has and does, in a myriad of ways, attempt to reduce racialization.

But this chapter, focusing on the structural arrangements of religion and their implications for groups, demonstrates the powerful countervailing influences of religion on racialization. These countervailing influences attenuate the impact of religion's positive actions, and ironically help generate and perpetuate the very conditions that these positive actions seek to end.

We examine two primary structural arrangements in this chapter— racially homogenous religious ingroups and the segmented religious market—and investigate their implications for racialization. We claim that these patterns not only generate congregational segregation by race, but contribute to the racial fragmentation of American society, generate and sustain group biases, direct altruistic religious impulses to express themselves primarily within racially separate groups, segregate social networks and identities, contribute to the maintenance of socioeconomic inequality, and generally fragment and drown out religious prophetic voices calling for an end to racialization.

Racially Homogenous Religious Groups, Divisions, Biases, and Loyalty

Macro-Level Division

We defined a racialized society as a society wherein race matters profoundly for life experiences, life chances, and social relationships. The racialized society of the United States, we said, is characterized by low intermarriage rates, de facto segregation, socioeconomic inequality, and personal identities and social networks that are racially distinctive.

Congregations that are racially homogenous are, by definition, part of the elaborate structure of racialization. But many people see racially separate congregations as a relatively innocuous contribution to racialization. It is a contribution that can eventually be overcome, if really necessary, by integration in other spheres—such as economics or politics. Or for others, such division can be mitigated with a little extra effort and attention, say, by having occasional joint worship services with a congregation of another race, or, as we have seen, by making a friend from another race.

Such views, however, miss the connections between simple segregation by race in places of worship and the many consequences that flow from this division. To reflect on this issue properly, we must keep in mind the distinction between macro and micro effects. Part of the irony of religion's role is that in strengthening micro bonds between individuals, religion contributes to within-group homogeneity, heightens isolation from different groups, and reduces the opportunity for the formation of macro bonds—bonds between groups—that serve to integrate a society. As sociologists Blau and Schwartz state:

> Social integration is often interpreted as resting on strong ingroup bonds. But this is a microsociological view, which looks at integration from the standpoint of the individual. What benefits ingroup bonds may have for individuals, from a macrosociological perspective they are a disintegrative force because, far from integrating the diverse segments of a society or community, they fragment it into exclusive groupings. The social integration of the various segments of a large population depends not on strong ingroup ties but on extensive intergroup relations that strengthen the connections among segments and unite them in a distinctive community, notwithstanding their diversity.[1]

The fact that various groups all serve different but necessary functions for society is not sufficient for social integration. Intergroup bonds are needed. Such bonds may eventually blur the distinctions between groups, but at the same time they integrate the larger community. The processes that create meaning and belonging within groups, according to Blau and Schwartz, fragment the larger community. This fragmentation is particularly acute when social factors are "consolidated," that is, when several social dimensions such as religion, place of residence, and class are closely associated with some other social dimension such as race.

Blau and Schwartz empirically demonstrate that a close association of social dimensions inhibits relationships between groups.[2] Race, they find, is the dimension most closely associated with differential income, education, residential location, occupation, and so on. Because religion is one dimension that separates social life along racial lines, it reduces opportunities for intergroup relations and social ties.

Moreover, Blau and Schwartz find that a lack of social ties between groups inhibits mobility between them, increasing the salience of group boundaries and social differences. The organization of American religion into racially homogenous groups lowers the probability of intergroup mobility (such as through marriage) and heightens the importance of racial boundaries, identities, and other differences between groups. Although many in the religious community call and work for an end to racial division, the organization of religion into homogenous groups often undercuts their efforts.

Categorization and Differentiation

Clearly, separate groups result in categorization, for separate groups must be categorized by something—region, religion, race, ethnicity, occupation, age, or some combinations of factors. For instance, two softball teams are categorized, at a minimum, by their unique team names, say the Las Vegas Lizards and the New Jersey Nasty Newts. Cognitive and social psychologists help us understand the implications of this categorization. According to psychologists Hamilton and Trolier:

> The social categories we develop are more than convenient groupings of individuals that simplify the actual diversities among the people we observe and encounter. They are also categories that can bias the way we process information, organize and store it in memory, and make judgments about members of those social categories.[3]

People consistently engage in social comparison,[4] and research links categorization to at least five biases. The purpose of these biases "is primarily to distinguish the ingroup positively from the position of the outgroup rather than to downgrade the outgroup." [5]

Merely knowing that people are classified into one group or another produces a rather consistent consequence: people tend to exaggerate the similarities of ingroup members and their differences from outgroup members.[6] And because people know the outgroup by its perceived differences, outgroup members are identified by these differences, overly homogenizing them.[7] This occurs even when the "difference" is merely temporary, arbitrary, and minimal, or even when the only basis for separate groups is random assignment.

What is more, people do not evaluate ingroup and outgroup members in the same way. Even when performing exactly the same actions, ingroup members are evaluated more positively and outgroup members more negatively.[8] Ingroup bias, it seems, is "built in" to the way we think.

According to this research, we also have different ways of experiencing positive and negative behavior based on the ingroup/outgroup dichotomy. Much as we tend to do in evaluating our own behavior, we attribute positive behavior of ingroup members to internal traits such as intelligence, and negative behavior to external causes such as a poor home life. Conversely, we tend to attribute the positive behavior of outgroups to external causes such as luck, and negative behavior to internal traits such as limited intelligence. Not only do we interpret behavior more positively for ingroup members and more negatively for outgroup members, but we also appear to have better memories for negative outgroup behaviors than for negative ingroup behaviors.[9] We are consistently positively biased toward our group.

Recalling our tendency to deindividualize outgroup members, researchers find that if categorical labels are available—male/female, Northsider/ Southsider—then the negative behavior of the outgroup member is likely to be perceived as a characteristic of the outgroup itself.[10] Our cognitive processes appear to make the leap from "Tamika and Sally shoplifted" to, for example, "Women shoplift."

And then, once people have preconceived stereotypes of an outgroup, they tend to recall only information that confirms the stereotypes, while contradictory evidence is dismissed as an exception and typically forgotten altogether.[11]

The categorization effect goes beyond mere perception and interpretation to influence actual behavior.[12] In numerous experiments, researchers find, again even when groups are created merely by random assignment, that people show favoritism to ingroup members. The net result—preferential treatment for the ingroup.

Despite the seeming inevitability of these results, the picture is not all gloomy. Thankfully, the world is much more diversified than two groups differing on all characteristics. When group characteristics overlap, outgroup discrimination and ingroup preference are mitigated.[13] For example, a Mexican lawyer is less likely to employ categorization biases when the comparison category is Korean lawyers rather than Korean shoeshiners. Bias toward the person of the other ethnicity is mitigated by the shared occupation. It is also mitigated if the Mexican lawyer has social associations with Koreans, which is more likely to occur when group memberships overlap, such as when both work for the same firm or attend the same place of worship.[14] Thus, in a society with multiple cross-cutting group memberships, ingroup/outgroup biases are reduced.

Herein lies the intractability of the black–white divide, however. Rather than extensively overlapping characteristics and group memberships, in this case multiple characteristics are, to use Professor Blau's term, consolidated along racial lines—from income, wealth, occupation, and neighborhood, to culture, dialect, religion, and more. This means that black and white Americans truly approximate the two separate groups of the psychologists' experiments and thus tend to exhibit the "natural" biases found in the ingroup/outgroup research.

Religion contributes to this consolidation along racial lines—and the stronger the religion, the more it contributes—and therefore increases racial categorization. Again, its individual participants and organizations do not intend this result, but it is a latent by-product of establishing meaning, belonging, and group strength. From our present perspective, religion, in the context of a racialized society, accentuates group boundaries, divisions, categorizations, and the biases that follow. Religion is of course only one mechanism that contributes to racial division, but an important mechanism. It both reinforces other aspects of racial identity and meaning, and is itself a product of racially separate identities and meanings. For example, as seen previously, the movement of blacks and whites from separate pews to separate churches led to the development of many other separate black and white institutions, more divergent social identities, and even further divergent ways of worshipping, musical styles, preaching styles, and church organization. These are the very differences that so many people now cite in justification of racially separate congregations. And these are differences that continue to be reproduced by racially distinct congregations.

The Ethical Paradox of Group Loyalty

Given human limitations, racially exclusive identities and congregations necessitate bias. We might call this the ethical paradox of group loyalty.[15] The paradox is that even if made up of loving, unselfish individuals, the group transmutes individual unselfishness into group selfishness.

Imagine two groups. Each member of each group is a deeply committed religious person, full of love and concern for others, and has even developed a friendship or two from the other group. For historical reasons, one group has more social goods—income, wealth, education, power—than the other group. Despite being made up entirely of unselfish individuals, the two groups will continue to be divided and unequal. How can this be?

This was a question that Reinhold Niebuhr explored back in 1932 in his book, *Moral Man and Immoral Society*. For one thing, he wrote, direct contact with members of the other group is limited, and always less than with one's own group. People thus know the members of their own group and their needs more deeply, fully, and personally than the members and needs of the other group. Therefore, they attend to the needs of their own group first, precisely because they are moral and loving. How can they turn their backs on the needs of their own group in favor of another group? For Neibuhr, who used the nation as his example of the group, even an entire nation composed of people with the greatest possible religious goodwill will still be "less than loving" toward other nations, "if for no other reason, because the individuals could not possibly think themselves into the position of the individuals of another nation in a degree sufficient to insure pure benevolence. Furthermore such good will as they did possess would be sluiced into loyalty to their own nation [due to the ethical paradox of group loyalty] and tend to increase that nation's selfishness."[16] At the individual level, selfishness is usually considered negative, but at the group level, it is considered moral and just. Indeed, at the group level, it is not called selfishness, but morality, service, sacrifice, or loyalty.

We find evidence of this every day. Consider the family group. Although we are selfish if we always look out for our own individual needs first, it is considered wrong and immoral if we do not consider the needs of our family first, ahead of other families. We house our families first, and only if we can spare extra do we help house other families. To do otherwise is considered immoral, or, at a minimum, a sad case of misplaced priorities.

This phenomenon works at many levels. Neighborhood associations can be an effective tool for building cohesion and the health of a local area, but, as the evidence repeatedly shows, they are a poor means for integrating a larger community and producing the greatest good for the greatest number. To the extent that their power allows, they will not only look out for their own interests, but will do so even if at the expense of others. If someone is looking to locate a halfway house for convicted child molesters in a residential neighborhood, every local neighborhood association will likely oppose its location in its specific neighborhood. Each will look out for its own wellbeing. Even people without children might sacrifice time and energy to fight the halfway house, out of concern for the children in their neighborhood. If there were no power imbalances, this might be acceptable. But given power imbalances, stronger associations will succeed in looking out for the best interest of their own neighborhood, as they are supposed to do, but with the unintended result that the halfway house will end up in a less powerful neighborhood. This is one outcome of the ethical paradox of group loyalty.

Given this paradox, because members of a group cannot understand and feel the needs and wants of another group as completely and deeply as those of their own group, reliance on love, compassion, and moral and rational suasion to overcome group divisions and inequalities is, in Niebuhr's words, "practically an impossibility." For this reason, relations between groups are always mainly political rather then ethical or moral. As Niebuhr says, "They will always be determined by the proportion of power which each group possesses at least as much as by any rational and moral appraisal of the comparative needs and claims of each group." [17]

We see this in white evangelicals' assessment of the race problem and racial inequality. Although they can perhaps talk with empathy about a black friend's situation, when they assess the group, they speak in ways, as we have seen, that largely justify division and inequality. They know that most of their friends and relatives—who are predominately white—are not hate-mongering racists bent on keeping blacks down. And they know this much better than they can know the experiences of black Americans. So, when they must assess the "race problem," given their cultural tools, they conclude that it must be blacks exaggerating, or to the advantage of some to claim there is a race problem, or that the race problem is but individual problems between some individuals of different races. In short, they speak in ways that support their own racial group and the American system. Almost no white evangelical suggests that inequality between groups is immoral and ought to disappear, for example. And, largely isolated in their own racial group, they fail to see their advantages. The exceptions are those white evangelicals so immersed in black social networks that they appear to identify more with black Americans than with white Americans. That is, they are less a part of their racial birth group than they are a part of their "adopted" group, and they therefore have a perspective on racial issues closer to the perspectives of many black Americans.

RACIALLY HOMOGENOUS RELIGIOUS GROUPS, SEPARATE NETWORKS, AND INEQUALITY

At its core, contemporary racialization is characterized by separate networks and differential access to valued resources, such as health, wealth, and status. The mere existence of racially homogenous religious groups contributes to racially separate networks. Racially homogenous religious groups, especially strong religious groups, also contribute to differential access to resources, given the preexisting context of inequality by race.[18]

Separate Networks

To a substantial degree, social networks are formed and maintained in social groups.[19] Feld argues that almost all social ties are formed within organized social activity.[20] Much of this results from the proximity principle— we have to meet people to form relationships with them. Therefore, our relationships form within groups. We rarely become connected with a person from another part of our community unless we meet in organized group activity. As research demonstrates, much of the reason people's networks consist of people so similar to themselves is due to the homogenous nature of their social groups.[21] This is even true of marriage. People marry from a very limited pool, usually people in their own social groups.[22] The greater the distance between groups, the lower the probability of intermarriage, and the lower the probability that any such marriage will survive.

As a group becomes more central for its members, its members more often find friendship within the group. As Olson shows, the processes that make religious groups strong result in "denser" network ties. For example, for moderate and liberal Protestants, the average proportion of good friends who also belong to a similar denomination is 35 percent.[23] For conservative Protestants—a stronger religious movement[24]—the percentage of good friends who are also conservative Protestants increases to 48 percent.[25] Considering that these categories are crudely measured by denominational affiliation, this gap may be understated. But the point is illustrated. The "stronger" the religion, the more it segregates networks by increasing the density of one's ingroup ties. Church growth specialists capitalize on this; by appealing to and using segregated networks (the "homogenous units" principle), churches grow, and religious strength is increased. This approach, though effective for congregational and denominational growth, also helps to strengthen and affirm homogenous networks, thereby consolidating racial division.

The basic workings of American religion promote more ingroup friends, marriages, and acquaintances. Thus, religion—especially "strong" religion—both helps to create racially distinctive networks and, in using them as the basis for congregational and denominational growth, helps maintain and justify them.[26]

Racial Inequality

The facts just considered, together with the findings of cognitive psychologists and macrostructural sociologists, have considerable implications for the perpetuation of racial inequality and stratification. The logic is straightforward: (1) In the United States there is racial inequality in access to valued resources (see Chapter One). (2) Access to valued resources—such as jobs, prestige, wealth, and power—is gained in significant part through social ties.[27] (3) As we have previously discussed, for reasons such as social categorization and comparison, people have positive bias for their ingroups and negative bias for outgroups. These three facts suggest that, other factors being equal, any social structure or process that both increases the saliency of group boundaries and reduces interracial ties necessarily reproduces racial inequality.[28]

Because the organization of religion in the United States does heighten the salience of racial boundaries and reduce interracial ties, it necessarily reproduces racial inequality.[29] We look at this proposition more closely by way of an apparently unrelated example.

Sociologists Fernandez and Weinberg studied the hiring process at a large retail bank.[30] Unlike previous studies, which looked at the influence of social ties for employees, they were able to examine the hiring process from the employer's perspective. In other words, they were able to consider both those who were hired and those who were not, allowing them to see if a social-tie disparity existed between those hired and those not hired. They also examined the role of personal contacts at each stage of the hiring process, not just at the decision-to-hire stage. Their results uncover the central role social ties play in obtaining employment. Social contacts refer better qualified applicants for the open positions, and they provide "inside" information to the applicant about the organizational screening process—such as how to write an appropriate résumé and what to say in an interview. They also increase the employer's awareness of the applicant and the perception of the applicant's quality. Referred applicants—those with pertinent social ties—were at an advantage over nonreferred applicants at every step of the hiring process. Even after removing the effect of observable factors thought to give applicants an advantage, such as training and skills, the influence of social ties remained strong. By having a personal contact, an applicant went from being a vague other to an associate of an ingroup member, creating a positive bias among employers for such applicants (recall our preceding discussion of group biases). This increased their likelihood of being hired.

Because social *networks* are highly segregated along racial lines,[31] we can easily see that referrals and personal ties will be segregated as well.[32] This would perhaps be of minimal consequence under the condition of equality between racial groups. But for black and white Americans, as we know, this is far from the case. Because people must use social ties and referrals from people in higher social positions to move to higher positions,[33] the segregation of networks by race has direct consequences for producing racial inequality and stratification.[34]

But does religion have anything to do with employment? Given that humans are finite in time and space, network size is limited. As a result, any time spent developing one network set necessarily limits time to develop other network sets. A network, increasingly made up of other religiously and racially similar people as the importance of religion to the individual increases, heightens the segregation of networks not just in the religious sphere, but in other spheres as well. Perhaps this is why, according to our analysis of the 1996 General Social Survey, 42 percent of white Conservative Protestants, compared to 27 percent of other whites, work in all-white places of employment. Because Conservative Protestants have denser network ties, and hiring often occurs via social ties, white conservative Protestants end up in more homogenous places of work as well. To the extent that inequality by race exists, then, religion helps perpetuate racial inequality.

THE SEGMENTED MARKET AND THE FRAGMENTED VOICE

In 1931, sociologist and co-founder of the NAACP W. E. B. DuBois minced no words in his analysis of the Christian church and its role in black–white relations: "It is mainly a social organization, pathetically timid and human; it is going to stand on the side of wealth and power; it is going to espouse any cause which is sufficiently popular, with eagerness."[35]

Hindsight tells us that DuBois is both wrong and right in his analysis. Wrong in that he overlooked the potential of much of the black church for the Civil Rights movement, and wrong in that he overlooked a few exceptions in the white church. Yet with respect to the overall role of the institution called the white church, he has proven thus far correct. Using our understanding of the structure of religion and social relations, we now explore why the white church as a whole is, with respect to black–white relations, "pathetically timid and human."

The United States is of course not just composed of two groups, one black, one white. Apart from other important racial and ethnic groups, division also runs within racial and ethnic groups. In American religion, within the racial divide, are hundreds upon hundreds of denominations and sects, hundreds of thousands of congregations, and likely millions of ideas about what a "religious" person is, what is right and what is wrong.

The organization of American religion gives religious groups the freedom to compete for adherents, which appears to create a dynamic vitality. It also leads to competition, pluralism, and ultimately a very segmented market.

For our purposes, there is an important consequence of this segmented market. A key function in most religions is to proclaim what ought to be, what is universally true, what is right and just. We may call this the prophetic voice. But the organization of American religion fragments this prophetic voice, even within the same religion, into thousands of different voices. What are the effects of this? Ultimately, exactly what DuBois concluded.

One specific effect is illustrated by the work of sociologist Stephen Hart.[36] He interviewed American Christians—from a broad range of denominations and congregations—to understand their views on economic inequality, and how religion informed their views. He found that people use religion to come to every conceivable position on economic inequality—from extremely conservative to extremely liberal. Should economic inequality be overcome? Yes. Should economic inequality be preserved? Yes. It depends on who is asked, and the answer is often, but not always, associated with the respondent's religious tradition. Although most attempt to apply their faith, American Christians, even within the same race, run the gamut of possible positions on economic inequality. Thus, religious people, in such a context, compete ideologically against each other, fragmenting the religious voice. And given the relative equality of power, the different religious voices negate one another.

But it is not reasonable to assume equality of power. And we contend that, at least in race relations, the dominant white religious voices, amid the vast variety, are nearly always those that are least prophetic, most supportive of the status quo. It is not just that the prophetic voice is fragmented; the prophetic voices that call for overcoming group divisions and inequalities typically are ghettoized.

As we have seen, the organization of American religion encourages religious groups to cater to people's existing preferences, rather than their ideal callings. In trying to create meaning and belonging, even to teach religious truths and implications for social action, religious leaders must act within a limited range shaped by the social locations of their congregation. The congregation often looks to religion not as an external force that places radical demands on their lives, but rather as a way to fulfill their needs. Those who are successful in the world, those of adequate or abundant means, those in positions of power (whether they are aware of this power or not), rarely come to church to have their social and economic positions altered. If we accept the oftentimes reasonable proposition that most people seek the greatest benefit for the least cost, they will seek meaning and belonging with the least change possible. Thus, if they can go to either the Church of Meaning and Belonging, or the Church of Sacrifice for Meaning and Belonging, most people choose the former. It provides benefit for less cost. Prophetic voices calling for the end of group division and inequality, to the extent that this requires sacrifice or threatens group cohesion, are perfectly free to exist, but they are ghettoized. They will have followers, but they will be a minority voice, both in terms of size and strength. This is in part because, as seminary professor Charles Thomas Jr. has summarized, "In practice congregation members expect the minister to do nothing (such as taking a prophetic voice) which would interfere with the harmony and growth of the membership." [37]

As a result, many religious leaders, even if they desire change, are constrained. Unless their message is in the self-interest of the group, they must necessarily soften and deemphasize their prophetic voice in favor of meeting within-group needs. We have many historical examples illustrating this restriction. As religious historian C. C. Goen noted, early American evangelical leaders and denominations, "In embracing more and more of the 'grassroots' population ... were unwittingly jeopardizing their ability to function as disciplined communities of faith and to exercise moral leadership on controversial issues without alienating their constituencies." [38]

Sociologist Jeffrey Hadden in his classic book, *The Gathering Storm in the Churches*,[39] traced the clergy who participated in a one-month study program at the Urban Training Center for Christian Mission (UTC) in Chicago in 1965, and looked at those who were arrested in the Civil Rights protest marches that took place at the time. The program attended by these forty-eight Protestant clergy—all male and all white but one—was designed to better equip them to minister in the inner city. During that month, conflicts

over educational policy and leadership in Chicago's public schools, centering on racial issues, led Civil Rights leaders to schedule three days of
marches from Soldiers Field to City Hall. The day before the first march, the
UTC trainees were informed of the protests, encouraged to participate, and
told that the UTC curriculum would be suspended to enable them to do so.
Over the three-day period, conflict between the marchers and the police es-
calated. On the second and third days, police reportedly changed the
agreed-on routes for marching and did so during the middle of the march.
In protest, some of the marchers sat down in the street, blocking traffic and
refusing to move, even though they knew this would lead to arrest. When
Hadden examined the UTC trainees, he found that twenty-five of the forty-
eight clergy had been arrested.

Why did these twenty-five take the more extreme actions that led to arrest? Were they more committed to achieving social justice for African
Americans? Or were they perhaps constitutionally more inclined to risk-
taking? When Hadden compared the UTC clergy who were arrested with
the UTC clergy who were not arrested, he found no differences on these
characteristics. In fact, he could find no group differences on any personality characteristics or attitudinal variables. Instead, Hadden found that a key
variable was the extent of the clergy member's "structural freedom." Of the
four clergy who pastored integrated inner-city churches, and thus had congregations sympathetic to the purpose of the marches, all were arrested. Of
the nine clergy who were not pastors of churches, and thus not constrained
by the wishes of parishioners, all but two, or 78 percent, were arrested. In
contrast, of the clergy who pastored white city churches, only 37 percent
were arrested, and of the ten clergy pastoring white suburban churches, just
one was arrested. The deviant suburban pastor told Hadden in an interview
afterward that he was highly ambivalent about staying at his suburban congregation. Hadden also found that four of the ten suburban ministers not
only failed to be arrested, but did not march in any of the demonstrations.

"Thus," wrote Hadden, "independent of their own personal views, the
positions of their respective denominations, the position of the UTC staff,
and the views and actions of fellow ministers in the training program, [the
clergy] appear to have responded to this choice in terms of their congregations' expectations."[40] What the clergy believed was right—in other words,
what they believed the prophetic voice should be—was ultimately
constrained and shaped by the wishes of their congregations. Although
this influence can be attenuated to some degree for clergy in hierarchically
structured traditions and denominations—such as Catholicism and
Methodism—the congregations still appear to constrain and shape actions.

And the shape the laity want the prophetic voice to take is usually that
which supports their own felt needs. As Hadden concluded, "Clergy have

come to see the church as an institution for challenging [people] to new hopes and new visions of a better world. Laity on the other hand, are in large part committed to the view that the church should be a source of comfort for them in a troubled world. They are essentially consumers rather than producers of the church's love and concern for the world, and the large majority deeply resent [the clergy's] efforts to remake the church."[41] This pattern apparently continues today.

For these reasons, we claim that the dominant religious voices, or at least those that receive the most support, on issues of race relations are those most supportive of the status quo. Surveying the research, we discover important confirmation. Scholars find that the more clergy have to lose by speaking and acting prophetically on race issues, the less likely they are to do so.[42] What is more, researchers find that the most popular religious groups in a local area—as measured by membership numbers—are the least likely to take social activism stands on racial issues, as they have more to lose in the community by challenging the status quo.[43] This effect appears to hold regardless of whether the numerically dominant group is Protestant or Catholic.[44] Thus, the numerically strongest voices, because structural forces push them to favor the racial status quo, serve to ghettoize the weaker voices calling for change.

Quite simply, the structure of American religion, and the values that both guide that structure and grant influence to individuals, result in significant limits to religious authority. This is true regardless of the religion. Catholicism, with its worldwide hierarchical structure and multiple centuries of tradition, might be expected to offer an exception. Popes speak ex cathedra, bishops vote, and pronouncements are made on various issues. But religious leaders, at least in the United States, are relatively powerless to compel their members to do or think anything. They cannot fine them, tax them, or restrain their religious attitudes, beliefs, and behavior except to remove them from official membership, influence others to shun them, or close and sell church properties (which they are loath to do). The Pope no longer has armies, and even the threat of excommunication may not deter because many U.S. Catholics do not recognize the Pope's authority to remove someone from the grace of God. Moreover, in the United States religious organizations are almost entirely dependent on their members for support, rather than on tax money collected with the ultimate backing of state-sanctioned force. So, for instance, although the Catholic hierarchy condemns the use of artificial birth control (they are "structurally free" to do so), not only do most Americans Catholics not condemn other people's use of it, but in direct opposition to the hierarchy, use artificial birth control themselves. Personal choices in the context of one's social network, not official church teachings, are the primary shapers of beliefs and actions for the religious of the United States and many other places. In Chapter Two, we found evidence of this throughout U.S. religious history. Denominations repeatedly issue proclamations calling for the end of some aspect of racialization; congregations and the people in the pews repeatedly ignore them. And when clergy or denominational leaders act in ways too deviant from the laity, the laity either leave or fire the religious officials.[45]

We do not wish to suggest that religious leaders have no power or authority. They often do. But as Max Weber noted nearly a century ago, religious authority is rooted in charisma, within the confines of a group's concerns. United States history is replete with charismatic religious leaders who have had the seeming ability to instill faith in their followers. This ability stems from the charismatic figure's gift to communicate people's felt needs and embody religious solutions to those needs. Leaders must both understand the social locations of their followers and speak their language. As Finke and Stark note, leaders thus must usually come from social locations similar to those of their parishioners.[46] And, as they also note, this hampers the prophetic role of religion.

Religious organizations therefore tend to be limited in the types of social change they can bring about. Change, as we have seen in American history, must come principally from within the group desiring change. The end of slavery came both from African Americans and from some northern whites, who saw slavery as an attack on their own way of life and were "structurally free" to argue against the institution. The end of slavery obviously did not come from southern white Christians, even if some personally desired it. Nor did it come from the majority of white northern Christians. Likewise, the end of Jim Crow segregation came from some within the black church and the Civil Rights movement that welled up from within.[47] It did not come from liberal white churches or any other group. It also came despite opposition from some in the larger black denominations.[48] And the changes that ensued succeeded only to the degree that they conformed to dominant American values such as individual freedom and equal opportunity.[49]

So, within groups, religious leaders possess power and authority, to be sure, but only to the extent that they embody a group's concerns and hopes. They can to some extent shape the direction of the group, yet if they stray too far from the felt needs of the group, from comforting and uplifting the group members, their authority and power are weakened and may be rejected. Evangelical leaders can call for an end to racialization, and are able to influence ordinary white evangelicals on race-relations issues, but only within a small range of possibilities, limited by the social positions and theological understandings of the mass of ordinary evangelicals. The radical message of the early racial reconciliation leaders, by the time it got to white, grassroots evangelicals, was minimized to little more than having re-spect for people of other races, or having a cross-race friendship. When a more radical message is pushed, as the leader of Promise Keepers, Bill McCartney, observed, the walls go up, and those in his conservative Chris-tian subculture tune him out.

FINAL THOUGHTS

Assessing the overall effect of religion on racialization is a complex task, as religion's influence operates on multiple and often contradictory levels. We can find numerous positive examples of religious people and groups work-ing to overcome racial division and inequality, but structural forces within the organization of religion undercut these positive actions. In fact, these structural forces often regenerate the very conditions the positive actions work to eliminate.

We have examined two primary structural arrangements—racially ho-mogenous ingroups and the segmented market—and their implications for racialization. These arrangements partially generate and reproduce the racial fragmentation of American society; they aid the formation and maintenance of group biases, direct altruistic religious impulses to express themselves primarily within racially separate groups, contribute to segre-gated social networks and identities, help perpetuate socioeconomic in-equality by race, and generally fragment and drown out religious prophetic voices calling for an end to racialization.

Most of these effects are intensified for "stronger" religious movements and groups. Evangelicalism, as perhaps the strongest Protestant religious movement in the United States,[50] relies heavily on marketing principles for its strength and growth, often intentionally segmenting its market, target-ing specific populations, and using homogeneity to its advantage to create religious meaning and belonging and dense ingroup social ties. Although this evangelical vigor can and is used to address racial division in unique ways, the movement also, by its heavy reliance on racially homogenous ingroups and the segmented market, ironically undercuts many of its own best efforts.

Conclusion

The journey toward justice and peace between black and white Americans, including black and white Christians, has been a long road. And, as this book reveals, much more of the road remains to be traveled to reach the destination of equality, interdependence, and mutual understanding. We may be able to shorten this journey, we think, by addressing some of the findings of this book.

Our aim has been to assess the influence of white evangelicalism on black–white relations in the United States. To accomplish this, we explored the historical relationship between white evangelicalism and black America, with a particular examination of the post-Civil Rights race-relations activities of white evangelicals. We then looked at ordinary evangelicals' views on the race problem in the United States, the ways white evangelicals explain racial inequality, and the kinds of solutions they propose to address America's race problem. Broadening our perspective beyond evangelicalism to American religion more generally, we also considered why congregations in the United States tend toward internal similarity, a characteristic feature of America's racialized society. And finally, we have reflected on the consequences of the organization of U.S. religion, and of internally similar congregations, for racialization.

Our analysis leads us to some key conclusions. Despite devoting considerable time and energy to solving the problem of racial division, white
evangelicalism likely does more to perpetuate the racialized society than to
reduce it. This, we have seen, is because of its history, its thorough acceptance of and reliance on free market principles, its subcultural tool kit, and,
more broadly, the nature of the organization of American religion. Our examination of a variety of data and consideration of a variety of levels of social influence suggest that many race issues that white evangelicals want to
see solved are generated in part by the way they themselves do religion, interpret their world, and live their own lives. These factors range from the
ways evangelicals and others organize into internally similar congregations,
and the segregation and inequality such congregations help produce; to
theologically rooted evangelical cultural tools, which tend to (1) minimize
and individualize the race problem, (2) assign blame to blacks themselves
for racial inequality, (3) obscure inequality as part of racial division, and (4)
suggest unidimensional solutions to racial division.

Despite the often very best intentions of most white American evangelicals, the complex web of factors explored in this book produce a rather dismal portrait of the realities of and prospects for positive race relations
among American Christians in the United States. Most white evangelicals,
directed by their cultural tools, fail to recognize the institutionalization of
racialization—in economic, political, educational, social, and religious systems. They therefore often think and act as if these problems do not exist.
As undetected cancer that remains untreated thrives and destroys, so unrec-
ognized depths of racial division and inequality go largely unaddressed and
likewise thrive, divide, and destroy. The solutions evangelicals propose and
practice—though in many ways unique in modern America, and much
needed as far as they go—simply cannot make much headway in the face of
these powerful countercurrents that undercut and fight against their well-
intentioned, individualistic solutions.

Is the situation hopeless? If white evangelicals continue to travel the same
road they have traveled thus far, the future does indeed look bleak. The issues are far too complex to be addressed by a homogenous subculture that
tends toward high-energy, but simplistic and unidimensional solutions to
complex social problems.

Evangelicals have some important contributions to offer for the solution
to racial division in the United States—such as their stress on the
importance of primary relationships, and the need for confession and forgiveness. These may be important because, given the long, tumultuous history of U.S. black–white relations, solutions that call only for structural
change are probably as naïve as solutions that merely ask individuals to
make some friends across race. The collective wounds over race run deep.

They need to be healed. And for healing to take place, there will have to be forgiveness.

But before there is healing, different racial groups of Americans will also have to stop injuring one another. Vast economic inequalities open deep wounds. Segregation—especially in neighborhoods and schools of unequal quality—opens the wounds further. The fact that Americans' health, life, and death are racialized make gaping wounds. And the immense divisions between social networks, cultures, and religions not only contribute to the rawness of these wounds, but make their healing that much more difficult.

Our analysis has not led us to specific solutions for ending racialization, and we will not attempt such a grandiose leap into policy. But this work does suggest some general paths that white evangelicals might want to explore in their quest for racial reconciliation.

In his 1994 book, *The Scandal of the Evangelical Mind*, evangelical historian Mark Noll powerfully argues that the American evangelical tradition and its culture direct evangelicals, because of their constant sense of urgency, to get busy doing things, without first adequately thinking through the issues. Evangelicals—like the broader American culture they helped shape—value action more than careful thought. As Noll puts it, "The evangelical ethos is activistic, populist, pragmatic, and utilitarian. It allows little space for broader or deeper intellectual effort because it is dominated by the urgencies of the moment." [1] Likewise N. K. Clifford argues: "The Evangelical Protestant mind has never relished complexity. Indeed its crusading genius, whether in religion or politics, has always tended toward an oversimplification of issues and the substitution of inspiration and zeal for critical analysis and series reflection." [2]

To address successfully the complexity of American race relations, this evangelical tendency toward quick-minded activism should be modified. With a few exceptions, evangelicals lack serious thinking on this issue. Rather than integrate their faith with knowledge of race relations, inequality, and American society, they generally allow their cultural constructions to shape one-dimensional assessments and solutions to multidimensional problems. This will not do. The first new step evangelicals might consider, therefore, is engaging in more serious reflection on race-relations issues, in dialogue with educated others: What are the problems? In what directions are the United States and its people heading? What influences will class, growing racial-ethnic diversity, changing occupational and political structures, and complex systems of stratification play in altering the landscape of American race relations? How is the problem understood from different racial and ethnic group perspectives? How do individual-level versus group-level phenomena operate differently and simultaneously in the problems of race relations? What solutions have already been tried? What else helpful is currently known about these questions and solutions?

Evangelicals might then bring together this knowledge with Christian understanding of freedom, love, universalism, justice, unity, and community. This could be done with the recognition that a Christian solution ought adequately to account for the complex of factors that generate and perpetuate the problems, and then faithfully, humbly, carefully, and cooperatively work against them. To do this will require attention to multiple factors—from historical forces to subcultural tools to the very organization of American religion. As we show elsewhere,[3] addressing racialization must involve replacing structural barriers—such as segregation, inequality, and group competition—with structural supports—such as equality and cooperation and mutual interdependence.

Trying to overcome racial divisions in America has been very difficult in the past, and we should not expect things to get much easier in the very near future. At the same time, the choices and actions that people make to deal with racial divisions do matter and can make a difference. Good intentions are not enough. But educated, sacrificial, realistic efforts made in faith across racial lines can help us together move toward a more just, equitable, and peaceful society. And that is a purpose well worth striving toward.

Appendix A

Table A-1

Explanations for the Black–White Socioeconomic Gap,
White Conservative Protestants and Other White Americans

Explanation		Other Whites	Conservative Protestants	N
Individual	Ability	10%	10%	1521
	Motivation	51%	62% [a]	1471
Structural	Education	46%	32% [a]	1524
	Discrimination	36%	27% [b]	1493

[a] Difference between conservative Protestants and other whites statistically significant (χ^2, $p < .01$, 2-tailed).

[b] χ^2, $p < .05$, 2-tailed.

Source: General Social Survey, 1996.

Table A-2
Logistic Regressions of Explanations for Black-White Socioeconomic Gap, White Americans

		Lack Motivation	Lack Educational Opportunities	Discrimination
Religious Identity[a]	Conservative Protestant	.50 (.19) [b]	−.62 (.19) [b]	−.40 (.20) [c]
Social Location	Male	.12 (.13)	−.32 (.12) [b]	−.44 (.13) [b]
	Age (x10)	.10 (.04) [b]	.15 (.04) [b]	.14 (.04) [b]
	Education	−.18 (.03) [b]	.12 (.03) [b]	.02 (.03)
	Income	.02 (.01)	−.02 (.01)	−.06 (.01) [b]
	Father's Socioeconomic Index (x10)	−.11 (.04) [b]	.10 (.04) [b]	.00 (.04)
	Town (2500 to 9999)	−.37 (.25)	.00 (.24)	.05 (.26)
	Rural (<2500)	.22 (.22)	−.36 (.21)	−.51 (.24) [c]
Region	Northeast	.24 (.27)	−.04 (.25)	−.06 (.26)
	Midwest	.03 (.25)	.07 (.24)	−.24 (.24)
	South	1.01 (.24) [b]	−.53 (.23) [c]	−.28 (.24)
Region at 16	Northeast	−.33 (.26)	−.14 (.25)	−.05 (.25)
	Midwest	−.08 (.25)	.04 (.23)	.16 (.24)
	South	−.67 (.26) [c]	−.16 (.25)	−.38 (.26)
Racial Attitudes	Traditional Prejudice [b]	.85 (.23) [b]	−.15 (.18)	−.40 (20) [c]
	Pseudo R^2	.13	.09	.06
	χ^2	166 [b]	112 [b]	77 [b]
	N	1165	1209	1184

[a] Comparison category is all non-conservative Protestants (including Catholics, those of other religions, those with no religious preference, and the nonreligious).

[b] $p < .01$.

^c p < .05.

^d The individual-level traditional prejudice index follows Kluegel's measure of traditional prejudice. A score of "2" was assigned if a respondent said "Yes," they favor a law against racial intermarriage and agreed (slightly or strongly) that whites should have the right to segregate neighborhoods. A score of "1" was assigned if a respondent said "Yes" to the intermarriage item or agreed with the segregation item, but not both. A score of "0" was assigned to respondents who said "No" to the intermarriage item, and disagreed with the segregation item.

Note: Values are betas. Standard errors are in parentheses.

Source: General Social Survey, 1996.

Table A-3
Explanations for the Black–White Socioeconomic Gap, White Theologically-Liberal Protestants and White Conservative Protestants

Explanation		Liberal Protestants	Conservative Protestants	N
Individual	Ability	7%	10%	300
	Motivation	40%	62% [a]	290
Structural	Education	58%	32% [a]	299
	Discrimination	43%	27% [a]	288

[a] Difference between the two groups statistically significant (χ^2, p < .01, 2-tailed).

Source: General Social Survey, 1996.

Table A-4

Explanations for the Black-White Socioeconomic Gap, White and Black Protestants Compared to White and Black Other Americans

Explanation	Other Americans			Conservative Protestants			Differences between W-Bs[c]
	White	Black	W-B[a]	White	Black	W-B[a]	
Individual Ability	10%	11%	−1	10%	7%	+3	+2
Motivation	51%	42%	+9 *	62%	31%	+31**	+22**
Structural Education	46%	53%	+7 *	32%	54%	+22 *	+15**
Discrimination	6%	63%	+27**	27%	72%	+45**	+18**

[a] Other whites percentage minus other blacks percentage.

[b] White conservative Protestant percentage minus black conservative percentage.

[c] Conservative Protestant racial difference minus absolute value of other Americans racial difference—these figures show how much wider is the gap between conservative Protestant whites and blacks than between other American whites and blacks.

* Difference statistically significant ($p < .05$, 2-tailed).

** $p < .01$, 2-tailed.

Source: General Social Survey, 1996.

Table A-5
Explanation of Black–White Socioeconomic Gap,
by Evangelical Ranking, Whites

Explanation	Weak-to-Moderate [a]	Strong [b]	Difference [c]
Anti-Structural			
Culture or Motivation (CM)	65%	80%	15
CM, History, or Welfare	75%	95%	20
Pro-Structural			
Education or Discrimination	35%	34%	−1
Education or Discrimination Only	21%	5%	−16

N=103 (Smaller N than in Table 4 result of 14 interviews not given evangelical ranking).

[a] Evangelical ranking of 1 to 7 on 10-point scale, with 10 indicating theologically consistency with evangelical hallmarks and closely connected with evangelical institutions (churches, colleges, para-church ministries).

[b] Evangelical ranking of 8 to 10 on 10-point scale.

[c] Strong minus Weak-to-Moderate percentage.

Note: The "no inequality" and "other" categories showed no sample differences.

Source: Pew Evangelical Interviews, 1996.

Table A-6
Explanation for Black–White Socioeconomic Gap by
Level of Contact with Blacks, White Conservative Protestants [a]

Explanation		Low Contact [b]	High Contact	N
Individual	Ability	25%	10% [c]	1184
	Motivation	73%	56% [c]	1181
Structural	Education	42%	52% [d]	1213
	Discrimination	32%	44% [c]	1196

[a] Those attending conservative denominations more than once a year. The religious identity question used to measure conservative Protestantism in previous tables is only available for 1996.

[b] Contact measured with two questions: (1) Are there any blacks living in this neighborhood now? and (2) During the last few years, has anyone in your family brought a friend who was black home for dinner? Persons classified as having low contact said 'no' to either or both questions.

[c] $p < .01$, 2-tailed.

[d] Difference between low and high contact groupings statistically significant ($p < .05$, 2-tailed).

Source: General Social Surveys, 1972–1994.

Appendix B

Table B-1
Solution-to-Racism Alternatives:
Percent Responding "Very Important," White Strong Evangelicals [a]

Alternatives	Very Important	N
Get to Know People of Another Race	89%	78
Work Against Discrimination in Jobs or Courts	83%	78
Racially Integrate Congregations	58%	76
Racially Integrate Neighborhoods	38%	76

[a] Those who assented to all evangelical hallmarks and said their main or only religious identity was evangelical.

Source: Pew Survey of Religious Identity and Influence, 1996.

Table B-2
Solution-to-Racism Alternatives:
Number of Mentions in Christianity Today, *1994–1998*

Alternatives	Number of Mentions
Get to Know People of Another Race	20
Work Against Discrimination in Jobs or Courts	2
Racially Integrate Congregations	8
Racially Integrate Neighborhoods	2

Source: Context Analysis, all issues of *Christianity Today* from January 1994 to November 1998.

Table B-3

Solution-to-Racism Alternatives:
Percent Responding "Very Important," Whites, Evangelical Type [a]

Alternatives	Not Evangelical	Moderate Evangelical	Strong Evangelical	Difference by Evangelical Type	N
Get to Know People	68%	79%	89%	Yes [b]	1598
No Discrimination in Job/Leg	78%	75%	83%	No	1568
Integrate Congregations	39%	50%	58%	Yes [b]	1563
Integrate Neighborhoods	35%	33%	38%	No	1537

[a] See Chapter 6 for measurement details.

[b] $p < .01$, chi-square test of linear difference.

Source: Pew Survey of Religious Identity and Influence, 1996.

Table B-4
Solution-to-Racism Alternatives:
Percent Responding "Very Important" [a]

Alternatives	Not Evangelical	Moderate Evangelical	Strong Evangelical	Difference by Evangelical Type?	N
Get to Know People					
White	68%	79%	89%	Yes [b]	1598
Black	72%	81%	93%	Yes [c]	231
No Discrimination in Job/Leg					
White	78%	75%	83%	No	1568
Black	80%	81%	93%	No	233
Integrate Congregations					
White	39%	50%	58%	Yes [b]	1563
Black	33%	55%	87% [d]	Yes [b]	231
Integrate Neighborhoods					
White	35%	33%	38%	No	1537
Black	50% [d]	51% [d]	64% [d]	No	226

[a] Catholics not included because survey did not ask them the questions needed to classify by evangelical type.

[b] $p < .01$, chi-square test of linear difference.

[c] $p < .05$, chi-square test of linear difference.

[d] Difference between whites and blacks by evangelical type significant (t-test, 1-tailed, $p < .05$).

Source: Pew Survey of Religious Identity and Influence, 1996.

Notes

Introduction

1. E.g., Scherer 1975; Wood 1991.
2. Marsden 1991; Woodbridge, Noll, and Hatch 1979.
3. Smith et al. 1998.
4. Woodberry and Smith 1998.
5. See Smith et al. 1998, Chapter 1 for a description of this movement.
6. E.g., see Marsden 1984; Olson 1995.
7. Smith et al. 1998.
8. For a full explanation and justification of this measurement method, see Smith et al. 1998.
9. E.g., see DeYoung 1995; 1997; Evans 1995; Pannell 1993; Perkins and Rice 1993; Washington and Kehrein 1993.

Chapter 1

1. Gunnar Myrdal 1964.
2. E.g., Feagin and Sikes 1994; Wellman 1977.
3. Loury 1995.
4. Bonilla-Silva 1997:474.
5. Allen 1994; Berkhofer 1978.
6. Omi and Winant 1994.
7. Brooks and Manza, 1997.
8. Van den Berghe 1967; Clara Rodriguez 1991.
9. "Jim Crow" refers to the pattern of racial discrimination resulting from state and local laws requiring segregation in everything from housing, work sites, bus seating, churches, cemeteries, theaters, hospitals, schools, restaurants, and much more. The term derives from a song referring to Jim Crow, a "happy slave," performed in the 1830s by Thomas D. Rice, a white performer in blackface. Jim Crow came to be a code word for segregation (McLemore and Romo 1998).
10. Wellman 1977.
11. Bonilla-Silva 1997:476.
12. Our thanks to Professor Karen McKinney for this definition.
13. Wellman 1977.
14. Emerson and Sikkink 1997.
15. Essed 1990.
16. Massey and Denton 1993.
17. Pettigrew 1988:23.
18. Kitano 1976; Tinker 1982.
19. Kantrowitz 1986; Kitano and Chai 1982; Kitano and Yeung 1982; Yuan 1980.
20. Alba and Golden 1986; Sandefur and McKinnel 1986.
21. McDaniel 1996.

22. Jaret 1995:394.

23. See, e.g., Farley and Frey 1994; Massey and Denton 1993.

24. Emerson 1994.

25. Clark 1992; Farley and Frey 1994; Massey and Gross 1991.

26. Alba and Logan 1993; Massey and Denton 1993.

27. Hurst 1998:147.

28. Oliver and Shapiro 1995:2.

29. Oliver and Shapiro 1995:94–95.

30. Wenneker and Epstein 1989.

31. Winslow 1992.

32. Henslin 1997.

33. Statistical Abstract of the U.S. 1995.

34. Roediger 1994.

35. Bonilla-Silva 1997; David Rodriguez 1991.

36. Binder 1993:765.

37. Binder 1993:765.

38. Binder 1993:762.

39. Binder 1993:766.

40. Zurawik 1996. The fourth quarter of 1998 (the latest period available before this book went to press) shows a slight narrowing of the TV-viewing gap, due largely to a few shows with multiracial casts. For example, *Touched by an Angel*—starring both black and white angels—ranked in the top twenty for both blacks and whites. *ER*, also with a mixed-race cast, continued to be number one among whites and moved to number fifteen among blacks. But the dominant pattern of separate TV viewing remained. The series *Friends* ranked number two among whites, but only 88th among blacks. The most-watched programs among blacks continued to be almost completely avoided by whites. *The Steve Harvey Show* and *The Jamie Foxx Show* ranked number one and two among blacks, but among whites, they ranked a dismal 127th and 120th respectively (Huff 1999).

41. Lincoln and Mamiya 1990:xii.

42. Although we suspect we are accurate in our figure for whites, based on the logic we used to derive the figure, it is technically more accurate to say "95 percent nonblack" rather than "white" given the presence of other groups in the United States.

43. See, for example, Berger 1967; Geertz 1973; Smith 1996. The ensuing discussion relies on Smith (1996:5–7).

44. Smith 1996:6.

45. For detailed discussion of methodological design and sample selection, see Smith et al. 1998, Appendix A.

Chapter 2

1. Discipleship means developing and training Christians in the beliefs and practices of Christian faith and life.

2. Scherer1975:105–106. This discussion relies heavily on Scherer's (1975) book, *Slavery and the Churches in Early America, 1619–1819*. Unless otherwise noted, quotations from figures of the 1700s are taken from Chapters Five and Six of this work.

3. Scherer 1975:64.

4. In Wood 1991:36.

5. In Scherer 1975:66.

6. Jordan 1968; Lincoln 1984.

7. Ahlstrom 1972; Marsden 1990.

8. Finke and Stark 1992:49.

9. In Finke and Stark 1992:50.

10. In Jordan 1968:214.

11. Marsden 1990:28.

12. Jordan 1968:213.

13. Wood 1991:274.

14. Scherer 1975:74.

15. In Scherer 1975:77.

16. Wood 1991:275.

17. In Wood 1991:78.

18. Berger 1967.

19. Essig 1982:20.

20. In Scherer 1975:127.

21. Jordan 1968:296.

22. Essig 1982:22–23.

23. Essig 1982:160.

24. Scherer 1975:134.

25. Quarles 1969:11.

26. Quarles 1969:13.

27. Marsden 1990:66.

28. Quarles 1969.

29. Essig 1982:139–140.

30. Handy 1984:52.

31. Quarles 1969:14.

32. Dayton 1976:29.

33. Cole 1954.

34. In Quarles 1969:17.

35. Cole 1954; Lesick 1980.

36. *Christian History* 1992.

37. Cole 1954; Lesick 1980:235.

38. In Cole 1954:208.

39. Dayton 1976:67.

40. Lesick 1980:162.

41. Cole 1954.

42. Wood 1991:40.

43. Boles 1988:1–2.

44. Quotes in Boles 1988:10.

45. Wood 1991:309.

46. Marsden 1990:9.

47. Wood 1991:276.

48. In Bennett 1982:217.

49. Bennett 1982:182.

50. Bennett 1982:215.

51. In Bennett 1982:215–16.

52. Through the latter part of the nineteenth century, these views were increasingly fueled by Social Darwinism, the pseudo-scientific understanding that some races were more advanced than others. Seen as part of God's design, Anglo-Saxons had been chosen as the most advanced race. Part of their responsibility was to help raise up and Christianize the less advanced races.

53. Massey and Denton 1993.

54. Marsden 1990; Ahlstrom 1972.

55. Using this argument, Lieberson (1980) provides an excellent historical analysis of the northern response to African-American population growth in northern cities. As the relative black population increased, so to did segregation, though not by force of law typically. By extension, then, northerners differed from southerners, at least in part, simply because of the vast differences in relative percentages of African Americans, further supporting a smaller difference between northern and southern attitudes and actions than is typically believed. Southern Jim Crow laws were essentially borrowed and "perfected" from the practices of the North, which had segregation laws and practices at least since the 1830s (Woodward 1955).

56. Reimers 1965.

57. Marsden 1990.

58. Lincoln and Mamiya 1990:27.

59. In Reimers 1965:33.

60. This decision to segregate churches shapes present-day race relations. The African-American churches became the cultural hub of an independent black culture and society: they gave rise to new institutions like banks, schools, and insurance companies, provided an arena for political activity, nurtured leaders and musical innovation, offered a place of socialization and development of unique theology, literature, humor, and more (Lincoln and Mamiya 1990). This has created differences in cultures that modern evangelicals often cite in support of continued separate churches and neighborhoods.

61. In Reimers 1965:36.

62. In Reimers 1965:38.

63. In Marsden 1990:150.

64. Marsden 1990.

65. During this period, the decades around the turn of the century, a split in personal piety and social reform occurred, so that evangelicals increasingly focused on personal piety while more liberal Protestants increasingly focused on the social gospel, deemphasizing personal conversion and piety.

66. Reimers 1965; Myrdal 1964.

67. Drake and Cayton 1945:178–79.

68. E.g., Oldham 1924.

69. Massey and Denton 1993:Chapter 2. The National Association of Real Estate Board's code of ethics for many years included the following: "A Realtor should never be instrumental in introducing into a neighborhood ... members of any race ... whose presence will clearly be detrimental to property values in that neighborhood."

This was aided by restrictive covenants. For example, restrictive covenants recorded in deeds for residential property and taken from the suburbs around Milwaukee included: "This land shall never be occupied by or conveyed to a colored person" (1925), "No race other than the Caucasian race shall use or occupy any building or any lot in said subdivision" (1945), and "No persons other than the white race shall own or occupy . . ." (1953) (in Taeuber 1989:129–31).

70. In Reimers 1965:100.

71. Loescher 1948:7.

72. Myrdal 1964:30.

73. Myrdal 1964:27.

74. Myrdal 1964:46.

75. Myrdal 1964:27.

76. Myrdal 1964:29.

77. Massey and Denton 1993.

78. Tapia 1997:55.

79. Martin 1991:168.

80. Martin 1991:169.

81. In Martin 1991:170.

82. In Martin 1991:296.

83. Over time, Billy Graham became much more concerned with racial and ethnic strife, calling them key barriers to evangelism and social harmony. See the Introduction and Chapter Three for quotes expressing Graham's more recent view of racial strife.

84. Myrdal 1964:48.

Chapter 3

1. This story is a composite description of several Promise Keeper events attended by the authors.

2. As Andrew Young notes in his book, *An Easy Burden* (1996:237–38), demonstrators in Civil Rights activities were required to sign written pledges. They pledged to follow the "ten commandments" of the nonviolent movement. These included meditating on the life and teachings of Jesus, praying, and remembering "always that the nonviolent movement seeks justice and reconciliation—not victory" (238).

3. Perkins 1976.

4. Perkins 1976.

5. The structure of the description of John Perkins is indebted to the work of Timothy Essenburg, "Urban Community Development: An Examination of the Perkins Model" (1998), unpublished manuscript.

6. Skinner 1968:37.

7. *Christianity Today* 11:66.

8. Skinner 1968:24.

9. Skinner 1968:39.

10. Hines 1995:xvi.

11. Perkins and Rice 1993.

12. E.g., Perkins 1976b.

13. Yancey 1998.

14. Hines 1993:26.

15. Perkins and Rice 1993:18.

16. In Martin 1991:170.

17. Kuchavsky 1966.

18. Kuchavsky 1965.

19. *Christianity Today* August 11:33.

20. Excerpted from "The Psychopathology of Racism," by Joseph Daniels, January 15, 1971:7–8. To maintain congruence with the following letter, "man" was changed to "person."

21. Excerpted from "Up From Ignorance: Awareness-Training and Racism," by Virginia Mollenkott, in *Christianity Today* March 26, 1971:6–8.

22. Sider 1977.

23. Salley 1970.

24. De Young 1995.

25. De Young 1997.

26. In Gilbreath 1996.

27. Morley 1997.

28. Perkins and Rice 1993; Washington and Kehrein 1993; Usry and Keener 1996; Perkins and Tarrants 1994.

29. Pannell 1993; De Young 1995; Hines 1995; Yancey 1996; Evans 1995; Park 1996; Volf 1996; Weary 1990.

30. Maxwell 1994.

31. Grady 1994.

32. Tragedy also found the evangelical reconciliation movement in the 1990s. After hosting the "College, Ethnicity, and Reconciliation" Conference in January 1998, Spencer Perkins, in his mid-forties, died of a massive heart attack. Previously, in 1994 and 1995, Tom Skinner, in his fifties, and Samuel Hines, in his sixties, also died. Some close to these men say the weight of their reconciliation struggles contributed to their early deaths.

33. Olsen 1996:67.

34. *Christianity Today* 1993:27.

35. Olsen 1997.

36. White 1996:88.

37. White 1996:88.

38. From Miller 1995:43.

39. Bray 1992:42.

40. Bray 1992:42.

41. Warner 1993:26.

42. De Young 1995:13, 106.

43. Rabey 1997:90.

44. Emerson 1998.

45. Murray 1993:20.

46. McCartney 1997.

Chapter 4

1. E.g., see Bobo and Hutchings 1996; Jaret 1995.

2. Martin 1991:168.

3. Swidler 1986.

4. Swidler 1986:281.

5. Sewell 1992.

6. E.g., see Sherkat and Ellison 1997.

7. Hunter 1991.

8. Fine 1997.

9. Stark and Glock 1969:80–81.

10. E.g., Bellah et al. 1985.

11. E.g., see Sider 1997.

12. It is important to keep in mind the theological context within which these cultural tools are set. They currently operate within the larger theological framework of pre-millenialism. As we defined this view in Chapter Two, the world is seen as evil and remaining so until Christ reappears. To devote time and energy to social reform, then, is largely futile. By extension, the influence of social structures tend to drop from conscious view, as the ultimate root of all trouble is individual sin and/or Satan, and while individuals may overcome them through Christ, non-Christians and institutions will not. In the 1800s, post-millenialism was the dominant theology. According to this view, Christians could hasten the return of Christ by creating a Christian society. In the context of this theology, the cultural tools operated differently, as we detailed in Chapter Two.

13. Swidler 1986.

14. We use acquaintance as an overarching term meant to include a friend, workmate, relative (such as a niece or a brother-in-law), or other.

15. By "daily experience" we mean the sum total of contacts with individuals and institutions. This includes, at the relational level, family, friends, acquaintances, workmates, neighbors, church attendees. At the institutional level, it includes schools, work, church, neighborhood organizations, political organizations, media, and more. Although individuals might have a nonwhite friend, have a few nonwhites in their church, have a child attend a mixed-race school, or shop in a grocery store frequented by many racial/ethnic groups, exceptionally few had more than one or two of these, thus leading, in sum, to nearly homogenous worlds.

16. Quoted in the Durham [North Carolina] *Herald Sun*, "Group Turns Focus to Racial Healing," by Addelle M. Banks, 1996, specific date unknown.

17. Allport 1954; Powers and Ellison 1995.

18. General Social Survey 1996.

19. Wellman 1977:218.

20. Wellman 1977.

21. For a visual illustration of this, see the video, *True Colors*, originally aired on *Prime Time Live* in 1991. Although we could cite many good books and articles on this topic and the other effects we discuss in the paragraph, we recommend two here: Theologian Cornel West's *Race Matters*, and *Living with Racism: The Black Middle Class Experience* by sociologists Joe Feagin and Melvin Sikes.

22. For a visual illustration of this, see the video, *Driving While Black*, originally aired on *20/20* in 1996.

23. Feagin and Sikes 1994:319.

24. West 1993:95.

25. Bakhtin 1986. When one of the authors read a draft of this conclusion to a family member, the response was: "It sounds like you are picking on whites." This is not our intention, as any group isolated from other groups, with an historical advantage, and with an individualistic perspective would essentially have similar views. We also must note that by focusing primarily on white evangelicals, we appear to render black Americans blameless in contributing to the racialized society. We find the position that only one race contributes to America's contemporary racialized character untenable.

Chapter 5

1. Oliver and Shapiro 1995.

2. Kluegel 1990.

3. Because evangelicals and fundamentalists share many of the same cultural tools, and all the same cultural tools that we argue are key to understanding explanations of racial inequality, it is not surprising that they do not differ in their explanations.

4. Essed 1996; Kluegal 1990; Sniderman and Hagen 1985; Wellman 1977.

5. Because respondents can cite more than one explanation, we also classified them as individualists only (cited only ability or motivation), intermediatists (cited both individual and structural reasons), and structuralists only (cited only education or discrimination). Following the same pattern, conservative Protestants are significantly more likely to be individualists only, and significantly less likely to be structuralists only when compared to others. We found no difference in the proportion who were intermediatists.

6. Hart 1992.

7. We return now to focusing on evangelicals rather than the broader focus on conservative Protestants. We only interviewed a few fundamentalists—the other group making up the conservative Protestant category—but analysis of their interviews did not reveal any differences between them and evangelicals on this question.

8. Stark and Glock 1969.

9. Festinger 1957.

10. After reading through each and every interview, we created ten categories that captured all the main themes in the responses. We then read through each interview again, coding the responses. Some evangelicals cited one reason, others as many as four. No matter how many they cited, we recorded them.

11. Because the interviews were not truly randomly sampled, we do not report significance tests. The differences, then, reflect the sample and caution should be exercised in generalizing to the population.

12. For all white Americans, we found very similar effects as those reported here for white conservative Protestants.

13. Put in the context of a logistic regression, the contact effect remains statistically significant even after controlling for age, sex, and education.

14. Jackman and Crane 1986.

15. In contrast, in a survey conducted in twelve European countries in 1990, only 17 percent felt that poverty was the result of laziness or lack of willpower. Two-thirds

of the Europeans thought poverty was due to social injustice, misfortune, or changes in the modern world (Wilson 1996:67).

16. The book, *Rich Christians in an Age of Hunger* (Sider 1997), suggests alternatives evangelicals could draw on. These range from the Year of Jubilee already mentioned; to the Sabbatical Year, the law calling for freeing the soil, debtors, and slaves every seven years (including the requirement that slaves be given provision enough to earn their own way when set free); the laws on tithing and gleaning; the community model of Jesus wherein all shared from a common purse; the original Christian church, whose members engaged in extensive economic sharing such that, "there was not a needy person among them ... distribution was made to each as any had need" (Acts 4:34–35); to the apostle Paul's developing interchurch economic sharing across the widely scattered congregations so "that there might be equality" (2 Cor 8:24).

17. Apostle et al., 1983.

18. Kluegel 1990.

19. 1995.

20. Apostle et al., 1983.

21. Kluegel and Smith 1986:37.

22. Kluegel 1990:521.

23. And, in an interesting corollary, people who are "successful" overestimate the importance of their own efforts.

24. West 1993:3, 12.

25. Wilson 1996.

26. West 1993:13.

Chapter 6

1. Stark 1971:102–3; Woodbridge, Noll, and Hatch 1979:246.

2. Hart 1992:50–52.

3. E.g., Kellstedt and Smidt 1991.

4. The articles in the "other" category were consistent with evangelical emphases. The articles ranged from discussing the need for black self-help, to what we call the "racial missionary" articles describing, typically, white Christians with ministries in cities to help minorities. For example, one article of the racial missionary variety is entitled, "Mrs. Dudley Goes to the Hood: How a White Suburban Mother Helped Transform an Inner-City Black Community" (*Christianity Today* Jan. 9, 1995:15–16).

5. Morris 1984.

6. The evangelical and race effects discussed in bivariate terms in this section remain even when controlling for other important factors, such as education, income, gender, and region. The exception, perhaps resulting from the small sample size of African Americans, is no significant interaction between race and evangelicalness for the integrating neighborhoods alternative.

7. We have edited Beth's comments for clarity and brevity.

8. Nash 1972.

9. Jackman and Crane 1986.

10. Smith et al. 1998:32–36.

11. Olson 1993.

Chapter 7

1. Chaves 1999.

2. We do not argue that only the current organization of American religion leads to internally similar congregations. Many other forms can and do as well. Rather, we merely seek to explore the dividing factors that operate within the context of the present organization of American religion.

3. Such as Durkheim, Marx, Simmel, Tonnies, and Weber.

4. E.g., Wagner 1979:Chapter 1.

5. E.g., Chaves 1994; Finke and Stark 1992; Hatch 1989; Marsden 1990; Stephen Warner 1993.

6. E.g., Berger 1967; Finke and Stark 1992.

7. Handy 1984:4.

8. Wright 1957:1.

9. Because religion was not left to personal choice, and thus seen more as a product of society rather than individuals, actual individual participation in religious worship attendance was less than it is today (Finke and Stark 1992).

10. Handy 1984:18.

11. Handy 1984:19.

12. In Handy 1984:20.

13. 1989.

14. 1992.

15. Stark, Finke, Iannaccone, Warner, and others.

16. Olson 1998.

17. We know of one church that tried to offer a "traditional" and "contemporary" service simultaneously on two floors of the same building, with one pastor running back and forth between them. It did not work, so they stopped the experiment.

18. Wagner 1979:11.

19. Smith et al., 1998:90–91.

20. Berger 1967.

21. Cohen 1985.

22. Smith et al., 1998.

23. Finke and Stark 1992; Iannaccone 1990; Kelley 1972; Stephen Warner 1993.

24. Hechter 1987.

25. Kelley 1972.

26. Wagner 1979:147.

27. Hechter 1987:41.

28. An exception of course is if people value internal diversity highly enough that the cost of not having it outweighs the typically greater costs in areas such as meaning, belonging, and unity.

29. Lazerfeld and Merton 1964; Hallinan and Williams 1989.

30. Verbrugge 1977.

31. Samuelson and Zeckhauser 1988.

32. Tversky and Kahneman 1990.

33. Tversky and Kahneman 1990; Quattrone and Tversky 1988.

34. Chaves and Montgomery 1996.

35. Roof and McKinney 1987:165–66.

36. Blau 1977, 1987, 1994; also see Blau and Schwartz 1984.
37. Popielarz and McPherson 1995.
38. E.g., Stark and Bainbridge 1985.
39. Popielarz and McPherson 1995.
40. McPherson, Popielarz, and Drobnic 1992.
41. Popielarz and McPherson 1995:703.
42. Blau 1977, 1987, 1994.
43. Blau and Schwartz 1984.

44. This is not to suggest that some congregations will not be racially heterogeneous. The religious economies model suggests that there should be a niche for mixed-race congregations. However, given the other factors explored in this chapter, without significant changes, the niche for mixed-race congregations will remain small.

45. As we shared drafts of this work with others, we were often asked to consider an important exception—Pentecostals. "Why," we were asked, "are Pentecostals more successfully able to integrate congregations across race?" Our response, "Though they may be somewhat more likely to be in mixed-race congregations, it would be hard to call their degree of integration successful."

Modern-day Pentecostalism is typically traced to the Azuza Street revivals of Los Angeles in 1906. It did share rather unique distinctions, especially for the time, in that it was led by an African-American preacher and its adherents were both black and white. This is perhaps the genesis of the "successful" exception Pentecostals supposedly represent. But within ten years of its founding, the American Pentecostal movement ripped apart along racial lines, as Pentecostals divided into black and white denominations. Today, the two major Pentecostal denominations—the Church of God in Christ and the Assemblies of God—share a typical American characteristic—one is almost exclusively black, the other almost exclusively white. And we are quite sure that whatever limited heterogeneity exists in the denominations is less at the congregational level. Harvey Cox, a Harvard theologian who traveled and attended Pentecostal churches extensively in preparation for his book on Pentecostalism, *Fires from Heaven*, writes about Pentecostalism idealic founding and present-day reality (1995:297):

> The revival that one visitor said was a demonstration of the power of the Spirit to "wash away the color line with the blood of the cross," and to purge the church of the sin of racism, had resegregated itself very quickly. Today pentecostalism stands in grave danger of losing the invaluable message it could bring to the other churches and to the rest of the world. What happened to the spirit of Azuza Street?

> He goes on to discuss the lack of cooperation between white and black Pentecostals. The divisions, he says, are hardly trivial, and often led to taking opposite sides of issues and supporting alternative causes (311). We thus do not view Pentecostalism as an important exception to the within-group homogeneity concept, but merely another example of it.

46. Wagner 1979.
47. Wagner 1979:15–16.
48. Wagner 1979:150.
49. Handy 1984; Marsden 1990.

Chapter 8

1. Blau and Schwartz 1984:12–13.

2. Blau and Schwartz 1984.

3. Hamilton and Trolier 1986:133.

4. Hogg 1992:91; Tajfel 1978: Chapter 3.

5. Turner 1978:249–50.

6. Hogg and Abrams 1988.

7. Hamilton and Trolier 1986:131; Linville, Salovey, and Fischer 1986.

8. Hewstone, Jaspers, and Lalljee 1982; Sager and Schofield 1980; Taylor and Jaggi 1974; Wang and McKillip 1978.

9. Howard and Rothbart 1980.

10. Taylor 1981.

11. Hamilton and Trolier 1986; Wilder 1981.

12. Billig and Tajfel 1973; Tajfel 1969, 1978; Rabbie and Horwitz 1969.

13. Blau 1977, 1994; Doise 1990.

14. Blau and Schwartz 1984.

15. Reinhold Niebuhr (1932), with his focus on nations, calls this the ethical paradox of patriotism.

16. Niebuhr 1932:75.

17. Niebuhr 1932:xxii–xxiii.

18. Our discussion of inequality assumes either that the amount of resources are fixed or, given the frequent condition that they are not, that those with greater resources desire more.

19. S. Feld/R. Feld 1981, S. Feld/R. Feld 1984; Fischer et al. 1977; McPherson and Smith-Loven 1987.

20. S. Feld/R. Feld 1982.

21. We must also keep in mind, though, as Chapter Seven made clear, that the social makeup of voluntary groups is not randomly created. People are more likely to join and stay in groups composed of people similar to themselves.

22. Blau and Schwartz 1984.

23. Olson 1993.

24. Smith et al. 1998.

25. Olson 1993.

26. This is a good example of the contradictory forces often at work in the social world. On the one hand, evangelical leaders advocate creating cross-race friendships, and even interracial networks. Yet, at the same time, uniracial networks are used for church growth and unintentionally affirmed.

27. E.g., Fernandez and Weinberg 1997; Lin, Vaughn, and Ensel 1981; Haines and Hurlbert 1992.

28. This statement implies neither a relative contribution to inequality nor the existence of countervailing influences. Only that other things held constant, religion contributes to the reproduction of racial inequality. We explore its significance after presenting the argument.

29. Knowing to what degree it reproduces inequality, and is counteracted through equality-producing actions taken by religious people and groups, must wait for future study.

30. Fernandez and Weinberg 1997.

31. Blau and Schwartz 1984; Jackman and Crane 1986; Marsden 1987.

32. Music groups, overwhelmingly uni-race, are an interesting example of this effect. The well-known (and all-white) rock band from the 1970s and 1980s, *Boston*, illustrates how bands are usually formed. According to lead singer Bradley Delp, "Fran knew Barry, and I knew Fran, and Fran had played with Sib, and Sib had played with Tom, and Barry knew Tom, and Tom knew me, but Fran didn't know that I knew that he knew Barry too . . ." (from 1976 album sleeve).

33. Lin, Vaughn, and Ensel 1981.

34. The common evangelical proposition that people need to form a cross-race friendship could positively contribute to reducing racial inequality, but the effect is, at best, small. Research indicates multilevel interracial networks, as opposed to a mere friendship or two, are needed (e.g., see Jackman and Crane 1986).

35. DuBois 1931:1556

36. Hart 1992.

37. Thomas 1985:382.

38. Goen 1985:47.

39. Hadden 1969.

40. Hadden 1969:170–71.

41. Hadden 1969:206–7.

42. Campbell and Pettigrew 1959; Martin 1972; Thomas 1985.

43. Campbell and Pettigrew 1959; Martin 1972; Thomas 1985.

44. Thomas 1985.

45. We do not exaggerate. Religious leaders are fired, or transferred because, from the congregation's perspective, they take controversial or incorrect stands. For example, see Wood and Zald 1966.

46. Finke and Stark 1992.

47. Morris 1984.

48. Clayton 1995; Silver 1966.

49. The Civil Rights movement appears to have made little or no impact on racially separate congregations, racially distinct social networks, or overall economic inequality.

50. Smith et al. 1998.

Chapter 9

1. Noll 1994:12

2. Clifford 1973:323.

3. Emerson 1998.

Bibliography

Abrams, Dominic, and Michael Hogg. 1988. "Comments on the Motivational Status of Self-Esteem" in *Social Identity and Intergroup Discrimination. European Journal of Social Psychology* 4(18):317–34.

Ahlstrom, Sydney E. 1972. *A Religious History of the American People.* New Haven: Yale University Press.

Alba, R. D., and R. M. Golden. 1986. "Patterns of Ethnic Marriage in the United States" in *Social Forces* 65:202–23.

Alba, Richard D., and John R. Logan. 1993. "Minority Proximity to Whites in Suburbs: An Individual Level Analysis of Segregation" in *American Journal of Sociology* 98:1388–1427.

Allen, Theodore W. 1994. *The Invention of the White Race, Vol. 1, Racial Oppression and Social Control.* ed. Nicholas Canny. London, England: Verso.

Allport, Gordon W. 1954. *The Nature of Prejudice.* Cambridge, MA: Addison-Wesley.

Apostle, Richard A., et al. 1983. *The Anatomy of Racial Attitudes.* Berkeley: University of California Press.

Bakhtin, M. M. 1986. *Speech Genres and Other Late Essays.* Trans. Vern. W. McGee; eds. Caryl Emerson and Michael Holquist. Austin: University of Texas Press.

Bellah, Robert N., et al. 1985. *Habits of the Heart: Individualism and Commitment in American Life.* Berkeley: University of California Press.

Bennett, Lerone. 1982. *Before the Mayflower: A History of Black America.* New York: Penguin Books.

Berger, Peter. 1967. *The Sacred Canopy: Elements of a Sociological Theory of Religion.* Garden City, NY: Doubleday.

Berkhofer, Robert E. 1978. *The White Man's Indian: Images of the American Indian from Columbus to the Present.* New York: Vintage.

Billig, Michael, and Henry Tajfel. 1973. "Social Categorization and Similarity in Intergroup Behavior" in *European Journal of Social Psychology* 1(3):9–26.

Binder, Amy. 1993. "Constructing Racial Rhetoric: Media Depictions of Harm in Heavy Metal and Rap Music" in *American Sociological Review* 58:753–67.

Blackmon, Douglas S. 1997. "Racial Reconciliation Becomes a Priority for the Religious Right" in *Wall Street Journal*, June 23, Section A, Page 1, Col. 1.

Blau, Peter M. 1977. *Inequality and Heterogeneity: A Primitive Theory of Social Structure.* New York: Free Press.

———.1987. *Bureaucracy in Modern Society.* New York: McGraw-Hill Companies.

———.1994. *Structural Contexts of Opportunities.* Chicago: University of Chicago Press.

Blau, Peter M., and Joseph E. Schwartz. 1984. *Crosscutting Social Circles: Testing a Macrostructural Theory of Intergroup Relations.* Orlando: Academic Press.

Bobo, Lawrence, and Vincent L. Hutchings. 1996. "Perceptions of Racial Group Competition: Extending Blumer's Theory of Group Position to a Multiracial Context" in *American Sociological Review* 61:951–72.

Boles, John B. 1988. *Masters and Slaves in the House of the Lord: Race and Religion in the American South, 1740–1870.* Lexington: University Press of Kentucky.

Bonilla-Silva, Eduardo, and Amanda Lewis. 1997. *The "New Racism": Toward an Analysis of the U.S. Racial Structure, 1960s–1990s.* Unpublished manuscript.

Bray, Hiawatha. 1992. "Evangelical Racism?" in *Christianity Today* 26:42–44.

Brooks, Clem, and Jeff Manza. 1997. "Social Cleavages and Political Alignments: U. S. Presidential Elections, 1960 to 1992" in *American Sociological Review* 62:937–46.

Campbell, Ernest Q., and Thomas F. Pettigrew. 1959. "Racial and Moral Crisis: The Role of the Little Rock Ministers" in *American Journal of Sociology* 64:509–16.

Chaves, Mark. 1994. "Secularization as Declining Religious Authority" in *Social Forces* 72:749–74.

Chaves, Mark. 1999. *National Congregations Study. Machine-readable file.* Department of Sociology. University of Arizona.

Chaves, Mark, and James D. Montgomery. 1996. "Rationality and the Framing of Religious Choices" in *Journal for the Scientific Study of Religion* 35:128–44.

Christian History. 1992. 11:24.

Clark, William A. 1992. "Residential Preferences and Residential Choices in a Multiethnic Context" in *Demography* 3(29):451–66.

Clayton, Obie. 1995. "The Churches and Social Change: Accommodation, Moderation, or Protest" in *Daedalus* 1(124):101–19

Clifford, N. K. 1973. "His Dominion: A Vision in Crisis" in *Sciences Religieuses/Studies in Religion* 2:323.

Cohen, Anthony P. 1985. *The Symbolic Construction of Community.* New York: E. Horwood; Tavistock Publications.

Cole, Charles Chester. 1954. *The Social Ideas of the Northern Evangelists.* New York: Columbia University Press.

Cox, Harvey. 1995. *Fire from Heaven: The Rise of Pentecostal Spirituality and the Reshaping of Religion in the Twenty-first Century.* Reading, MA: Addison-Wesley Publishing Company.

Daniels, Joseph. 1971. "The Psychopathology of Racism" in *Christianity Today* 15:7–8.

Dayton, Donald W. 1976. *Discovering an Evangelical Heritage.* New York: Harper and Row.

DeYoung, Curtiss P. 1995. *Coming Together: The Bible's Message in an Age of Diversity.* Valley Forge, PA: Judson Press.

———. 1997. *Reconciliation: Our Greatest Challenge—Our Only Hope.* Valley Forge, PA: Judson Press.

Doise, Willem. 1990. *Groups and Individuals: Explanations in Social Psychology.* Cambridge: Cambridge University Press.

Drake, Donald, St. Clair, and Horace R. Cayton. 1945. *Black Metropolis: A Study of Negro Life in a Northern City.* Chicago: University of Chicago Press.

DuBois, W. E. B. 1969. *The Souls of Black Folk.* New York: New American Library.

———. 1931. "Will the Church Remove the Color Line?" in *Christian Century* 48:1554–56.

Durkheim, Emile. 1915. *The Elementary Forms of the Religious Life.* Trans. Joseph Ward Swain. New York: Free Press.

Emerson, Michael O. 1994. "Is it Different in Dixie? Percent of Black and Residential Segregation in the South and Non-South" in *The Sociological Quarterly* 35:571–80.

———. 1998. "Why Individual Racial Reconciliation Alone Cannot End Racial Strife" in *Christian Scholar's Review* 28:58–70.

Emerson, Michael O., and David Sikkink. 1997. *What People Say, What People Do: Education, Racial Attitudes, and Racial Realities.* Paper presented at the annual meeting of the American Sociological Association. Toronto, Canada.

Essed, Philomena. 1990. *Everyday Racism: Reports from Women of Two Cultures.* Alameda, CA: Hunter House, Incorporated.

———. 1996. *Diversity: Gender, Color, & Culture.* Amherst: University of Massachusetts Press.

Essenburg, Timothy. 1998. *Urban Community Development: An Examination of the Perkins Model.* Unpublished manuscript.

Essig, James D. 1982. *The Bonds of Wickedness: American Evangelicals Against Slavery.* Philadelphia: Temple University Press.

Evans, Tony. 1995. *Let's Get to Know Each Other.* Nashville: Thomas Nelson Incorporated.

Farley, Reynolds, and William H. Frey. 1994. "Changes in the Segregation of Whites from Blacks During the 1980s: Small Steps Toward a More Integrated Society" in *American Sociological Review* 59:23–45.

Feagin, Joe R., and Melvin P. Sikes. 1994. *Living with Racism: The Black Middle-Class Experience.* Boston: Beacon Press.

Feld, Richard. 1984. "Governing Urban America: A Policy Focus" in *The Annals of the American Academy of Political and Social Science* 474:207–8.

Feld, Scott. 1982. "Social Structural Determinants of Similarity Among Associates" in *American Sociological Review* 47:797–801.

———. 1981. "The Focused Organizations of Social Ties" in *American Journal of Sociology* 86:1015–35.

Fernandez, Roberto, and Nancy Weinberg. 1997. "Sifting and Sorting: Personal Contacts and Hiring in a Retail Bank" in *American Sociological Review* 6(62):883–903.

Festinger, Leon. 1957. *A Theory of Cognitive Dissonance.* Stanford, CA: Stanford University Press.

Finke, Roger. 1997. "The Consequences of Religious Competition: Supply-side Explanations for Religious Change" in *Rational Choice Theories of Religion,* ed. Lawrence A. Young, 45–64. New York: Routledge Press.

Finke, Roger and Laurence R. Iannaccone. 1993. "Supply-Side Explanations for Religious Change" in *Annals, American Academy of Political and Social Science* 527:27–39.

Finke, Roger and Rodney Stark. 1992. *The Churching of America, 1776–1990: Winners and Losers in Our Religious Economy.* New Brunswick, NJ: Rutgers University Press.

Fischer, Claude. 1982. *To Dwell Among Friends: Personal Networks in Town and City.*

Chicago: University of Chicago Press.

Fischer, Claude S., R. M. Jackson, C. A. Stueve, K. Gerson, and L. M. Jones. 1977. *Networks and Places: Social Relations in the Urban Setting.* New York: Free Press.

Geertz, Clifford. 1968. *Islam Observed: Religious Development in Morocco and Indonesia.* New Haven: Yale University Press.

——. 1973. *The Interpretation of Cultures: Selected Essays.* New York: Basic Books.

Gilbreath, Edward. 1996. "A Prophet out of Harlem" in *Christianity Today* 40:36–43.

Gilens, Martin. 1995. "Racial Attitudes and Opposition to Welfare" in *Journal of Politics* 57:994–1014.

Goen, C. C. 1985. *Broken Churches, Broken Nation: Denominational Schisms and the Coming of the American Civil War.* Macon, GA.: Mercer University Press.

Grady, J. Lee. 1994. "Pentecostals Renounce Racism: Memphis Gathering Begins Mending Historic Rift" in *Christianity Today* 38:58.

Graham, Billy. 1993. "Racism and the Evangelical Church" in *Christianity Today* 37:27.

Hacker, Andrew. 1992. *Two Nations.* New York: Maxwell Macmillian International.

Hadden, Jeffrey K. 1969. *The Gathering Storm in the Churches.* Garden City, NY: Doubleday.

Haines, Valerie, and Jeanne Hurlbert. 1992. "Network Range and Health" in *Journal of Health and Social Behavior* 33:254–66.

Hallinan, Maureen, and Richard Williams. 1989. "Interracial Friendship Choices in Secondary Schools" in *American Sociological Review* 54:1–67.

Hamilton, David L., and Tina K. Trolier. 1986. "Stereotype and Stereotyping: An Overview of the Cognitive Approach" in In *Prejudice, Discrimination, and Racism*, eds. John F. Dovidio, and Samuel L. Gaertner, 127–63. Orlando: Academic Press.

Handy, Robert T. 1984. *A Christian America: Protestant Hopes and Historical Realities.* New York: Oxford University Press.

Hart, Stephen. 1992. *What Does the Lord Require? How American Christians Think about Economic Justice.* New York: Oxford University Press.

Hatch, Elvin. 1979. *Biography of a Small Town.* New York: Columbia University Press.

Hatch, Nathan O. 1989. *The Democratization of American Christianity.* New Haven: Yale University Press.

Hechter, Michael. 1987. *Principles of Social Solidarity.* Berkeley: University of California Press.

Henslin, James M. 1997. *Sociology: A Down-to-earth Approach.* Boston: Allyn and Bacon.

Hewstone, Miles, Jos Jaspars, and Mansur Lalljee. 1982. "Social Representations, Social Attribution and Social Identity: The Intergroup Images of 'Public' and 'Comprehensive'" in *European Journal of Social Psychology* 12:241–69.

Hines, Samuel, with Joe Allison. 1995. *Experience the Power.* Anderson, IN: Warner Press.

——. 1993. "We Need Each Other" in *Christianity Today* 37:26-27.

Hogg, Michael. 1992. *The Social Psychology of Group Cohesiveness.* New York: New

York University Press.

Hogg, Michael A., and Dominic Abrams. 1988. *Social Identifications: A Social Psychology of Intergroup Relations and Group Processes.* London, England: Routledge.

Howard, John W., and Myron Rothbart. 1980. "Social Categorization and Memory for In-group and Out-group Behavior" in *Journal of Personality and Social Psychology* 38:301–10.

Huff, Richard. 1999. "It's a Split Screen Racially for Television Viewing." Reported in *The Holland Sentinel*, On-Line Edition, February 9.

Hunter, James Davison. 1991. *Culture Wars: The Struggle to Define America.* New York: Basic Books.

Hurst, Charles E. 1998. *Social Inequality: Forms, Causes, and Consequences.* Boston: Allyn and Bacon.

Iannaccone, Laurence R. 1990. "Religious Practice: A Human Capital Approach" in *Journal for the Scientific Study of Religion* 29:297–314.

——. 1994. "Why Strict Churches Are Strong" in *American Journal of Sociology* 99:1180–1211.

Jackman, Mary R., and Marie Crane. 1986. "'Some of My Best Friends Are Black': Interracial Friendship and Whites' Racial Attitudes" in *Public Opinion Quarterly* 50:459–86.

Jaret, Charles. 1995. *Contemporary Racial and Ethnic Relations.* New York: Harper-Collins College Publishers.

Jordan, Winthrop. 1968. *White Over Black: American Attitudes Toward the Negro.* Chapel Hill: University of North Carolina Press.

Kantrowitz, B. 1986. "The Ultimate Assimilation" in *Newsweek*, Nov. 24, 80.

Kelley, Dean. 1972. *Why Conservative Churches Are Growing.* New York: Harper and Row.

Kellstedt, Lyman A., and Corwin Smidt. 1991. "Measuring Fundamentalism: An Analysis of Different Operational Strategies" in *The Journal for the Scientific Study of Religion* 30:259–78.

Kennedy, John W. 1994. "'Deeper Than a Handshake': Atlantans, Black and White, Strive for Racial Understanding" in *Christianity Today* 38:62–63.

Kitano, Harry H. 1976. *Japanese Americans: Evolution of a Subculture.* Englewood Cliffs, NJ: Prentice-Hall.

Kitano, Harry H., and L. K. Chai. 1982. "Korean Interracial Marriage" in *Marriage and Family Review* 1(5):75–89.

Kitano, Harry H., and W. Yeung. 1982. "Chinese Interracial Marriage" in *Marriage and Family Review* 1(5):35–48.

Kluegel, James R. 1990. "Trends in Whites' Explanations of the Black-White Gap in Socioeconomic Status, 1977–1989" in *American Sociological Review* 55:512–25.

Kluegel, James R., and Eliot R. Smith. 1986. *Beliefs about Inequality: Americans' Views of What Is and What Ought to Be.* Hawthorne, NY: Aldine de Gruyter.

Kuchavsky, David E. 1965. "Billy Graham in Montgomery: A Stride Toward Reconciliation" in *Christianity Today* 9:31–32.

——. 1966. "The Gospel with Candor" in *Christianity Today* 11:53–54.

Lazerfeld, Paul F., and Robert K. Merton. 1964. "Friendship as Social Process: A

Substantive and Methodological Analysis in Freedom and Control" in *Modern Society*, eds. Monroe Berger, T. Abel, and C. H. Page, 18–66. New York: Octagon Books.

Lesick, Lawrence Thomas. 1980. *The Lane Rebels: Evangelicalism and Antislavery in Antebellum America*. Metuchen, NJ: Scarecrow Press.

Lieberson, Stanley. 1980. *A Piece of the Pie: Blacks and White Immigrants since 1880*. Berkeley: University of California Press.

Lin, Nan, John Vaughn, and Walter Ensel. 1981. "Social Resources and Occupational Status Attainment" in *Social Forces* 59:1163–81.

Lincoln, C. Eric. 1984. *Race, Religion, and the Continuing American Dilemma*. New York: Hill and Wang.

Lincoln, C. Eric, and Lawrence Mamiya. 1990. *The Black Church in the African American Experience*. Durham, NC: Duke University Press.

Linville, Patricia W., Peter Salovey, and Gregory W. Fischer. 1986. "Stereotyping and Perceived Distributions of Social Characteristics: An Application to Ingroup-Outgroup Perception" in *Prejudice, Discrimination, and Racism*, eds. John F. Dovidio and Samuel L. Gaertner, 127–63. Orlando: Academic Press.

Loescher, Frank. 1948. *The Protestant Church and the Negro: A Pattern of Segregation*. Westport, CT: Negro Universities Press.

Loury, Glenn C. 1995. *One by One from the Inside Out: Essays and Reviews on Race and Responsibility in America*. New York: Free Press.

Marsden, George. 1984. *Evangelicalism and Modern America*. Grand Rapids, MI: Eerdmans.

——. 1990. *Religion and American Culture*. San Diego: Harcourt Brace Jovanovich.

——. 1991. *Understanding Fundamentalism and Evangelicalism*. Grand Rapids, MI: Eerdmans.

Marsden, Peter. 1987. "Core Discussion Networks of Americans" in *American Sociological Review* 52:122–31.

Martin, Marty. 1972. "Ethnicity: The Skeleton of Religion in America" in *Church History* 41:5–21.

Martin, William. 1991 *A Prophet with Honor: The Billy Graham Story*. New York: W. Morrow and Co.

Massey, Douglas S. 1992. "Overview I" in *Race: How Blacks and Whites Think and Feel About the American Obsession*, ed. Studs Terkel, 95–96. New York: The New Press.

Massey, Douglas S., and Nancy A. Denton. 1993. *American Apartheid: Segregation and the Making of the Underclass*. Cambridge, MA: Harvard University Press.

Massey, Douglas S., and Andrew B. Gross. 1991. "Explaining Trends in Racial Segregation, 1970–1980" in *Urban Affairs Quarterly* 27(1):13–35.

Maxwell, Joe. 1994. "Racial Healing in the Land of Lynching: How 24,000 Mississippi Christians Are Beating Racism One Friendship at a Time" in *Christianity Today* 38:24–26.

McCartney, Bill, with David Halbrook. 1997. *Sold Out: Becoming Man Enough to Make a Difference*. Waco, TX: Word Publishing.

McDaniel, Antonio. 1996. "The Dynamic Racial Composition of the United States" in *An American Dilemma Revisited: Race Relations in a Changing World*, ed. Obie

Clayton, Jr., 269–87. New York: Russell Sage Foundation.

McLemore, S. Dale, and Harriett Romo. 1998. *Racial and Ethnic Relations in America*. Needham Heights: Allyn & Bacon.

McPherson, J. Miller, Pamela A. Popielarz, and Sonja Drobnic. 1992. "Social Networks and Organizational Dynamics" in *American Sociological Review* 57:153–70.

McPherson, J. Miller, and Lynn Smith-Loven. 1987. "Homophily in Voluntary Organizations" in *American Sociological Review* 52:370–79.

Miller, Kevin A. 1995. "McCartney Preaches Reconciliation" in *Christianity Today* 39:43.

Mollenkott, Virginia. 1971. "Up From Ignorance: Awareness-Training and Racism" in *Christianity Today* 15:6–8.

Mooneyham, W. Stanley. 1965. "Billy Graham in Alabama" in *Christianity Today* 9:44–45.

Morley, Patrick. 1997. "An Open Letter to Men of Color" in *New Man*, June, 60–61.

Morris, Aldon. 1984. "The Black Church in the Civil Rights Movement: The SCLC as the Decentralized, Radical Arm of the Black Church" in *The Origins of the Civil Rights Movement: Black Communities Organizing for Change*, ed. Aldon Morris. New York: Free Press.

Murray, Cecil. 1993. "Needed: An At-Risk Gospel" in *Christianity Today* 37:20.

Myrdal, Gunnar. 1964. *An American Dilemma: The Negro Problem and Modern Democracy.* Rev. ed. New York: McGraw-Hill Co.

Nash, Lee. 1972. "Evangelism and Social Concern" in *The Cross and the Flag*, eds. Robert G. Clouse, Robert D. Linder, and Richard V. Pierard, 133–55. Carol Stream, IL: Creation House.

Niebuhr, Reinhold. 1932. *Moral Man and Immoral Society; A Study in Ethics and Politics.* New York & London: C. Scribner's.

Noll, Mark A. 1994. *The Scandal of the Evangelical Mind.* Grand Rapids, MI: Eerdmans.

Oldham, Joseph H. 1924. *Christianity and the Race Problem.* London: Student Christian Movement.

Oliver, Melvin L., and Thomas M. Shapiro. 1995. *Black Wealth/White Wealth: A New Perspective on Racial Inequality.* New York: Routledge.

Olsen, Ted. 1996. "Lutheran, Catholic, and Black Churches Join Graham Effort" in *Christianity Today* 40:67.

———. 1997. "Racial Reconciliation Emphasis Intensified" in *Christianity Today* 41:67.

Olson, Daniel V. A. 1993. "Fellowship Ties and the Transmission of Religious Identity" in *Beyond Establishment*, eds. Jackson W. Carroll and Wade Clark Roof, 32–53. Louisville, KY: Westminster/John Knox Press.

———. 1998. "Religious Pluralism in Contemporary U.S. Counties" in *American Sociological Review* 63:759–61.

Olson, Roger E. 1995. "Postconservative Evangelicals Greet the Postmodern Age" in *Christian Century* 112:480–81.

Omi, Michael, and Howard Winant. 1994. *Racial Formation in the United States: From the 1960s to the 1990s.* New York: Routledge.

Pannell, William E. 1993. *The Coming Race Wars? A Cry for Reconciliation.* Grand Rapids, MI: Zondervan Publishing House.

Park, Andrew Sung. 1996. *Racial Conflict and Healing: An Asian–American Theological Perspective.* Maryknoll, NY: Orbis Books.

Perkins, John M. 1976. *Let Justice Roll Down: John Perkins Tells His Own Story.* Glendale, CA: Regal Books.

Perkins, John, and Thomas Tarrants, III., 1994. *He's My Brother: Former Racial Foes Offer Strategy for Reconciliation.* Grand Rapids, MI: Chosen Books.

Perkins, Spencer, and Chris Rice. 1993. *More Than Equals: Racial Healing for the Sake of the Gospel.* Downers Grove, IL: InterVarsity Press.

Pettigrew, Thomas F. 1988. "Integration and Pluralism" in *Eliminating Racism: Profiles in Controversy,* eds. Phyllis A. Katz and Phyllis, Dalmas A. Taylor, 19–30. New York: Plenum Press.

Popielarz, Pamela, and J. Miller McPherson. 1995. "On the Edge or in Between: Niche Position, Niche Overlap, and the Duration of Voluntary Association Memberships" in *American Journal of Sociology* 101:698–721.

Powers, Daniel A., and Christopher G. Ellison. 1995. "Interracial Contact and Black Racial Attitudes: The Contact Hypothesis and Selectivity Bias" in *Social Forces* 74:205–26.

Quarles, Benjamin. 1969. *Black Abolitionists.* New York: Oxford University Press.

Quattrone, George, and Amos Tversky. 1988. "Contrasting Rational and Psychological Analyses of Political Choice" in *American Political Science Review* 82:719–36.

Rabbie, J. M., and M. Horwitz. 1969. "The Arousal of Ingroup-outgroup Bias by a Chance Win or Loss" in *Journal of Social Psychology* 1:215–34.

Rabey, Steve. 1997. "Seedbed for Revival?" in *Christianity Today* 41:90.

Reimers, David M. 1965. *White Protestantism and the Negro.* New York: Oxford University Press.

Rodriguez, Clara. 1991. *Puerto Ricans: Born in the U. S. A.* Boulder, CO: Westview.

Rodriguez, David. 1991. *The Wages of Whiteness: Race and the Making of the American Working Class.* London, England: Verso.

Roediger, David. 1994. *Towards the Abolition of Whiteness: Essays on Race, Politics, and Working Class History.* London, England: Verso.

Roof, Wade Clark, and William McKinney. 1987. *American Mainline Religion.* New Brunswick, NJ: Rutgers University Press.

Sager, H. A., and J. W. Schofield. 1980. "Racial and Behavioral Cues in Black and White Children's Perceptions of Ambiguously Aggressive Acts" in *Journal of Personality and Social Psychology* 39:590–98.

Salley, Columbus, and Ronald Behm. 1970. *Your God Is Too White.* Downers Grove, IL: InterVarsity Press.

Samuelson, William, and Richard Zeckhauser. 1988. "Status Quo Bias in Decision Making" in *Journal of Risk and Uncertainty* 1:7–59.

Sandefur, G. D., and T. McKinnel. 1986. "American Indian Intermarriage" in *Social Science Research* 15:347–71.

Scherer, Lester B. 1975. *Slavery and the Churches in Early America, 1619–1819.* Grand Rapids, MI: Eerdmans.

Sewell, William H. 1992. "A Theory of Structure: Duality, Agency, and Transformation" in *American Journal of Sociology* 98:1–29.

Sherkat, Darren E., and John Wilson. 1995. "Preferences, Constraints, and Choices in Religious Markets: An Examination of Religious Switching and Apostasy" in *Social Forces* 3(73):993–1026.

Sider, Ronald J. 1977. *Rich Christians in an Age of Hunger: A Biblical Study.* Downers Grove, IL: InterVarsity Press.

———. 1997. *Rich Christians in an Age of Hunger: Moving from Affluence to Generosity.* Dallas: Word Publishing.

Silver, James. 1966. *Mississippi: The Closed Society.* 2nd ed. New York: Harcourt, Brace, and World.

Skinner, Tom. 1968. *Black and Free.* Grand Rapids, MI: Zondervan Publishing House.

Smith, Christian, ed. 1996. *Disruptive Religion: The Force of Faith in Social-Movement Activism.* New York: Routledge.

Smith, Christian, with Michael Emerson, Sally Gallagher, Paul Kennedy, and David Sikkink. 1998. *American Evangelicalism: Embattled and Thriving.* Chicago: University of Chicago Press.

Smith, Robert Edwin. 1922. *Christianity and the Race Problem.* New York: Fleming H. Revell.

Sniderman, Paul, and Michael G. Hagen. 1985. *Race and Inequality: A Study in American Values.* Chatham, NJ: Chatham House Publishers.

Stark, Rodney. 1971. *Wayward Shepherds: Prejudice and the Protestant Clergy.* New York: Harper and Row.

Stark, Rodney, and William Sims Bainbridge. 1985. *The Future of Religion: Secularization, Revival, and Cult Formation.* Berkeley: University of California Press.

Stark, Rodney, and Charles Y. Glock. 1969. "Prejudice and the Churches" in *Prejudice U.S.A.,* eds. Charles Y. Glock and Ellen Siegelman, 70–95. New York: Praeger.

Swidler, Ann. 1986. "Culture in Action: Symbols and Strategies" in *American Sociological Review* 51:273–86.

Taeuber, Karl. 1989. *Residence and Race: 1619 to 2019.* In *Race: Twentieth Century Dilemmas—Twenty-first Century Prognoses,* vol. 3, ed. Winston Van Horne. Madison: Board of Regents, The University of Wisconsin System.

Tajfel, Henri. 1969. "Cognitive Aspects of Prejudice" in *Journal of Social Issues* 25:79–97.

———. 1978. "Social Categorization, Social Identity and Social Comparison" in *Differentiation Between Social Groups: Studies in the Social Psychology of Intergroup Relations,* ed. Henri Tajfel, 61–76. London: Academic Press.

Tapia, Andrés T. 1997. "After the Hugs, What?" in *Christianity Today* 41:54–55.

Taylor, D. M., and V. Jaggi. 1974. "Ethnocentrism and Causal Attribution in a South Indian Context" in *Journal of Cross-Cultural Psychology* 5:162–71.

Taylor, S. E. 1981. *A Categorization Approach to Stereotyping. Cognitive Processes in Stereotyping and Intergroup Behavior,* ed. D. L. Hamiltion, 83–114. Hillsdale, NJ: Erlbaum.

Thomas, Charles B., Jr. 1985. "Clergy in Racial Controversy: A Replication of the

Campbell and Pettigrew Study" in *Review of Religious Research* 26:379–90.

Tinker, J. N. 1982. "Intermarriage and Assimilation in a Plural Society: Japanese-Americans in the United States" in *Marriage and Family Review* 5(1):61–73.

Turner, James. 1978. "The Founding Fathers of American Sociology: An Examination of Their Sociological Theories of Race Relations" in *Journal of Black Studies* 9:3–14.

———. 1991. "Loss Aversion in Riskless Choice: A Reference-dependent Model" in *The Quarterly Journal of Economics* 106:1039–61.

Tversky, Amos, and Daniel Kahneman. 1990. "Rational Choice and the Framing of Decisions" in *The Limits of Rationality*, eds. Karen Cook and Margaret Levi, 60–89. Chicago: University of Chicago Press.

U. S. Bureau of the Census. 1995. *Statistical Abstract of the United States: 1995*. Washington, D. C.: U. S. Government Printing Office.

Usry, Glenn, and Craig S. Keener. 1996. *Black Man's Religion: Can Christianity be Afrocentric?* Downers Grove, IL: InterVarsity Press.

Van den Berghe, Pierre L. 1967. *Race and Racism: A Comparative Perspective*. New York: Wiley, 1967.

Verbrugge, Lois M. 1977. "The Structure of Adult Friendship Choices" in *Social Forces* 56:576–97.

Volf, Miroslav. 1996. *Exclusion and Embrace: A Theological Exploration of Identity, Otherness, and Reconciliation*. Nashville: Abingdon Press.

Wagner, C. Peter. 1979. *Our Kind of People: The Ethical Dimensions of Church Growth in America*. Atlanta: John Knox Press.

Wang, G., and J. McKillip. 1978. "Ethnic Identification and Judgements of an Accident" in *Personality and Social Psychology Bulletin* 4:296–99.

Warner, Stephen. 1993. "Work in Progress toward a New Paradigm for the Sociological Study of Religion" in *American Journal of Sociology* 98:1044–93.

Warner, Tony. 1993. "Learn from Us" in *Christianity Today* 37:26.

Washington, Raleigh, and Glen Kehrein. 1993. *Breaking Down Walls: A Model for Reconciliation in an Age of Racial Strife*. Chicago: Moody Press.

Weary, Dolphus. 1990. *I Ain't Comin' Back*. Wheaton, IL: Tyndale House Publishers.

Wellman, David T. 1977. *Portraits of White Racism*. New York: Cambridge University Press.

Wenneker, Mark B., and Arnold M. Epstein. 1989. "Racial Inequalities in the Use of Procedures for Patients with Ischemic Heart Disease in Massachusetts" in *Journal of the American Medical Association* 261:253–57.

West, Cornel. 1993. *Race Matters*. Boston: Beacon Press.

White, Gayle. 1996. "Clergy Conference Stirs Historic Show of Unity" in *Christianity Today* 4(40):88.

Wilder, D. A. 1981. "Perceiving Persons as a Group: Categorization and Intergroup Relations" in *Cognitive Processes in Stereotyping and Intergroup Behavior*, ed. D. L. Hamilton, 213–57. Hillsdale, NJ: Erlbaum.

Wilson, William J. 1996. *When Work Disappears: The World of the New Urban Poor*. New York: Random House.

Winslow, Ron. 1992. "Study Finds Blacks Get Fewer Bypasses" in *Wall Street Journal*, March 18, B1.

Wood, Forrest. 1991. *Arrogance of Faith.* New York: Alfied A. Knopf.

Wood, James R., and Mayer N. Zald. 1966. "Aspects of Racial Integration in the Methodist Church: Sources of Resistance to Organizational Policy" in *Social Forces* 45:255–64.

Woodberry, Robert D., and Christian S. Smith. 1998. "Fundamentalism et al.: Conservative Potestants in America" in *Annual Review of Sociology* 24:25–56.

Woodbridge, John D., Mark A. Noll, and Nathan O. Hatch. 1979. *The Gospel in America: Themes in the Story of America's Evangelicals.* Grand Rapids, MI: Zondervan Publishing House.

Woodward, C. Vann. 1955. *The Strange Career of Jim Crow.* New York: Oxford University Press.

Wright, Louis B. 1957. *The Cultural Life of the American Colonies, 1607–1763.* New York: Harper.

Yancey, George. 1996. *Beyond Black and White: Reflections on Racial Reconciliation.* Grand Rapids, MI: Baker Books.

———. 1998. *Reconciliation Theology: Results of a Multiracial Evangelical Community.* Paper presented at the Color Lines in the Twenty-first Century conference, Chicago, IL.

Yuan, D. Y. 1980. "Significant Demographic Characteristics of Chinese Who Intermarry in the United States" in *California Sociologist* 3:184–96.

Zurawik, David. 1996. *A New Study Finds a Growing Chasm Between the TV Viewing Habits of Black and White Audiences.* St. Paul Pioneer Press, May 4, Express, 10D.

Index

Aid to Families with Dependent Children. *See* Welfare.
Aaron, Levorn, 61
Abernathy, Ralph, 45
Abolition. *See* Abolitionists; Slavery
Abolitionists, 28–34; evangelical, 29–30, 32, 33–34
Affirmative action, 47, 70, 87, 154
Alabama Baptist, 40
Alstrom, Sydney, 25
American Indians, 12, 72–73
Anderson College, 60; School of Theology, 62
Artificial birth control, 166
Atlanta Exposition, 41
Awakening, Great, 25, 138–39

Bakhtin, M.M., 91
Behm, Ronald, 59
Berger, Peter, 27, 142
Berkeley, George, 23
Bible, 3, 23, 43, 47, 78, 109; defense of slavery, 34–36; measuring evangelicalism, 94; solution to the race problem, 117–18
Black power movement, 47
Blau, Peter, 146, 149, 155, 157
Born again, 3
Boundaries, symbolic, 142–44
Brooks, Clem, 8
Bruce, Blanche Kelso, 38

Campolo, Tony, 59
Carmichael, Stokely, 130
Categorization, 156–58, 161
Chaves, Mark, 146
Chicago, 42
Christ. *See* Jesus Christ
Christian Advocate, 39–40
Christian America, 30–31, 36, 38, 41, 100; defined, 30
Christian History, 35
Christianity Today, 46, 56–58, 63–64, 66; in figure, 35; in table, 189; solutions to the race problem, 115, 123–24
Civil Rights movement, 2, 45, 46, 48, 153,

163, 195n.49; and protest marches, 164–65
Civil War. *See* War
Class, 8 13, 60, 62, 133; dependent, 80; dominant, 36; lower, 7, 13; middle, 7, 13, 70, 90, 94
Clemmons, Ithiel, 64
Clifford, N.K., 171
Cognitive processes, 157
Cole, Charles, 34
Colonization societies, 29
Commission on Interracial Cooperation, 42, 44
Commission on Race Relations, 43
Consolidated, 155, 157
Contact theory, 83–84
Cox, Harvey, 193n.45
Crane, Marie, 107–08, 131, 195n.34
Cultural tools, 21, 170; and the race problem, 76–80, 82–86, 89, 159–60; and racial inequality, 95–97, 98–106; and solutions to the race problem, 117–19, 130, 132
Cuney, Norris Wright, 38

Darwinism, Social, 39, 186n.52
Davies, Samuel, 24
Denton, Nancy, 43, 45
de Tocqueville, Alexis, 1, 16
DeYoung, Curtiss, 60–63, 66–67
Differentiation, 156–58
Discipleship, definition, 184n.1
Discrimination, 9, 183n.1
Disestablishment, 138–39, 140
Douglas, Frederick, 31
DuBois, W.E.B., 41, 162, 163

Eisenhower Foundation Commission, 17
Ellis, Carl, 67
Engaged orthodoxy, 3
Enlightenment, 136–39
Essenburg, Timothy, 187n.5
Evangelicals, definition, 2–4; measurement of, 94, 105, 121
Evangelizing, 3
Evans, Tony, 63, 66

Farrakhan, Lewis, 82
Feagin, Joe, 90, 189n.21
Federal Council of Churches, 43
Feld, Scott, 160
Fernandez, Roberto, 161–62
Finke, Roger, 25, 139, 167, 192n.9
Finney, Charles, 31, 32–33
Fitzpatrick, Sarah, 36
Fragmentation, 155, 162–68
Franklin, Ben, 25, 26, 93
Freedom, structural, 165, 166, 167

Garrison, William, 32
Gates, Bill, 93
Geertz, Clifford, 153
General Social Survey, 94, 98, 99, 100, 106,
    119, 162; in tables, 169, 175, 176, 178
Ghetto, 42, 45, 47
Gilens, Martin, 110
Glock, Charles, 76–77, 93
Goen, C.C., 164
Graham, Billy, 3, 46–47, 55–56, 64–65, 187
    n.83
Great Awakening, 25
Grimes, William, 27
Group Loyalty, paradox of, 158–60

Hacker, Andrew, 17
Hadden, Jeffrey, 164, 165–66
Hamilton, David, 156
Hampton Institute, 40
Hart, Stephen, 117, 163
Health, 14
Hechter, Michael, 143–45
Henry, Patrick, 28
Hill, E. V., 54, 56
Hines, Samuel, 53–54, 55, 56, 62, 188n.32
Holloway, Scottye, 59
Homogenous units principle, 150–51, 161
Homophily principle, 147, 149
Howe, Mark DeWolfe, 129
Howard University School of Divinity, 60,
    62
Hunter, James, 76
Hybels, Bill, 137

Immigrants, 14–15, 41, 86, 126
Immigration, 26, 41, 44
Indians. *See* American Indians
Industrialization, 39, 44
Integration. *See* Segregation
Interracial contact. *See also* Segregation;

measure of, 106–7
Interracial marriage, 39, 85
Intervarsity Christian Fellowship, 66
Isolation. *See* Segregation

Jackman, Mary, 107–8, 131, 195n.34
Jackson, Jesse, 80
Jefferson, Thomas, 27, 138, 139
Jesus Christ, 3, 24, 56, 77, 86, 104; solution
    to the race problem, 116, 118, 187n.2
Jim Crow 8, 9, 33, 38–39, 40, 41, 43, 47, 48,
    90, 167; borrowed from the North, 186
    n.55; defined, 183n.1; likened to, 132
Johns, Vernon, 45
Johnson, James, 56

Kelley, Dean, 144
Kerner Report, 17
King, Coretta Scott, 64
King, Martin Luther, Jr., 45, 47, 52, 54,
    60
Ku Klux Klan, 8, 42, 72, 87

Lane Rebels, 33
"Lazy-butt account," 102–103
LeJau, Francis, 24
Loescher, Frank, 44
Loss aversion, 146
Lynching, 40, 42, 44

Macro bonds, 155
Manza, Jeff, 8
Marriage, 11–12; interracial, 7, 11–12
Marsden, George, 25, 39
Martin, William, 46
Massey, Douglas, 43, 45
Massey, James Earl, 54, 56, 60, 61, 62
Mather, Cotton, 23, 24
May, Samuel, 32
Mays, Benjamin, 45
McCartney, Bill, 65–68, 168
McKinney, Karen, 183n.12
McPherson, J. Miller, 148, 149
Memphis Miracle, 3, 64
Migration, 45
Millennialism, post-, 30, 189n.12; pre-, 47,
    189n.12
Million Man March, 67, 70
"Miracle motif," 117–18, 126, 130–31
Mission Mississippi, 63
Montgomery, James, 146
Moody, D.L., 41

Morley, Tom, 62–63
Morse, Jedidiah, 29
Murray, Cecil, 67
Music, 15
Myrdal, Gunnar, 6, 10, 16, 41, 44, 48, 132

National Black Evangelical Association, 66
National Congregations Study, 135–36
National Opinion Research Center, 94
Native Americans. *See* American Indians
Networks, separate, 160–61
Niche edge effect, 148–50
Niche overlap effect, 149–50
Niebuhr, Reinhold, 158–59
Noll, Mark, 171

Occupation, 3, 12,13–14, 109, 155
Oliver, Melvin, 13, 14
Olson, Daniel, 160

Pannell, William, 54, 56, 58
Pentecostal Churches of North America, 3, 64
Pentecostal Fellowship of North America, 3, 64
Perkins, John, 50, 51, 52, 53, 56, 59, 129, 187n.5
Perkins, Spencer, 63, 64, 188n.32
Personal piety, 186n.65
Pettigrew, Thomas, 11
Pew Evangelical Interviews, in table, 177
Pew Survey of Religious Identity and Influence, in tables, 179–81
Pike, James, 38
Pinchback, Pinckney Benton Stewart, 38
Popielarz, Pamela, 148, 149
Post-Civil Rights, 11
Poverty, 12, 38, 40, 52, 53, 60, 112; compared to Europe, 190n.15; views of, 93–98, 104, 108, 110;
Presbyterian General Assembly, 29
President's Commission, 16
Project Joseph, 67
Promise Keepers, 3, 50, 65–68, 119, 127–28, 129, 168, 187n.83
Puerto Ricans, 61

Race relations scholars, 2
Racialized, definition of, 7, 154; evidence for, 11–17
Racial reconciliation, 52–68; evangelicals'

definitions, 127–29
Racial steering, 42, 43
Racism: definition of, 9; evangelicals' examples of, 86–88; ways to address, 120–27
Reconcilers Fellowship, 64
Reconstruction, 37
Redlining, 43
Reimer, David, 41
Religious affiliation, 16
Religious authority, limits to, 162–68
Religious marketplace, 136–42, 150; and segmentation, 162–68
Religious pluralism, 141
Restrictive covenants, 43
Revolutionary War. *See* War
Rice, Chris, 63, 64
Rice, Thomas, 183n.1
Riots, 16

Salley, Columbus, 59
Salvation, 3
Schwartz, Joseph, 155
Segmented religious market, 162–68
Segregation, 78 131, 162, 171. *See also* Jim Crow; as isolation 80–81, 83–86, 89, 106–09; congregational 16, 39, 43, 71; 121–25, 132, 133, 154–62, 186n.60; de facto 44; desegregation, 43, 120–21, 125–27; residential 10, 71, 112; 122–25, 126, 132; northern 43; school 72
Separate networks, 160–61
Sewell, William, 76
Shapiro, Thomas, 13, 14
Sharecropping, 37
Shea, George Beverly, 56
Sider, Ronald, 59
Sikes, Melvin, 90, 189n.21
Skinner, Tom, 53, 56, 58, 62–63, 188n.32
Slavery, 81–82, 154, 167; abolition, 27–34, 36, 37, 48; defense of, 22; divided by, 31, 33–34, 36–37; problematic, 27–28, 31, 33–36
Slaves, 40, 48; baptismal vow, 24; Christianizing, 22–25, 26, 27; former, 37, 38; likened to welfare, 104; need for, 26–27; size, 22, 28, 36
Smith, Robert, 43
Social Darwinism, 39, 185n.52
Social gospel, 185n.65
Social integration, 155
Social reform, 185n.65

Social solidarity, 142–44
Socially constructed, 7–8, 14, 89, 145
Society of Negroes, 23
Stand in the Gap, 67
Stark, Rodney, 25, 77, 93, 139, 167, 192n.9
Status-quo bias, 146
Strikebreakers, 42
Strong, Josiah, 38
Structural freedom, 165, 166, 167
Sunday, Billy, 41
Survey of Income and Program Participation, 13
Swidler, Ann, 75–76, 79
Symbolic boundaries, 142–44

Tapan, Arthur, 32, 33
Tapan, Lewis, 32, 33
Television viewing, 16, 184n.40
Tennent, Gilbert, 25
Thomas, Charles Jr., 164
Tools. *See* Cultural tools
Transposing, 77
Trolier, Tina, 156
Truth, Sojourner, 31
Tubman, Harriet, 31
Turner, Nat, 31
Tuskegee Institute, 40

Unemployment, 12
Union Theological Seminary, 62
Urbanization, 44
Urban Training Center for Christian Mission, 164

Verbrugge, Lois, 145
Violence, 42

Virginia Bill for Establishing Religious Freedom, 138, 139
Voice: fragmented, 162–68; prophetic, 162–68

Wagner, C. Peter, 144, 150
Walker, David, 32
Wall Street Journal, 3, 63
War: Civil, 34, 36, 146; Revolutionary, 27; World War I, 41; World War II, 45
Warner, Tony, 66
Washington, Booker, 40–41
Washington, Raleigh, 63, 65
Wealth, 13, 93, 94, 108, 109
Weary, Dolphus, 59
Weber, Max, 167
Weinberg, Nancy, 161–62
Weld, Theodore, 31
Welfare, 102–04
Welman, David, 88–89
West, Cornel, 90, 112–13, 189n.21
Whitefield, George, 25–27
Willow Creek Association, 137, 140, 141
Wilson, William Julius, 113, 190n.15
Wood, Forrest, 26
Wood, James, 195n.45
Wood, Robert, 38
World War I. *See* War
World War II. *See* War
Wright, Louis, 138

Yancey, George, 54
Year of Jubilee, 108–09, 190n.16
Young, Andrew, 187n.2

Zald, Mayer, 195n.45